Why Containment Works

A VOLUME IN THE SERIES

Cornell Studies in Security Affairs

Edited by Robert J. Art, Robert Jervis, and Stephen M. Walt

A list of titles in this series is available at cornellpress.cornell.edu.

Why Containment Works

Power, Proliferation, and Preventive War

WALLACE J. THIES

Cornell University Press

Ithaca and London

First published 2020 by Cornell University Press

Library of Congress Cataloging-in-Publication Data

Names: Thies, Wallace J., author.
Title: Why containment works : power, proliferation, and preventive war / Wallace J. Thies.
Description: Ithaca [New York] : Cornell University Press, 2020. | Series: Cornell studies in security affairs | Includes bibliographical references and index.
Identifiers: LCCN 2020022151 (print) | LCCN 2020022152 (ebook) | ISBN 9781501749483 (cloth) | ISBN 9781501749490 (epub) | ISBN 9781501749506 (pdf)
Subjects: LCSH: Balance of power. | Deterrence (Strategy) | United States—Foreign relations—Philosophy. | Libya—Foreign relations—United States. | Iraq—Foreign relations— United States. | Iran—Foreign relations—United States.
Classification: LCC JZ1313 .T45 2020 (print) | LCC JZ1313 (ebook) | DDC 956.7044/31—dc23
LC record available at https://lccn.loc.gov/2020022151
LC ebook record available at https://lccn.loc.gov/2020022152

Contents

Preface   *vii*

1. Preventive War and Containment   1
2. Containing Qaddafi's Libya   20
3. Dual Containment of Iraq and Iran   55
4. Containing Iraq   87
5. Invading Iraq   119
6. Containing Iran   150
7. Containment Reappraised   174

    Notes   195
    Index   221

Preface

The subject of this book is the strategy of containment, and why, under the proper conditions, it can serve as a viable alternative to the strategy of preventive war.

As I define it, containment is not a passive strategy, nor is it one that necessarily seeks regime change in a targeted state, although it often does. Nor is it one that seeks to prevent the target from doing anything and everything. Containment assumes that hostility exists between the "container" and the target, and so the strategy should be seen as a form of managed conflict that seeks to prevent the target state from overturning the local, regional, or global distribution of power. Containment aims for eventual victory over the targeted state, but it will settle for stalemate for a long, long time if necessary. Containment does not have to be practiced everywhere that two states' interests bump up against each other. Instead, a state engaging in a containment strategy seeks to thwart, deny, or prevent the target state from doing only those things that the container would find dangerous and unacceptable. The criterion for judging whether a containment policy has succeeded is not whether the target state continues to put up resistance, but whether the target has actually achieved anything that the container opposes.

Seen in this light, containment is the obverse of the strategy of preventive war. Those who hold to the latter strategy see war as inevitable down the road, believe that at that point the balance of forces between the container and the target will be unfavorable for the former, and therefore that action sooner is better than action later. Unlike containment, preventive war is an impatient strategy, one that sees a need to act quickly lest the threat grow too large to handle successfully. A containment strategy believes that the restraints imposed on the targeted state, and any additional ones added in the future, are sufficient to hold it in check. A preventive war strategy, to the contrary, believes that only a swift, decisive war can remove the threat. Prompt eradication of the threat versus patiently holding it in check—this is the crucial distinction between the two strategies.

In this book I do not claim that containment should always be the preferred strategy when a state confronts another state that poses a threat. There may well be instances when preventive war makes more sense, although I personally believe that those instances are rare. Instead, what I claim is that, when seen in historical perspective, containment has been a remarkably successful strategy for the United States. In the cases I examine containment worked in the sense that I earlier defined success.

If the goal of this book is not to demonstrate that containment is a strategy for all seasons, then what is its purpose? Simply put, to show that under the proper circumstances containment can work *because it has worked*. It should therefore be considered a viable alternative and taken seriously as such when the United States once again, as it inevitably will, contemplates preventive war. In short, I examine cases where containment succeeded in order to locate those factors that made it work and that can enable it to work again should the need arise.

I proceed as follows. In chapter 1, I recast the Bush Doctrine as a *theory of victory*, that is, a coherent strategic view that tells a state how best to transform the scarce resources available to it into useful military assets, and how to employ those assets in conflicts with other states or nonstate actors. I then compare and contrast these prescriptions derived from the Bush Doctrine with an alternative theory of victory—namely, one based on containment and deterrence. I argue that there were multiple convincing reasons for believing that the combination of containment and deterrence was working—indeed, working very well—against Saddam Hussein's Iraq as of 2002 and 2003, and thus there was no need to invade Iraq, certainly not in 2003 and probably not for years to come.

Having introduced these two rival theories of victory—one based on the Bush Doctrine, the other on traditional notions of containment and deterrence—I then reexamine, in chapters 2 through 6, five cases of containment drawn from the Cold War and the post–Cold War world. The Cold War cases include containing Libya and the dual containment of Iraq and Iran. The post–Cold War cases include containing Iraq, invading Iraq, and containing Iran. I picked these five cases because they each offered US officials a choice between reliance on traditional notions of containment and deterrence and reliance on a more forceful approach akin to the Bush Doctrine. For each of these five cases, I explore the extent to which reliance on these rival theories of victory—containment and deterrence versus striking first—contributed to a successful resolution of the issues at stake. I also pose a counterfactual question: Would these cases have been resolved more quickly, at less cost, and in a manner more favorable to American interests if US officials had chosen a different mix of the coercive and deterrent tools available to them? In chapter 7, I review the relative merits of these two theories of victory based on evidence drawn from my five case studies and the Cold War too. I also assess the new knowledge made possible by comparing and contrasting these two alternative theories of victory.

Acknowledgments

An author who undertakes a project of this size and scope inevitably incurs debts to numerous individuals. Several colleagues took it upon themselves to read some or even all of the manuscript. Before the manuscript was submitted to a publisher, Mark Randol read it cover to cover and offered numerous suggestions and lots of encouragement, which was greatly appreciated. Robert Art and Roger Haydon reviewed the manuscript on behalf of the Cornell Studies in Security Affairs program. Robert and Roger went above and beyond their duties as editors and reviewers to bring the book to publication. *Appreciation* is an inadequate word to express my debt to them for their contributions. Robert Jervis and Stephen Walt likewise evaluated the manuscript in their role as editors of the Cornell Studies in Security Affairs.

Why Containment Works

Preventive War and Containment

On March 18, 2003, US forces attacked Iraq with air strikes followed a few days later by a ground invasion launched from Kuwait. The purpose of both the air war and the invasion was regime change in Iraq—overthrowing the regime of the Iraqi president Saddam Hussein and replacing it with a democratic government. A democratic Iraq, the administration of George W. Bush claimed, would forgo pursuit of weapons of mass destruction (WMDs), forswear links with terrorist groups like al-Qaeda, and set an example of democratic rule that would encourage further democratization in the rest of the Middle East.

The 2003 invasion of Iraq was in many respects the culmination of a rhetorical campaign intended to redirect US foreign policy and defense policy—a campaign set in motion by the George W. Bush administration in the aftermath of the 9/11 terrorist attacks. Instead of containment and deterrence, the Bush Doctrine, as it came to be known, stressed preemption and even prevention. Instead of retaliating *after* being attacked, the Bush Doctrine called for the US to strike first. Instead of waiting to see what an opponent would do, the Bush Doctrine stressed acting—indeed, acting vigorously—to prevent potential terrorist attacks before they could be carried out.

The Bush Doctrine proved to be very controversial, not only in the United States but also among America's allies and friends worldwide.[1] In the United States, the Bush Doctrine was criticized by Democrats in Congress as a violation of traditional American norms, which called for responding firmly to provocations but not for striking the first blow ourselves. Within the Atlantic Alliance, the Bush Doctrine was likewise attacked—most prominently by the French and German governments—as reckless and provocative.

The Bush Doctrine

Viewed as a theory of victory, the Bush Doctrine includes six main points.

1. CONTAINMENT CANNOT HOLD INDEFINITELY

Containment worked during the Cold War, the George W. Bush administration argued, because "especially following the Cuban Missile Crisis, we faced a generally status quo, risk averse adversary."[2] That situation no longer holds. Instead, "the security environment confronting the United States . . . is radically different from what we have faced before."[3] New threats, President Bush told the graduating class at West Point on June 1, 2002, "require new thinking." He cautioned that "containment is not possible when unbalanced dictators with weapons of mass destruction can deliver those weapons on missiles or secretly provide them to terrorist allies."[4] President Bush expanded on this theme during some impromptu remarks at a political reception in Houston on June 14, 2002. "In the past," he explained, "we used to have a doctrine called containment and deterrence. You can't contain a shadowy terrorist network. You can't deter somebody who doesn't have a country. And you're not going to be able—future Presidents won't be able to deter or contain one of these nations which harbors [sic] weapons of mass destruction, nations who hate America."[5]

"Nations who hate America" existed during the Cold War, too, but memories of that bygone era were largely eclipsed by the shock and horror that followed the 9/11 attacks.[6] "After September 11," President Bush explained in January 2003, "the doctrine of containment just doesn't hold any water. . . . My vision shifted dramatically after September 11, because I now realize the stakes, I realize the world has changed."[7] Secretary of Defense Donald Rumsfeld offered a similar rationale. The United States, he explained, "did not act in Iraq because of dramatic new evidence of Iraq's pursuit of weapons of mass murder. We acted because we saw the existing evidence in a new light, through the prism of our experience on September 11."[8] The British prime minister Tony Blair made a similar argument in 2004 when he said, "Containment will not work in the face of the global threat that confronts us. . . . The terrorists have no intention of being contained. The states that proliferate or acquire [weapons of mass destruction] illegally are doing so precisely to avoid containment."[9]

2. DETERRENCE IS NOT ENOUGH

Deterrence worked during the Cold War, the George W. Bush administration claimed, because the Soviet Union and China were "status quo, risk-averse" adversaries that were susceptible to deterrent threats.[10] In the post-9/11 world, the Bush administration claimed, "the gravest danger facing America and the world is outlaw regimes that seek and possess nuclear, chemical, and biological weapons."[11] The deterrent threats that kept the Soviet Union and China at bay are not likely to work as well against these "outlaw regimes." The former US undersecretary of state John Bolton told an interviewer in 2007 that, regarding Iran, "when you have a regime that would be happier in the afterlife than in this life, this is not a regime that is subject to classic theories of deterrence. Retaliation, for them, which would obliterate their society, doesn't have the same negative connotations for their leadership."[12] In the post-9/11 world, "deterrence based only upon the threat of retaliation is less likely to work against leaders of rogue states more willing to take risks, gambling with the lives of their people and the wealth of their nations."[13]

As seen by the George W. Bush administration, a strategy based solely or even largely on deterrence had three obvious flaws. First, it was reactive, based on the "threat of retaliation" but little more.[14] This kind of deterrence, President Bush claimed in his 2002 commencement address at West Point, "means nothing against shadowy terrorist networks with no nations or citizens to defend."[15] "Given the goals of rogue states and terrorists," a senior official told reporters in a briefing accompanying the release of the Bush administration's first national security strategy document in September 2002, "the United States can no longer solely rely on a reactive posture as we have in the past."[16] Instead of reacting to what others did, in the post-9/11 world it was the ability to act quickly and decisively that counted most. "We must be prepared to stop rogue states and their terrorist clients before they are able to threaten or use weapons of mass destruction against the United States and our allies and friends."[17]

Second, deterrence as practiced prior to 9/11 was too static, too unimaginative, and too indiscriminate to work effectively against the new threats the United States was facing. "After September 11, a dramatically lowered tolerance for threats helps explain why realists such as [Vice President] Cheney, who had earlier believed that Saddam could be both deterred and contained, suddenly felt differently."[18] In the words of the 2006 *Quadrennial Defense Review Report*, the United States, while still needing the forces and capabilities acquired for old-style deterrence, also required a shift from a "one size fits all" kind of deterrence toward "more tailored capabilities to deter advanced military powers, regional WMD states armed with weapons of mass destruction, and non-state terrorists."[19]

Third and most important, old-style deterrence conceded the initiative to America's foes, in effect making US national security dependent on what others did or did not do. Conceding the initiative to others, waiting to see what they would do, acting only after others had acted to initiate or intensify hostilities—all these were hallmarks of an intellectually bankrupt policy that would likely fail again unless something new was added to the policy mix. Any policy that conceded to others the choice of where and when the next deterrence failure would occur was simply unacceptable to the Bush administration. "Perhaps the clearest lesson" that could be drawn from 9/11 was the "need to act swiftly and firmly before threats become attacks."[20] "The greater the threat, the greater is the risk of inaction—and the more compelling the case for taking anticipatory action to defend ourselves, even if uncertainty remains as to the time and place of the enemy's attack."[21] On the other hand, "if we wait for threats to fully materialize, we will have waited too long."[22] Above all, "we cannot let our enemies strike first."[23]

In fairness to members of the Bush administration, they were not the only responsible parties to question the relative merits of waiting versus acting. David Ben-Gurion of Israel, to cite one example, believed that a "negative attitude of 'waiting it out'" was "not enough. In the long run," he believed, "doing nothing may be far more dangerous than any bold deed—such as fomenting a war."[24] President Bill Clinton's first secretary of defense, Les Aspin, suggested that the primary threat to the United States came from nuclear-armed terrorists and pariah states, and these "new possessors of nuclear weapons may not be deterrable."[25] Tony Blair, in a speech delivered on March 5, 2004, claimed that "it is a matter of time unless we act and take a stand before terrorism and weapons of mass destruction come together, and I regard them as two sides of the same coin."[26] President Clinton's second secretary of defense, William Perry, in 2006 advocated a US strike on a North Korean missile launch site to prevent launch of a Taepodong long-range missile, lest a successful test embolden North Korea to search for new ways to threaten the United States.[27]

Neither was the Bush administration monolithic in its view of deterrence. Prior to joining the George W. Bush administration as national security adviser and, later, secretary of state, Condoleezza Rice believed that even an Iraq armed with WMDs would still be deterrable. Iraqi WMDs, she wrote a year before becoming national security adviser, "will be unusable because any attempt to use them will bring national obliteration."[28] President Bush personally described US foes as "unbalanced dictators" and terror networks, both of which he claimed were largely undeterrable. Yet the US Department of Defense, in its 2006 *Quadrennial Defense Review Report*, viewed US adversaries as highly rational and sensitive to the imposition of costs and risks upon them. "In confronting the range of security challenges [the United States] will face in the twenty-first century," the report advised, "the United States must constantly strive to minimize its own costs in terms of lives and treasure, while imposing unsustainable costs on its adversaries. The United States, NATO, other allies and partners can impose costs by taking actions and making investments that complicate an adversary's decision-making or promote self-defeating actions. Effective cost-imposing strategies also heighten an adversary's sense of uncertainty, potentially creating internal fissures in its leadership."[29]

3. TIME IS NOT ON OUR SIDE

In his 2002 State of the Union address, President Bush stated, "We must prevent the terrorists and regimes who seek chemical, biological, or nuclear weapons from threatening the United States and the world . . . yet time is not on our side. I will not wait on events while dangers gather. I will not stand by, as peril draws closer and closer."[30] As seen by the George W. Bush administration, the United States post-9/11 "could wait to be struck again, or adopt proactive strategies to prevent another September 11."[31] This made it imperative not just to act but to act quickly and decisively. Hence President Bush, in his commencement address at West Point a few months later, warned of the need to "take the battle to the enemy, disrupt his plans, and confront the worst threats before they emerge."[32] In similar fashion National Security Adviser Condoleezza Rice told CNN's Wolf Blitzer on September 8, 2002, "We don't want the smoking gun to be a mushroom cloud."[33]

4. ACTING IS BETTER THAN WAITING

"In the world we have entered," President Bush said in his West Point commencement address in June 2002, "the only path to safety is the path of action."[34] According to the Bush Doctrine, there were at least two reasons why a state with the size and might of the United States should prefer action to a wait-and-see approach. First, acting was preferable to waiting because the costs and risks of inaction would likely prove unacceptably high.[35] "If we wait for threats to fully materialize," President Bush explained in his West Point address, "we will have waited too long."[36] "Facing clear evidence of peril," he told an audience in Cincinnati on October 7, 2002, "we cannot wait for the final proof—the smoking gun—that could come in the form of a mushroom cloud."[37] "The United States," the George W. Bush administration argued in its first national security strategy document, could not "remain idle while dangers gather."[38] To do so would be to "permit the world's most dangerous regimes and terrorists to threaten [the United States] with the world's most destructive weapons."[39]

Second, as explained by Jeffrey Laurenti, in the aftermath of the 9/11 attacks, there was in the United States "little high-level interest in tightening multilateral controls, which were widely thought to be ineffective against America's adversaries but all too constraining of U.S. power." In the Bush administration's view, "powerful nations could best protect their security by acting on their own, rather than by trusting easily paralyzed multilateral mechanisms and talk shops."[40]

5. OFFENSE IS BETTER THAN DEFENSE

"The war on terror," President Bush asserted during his 2002 West Point commencement address, "will not be won on the defensive."[41] This was because the United States could "no longer simply rely on deterrence to keep the terrorists at bay or defensive measures to thwart them at the last moment." Instead, the "fight must be taken to the enemy, to keep them on the run." As Bush saw it, the United States "must join with others to deny the terrorists what they need to survive: safe haven, financial support, and the support and protection that certain nation-states historically have given them."[42] Offense and defense were not equally plausible alternatives. "It is not possible," Donald Rumsfeld explained, "to defend against every conceivable type of attack in every conceivable location at every minute of the day or night. . . . The best, and in some cases, the only defense, is a good offense."[43] In practical terms, this meant a "war without boundaries would now be taken to the enemy; preemptive strikes and preventive wars were preferable to waiting to take another hit."[44]

6. PREVENTIVE ACTION WORKS (BETTER THAN THE ALTERNATIVES)

Adherents of the Bush Doctrine saw preventive action as preferable to inaction for two reasons. First, if rogue states were able to acquire weapons of mass destruction, then those weapons might "also allow these states to attempt to blackmail the United States" and its allies, thus complicating the task of "deterring or repelling the aggressive behavior of rogue states."[45] Second, preventive action meant denying weapons of mass destruction to rogue states and their terrorist allies *before* those weapons could be used against the United States.[46] The United States, in the Bush administration's view, "must be prepared to stop rogue states and their terrorist clients before they [could] threaten or use weapons of mass destruction against the United States and [its] allies and friends."[47] Conversely, prompt anticipatory action by the United States would have the considerable advantage of allowing the United States to confront "emerging threats before they [were] fully formed" and thus were less costly and risky to confront.[48]

Was Containment Failing?

As practiced by the United States against the Soviet Union during the Cold War, containment was "a form of balance-of-power diplomacy," centered on "the creation of political, military, and economic counterweights around a potentially hostile or aggressive state."[49] Containment during the Cold War "sought to deny the Soviet Union the ability to expand its sphere of influence. Order was maintained by managing the bipolar balance between the American and Soviet camps. Stability was achieved through nuclear deterrence."[50]

In the post–Cold War world, in contrast, the United States so towers over relatively small states like Libya, Iraq, and Iran that it doesn't seem particularly useful to view containment as just another form of balancing behavior. Instead, I treat containment as a set of policies, each of which constitutes an instrument that can be employed against a rogue state or held in reserve, depending on circumstances. Containment, broadly defined, is thus the art of thwarting an adversary's plots and schemes, and not just once but again and again, through some combination of threats (verbal and nonverbal), sanctions or rewards, and if need be, forceful actions.

In the case of Iraq in 2002 and 2003, the George W. Bush administration took it as self-evident that containment could not hold indefinitely; that deterrence would likely fail; that time was not on our side; that action—especially offensive action—was preferable to a wait-and-see approach; that going on the offensive was preferable to standing on the defensive; and that preventive action could and should be used to disarm rogue states, especially Iraq. There are, however, multiple reasons for questioning whether the challenge posed by so-called rogue states[51] post-9/11 was anywhere near as dire as the Bush administration claimed. In this section, I reexamine those claims that collectively constitute the Bush Doctrine, beginning with the question of whether containment was working or failing.

1. WAS CONTAINMENT FAILING?

The George W. Bush administration took it as a given that the sanctions imposed on Iraq in order to thwart or at least impede its WMD programs could not be kept in place indefinitely, nor could United Nations weapons inspectors be kept in Iraq until Saddam's regime mellowed or fell apart. Similarly, the Bush administration took it as a given that Saddam would attempt to reconstitute his WMD programs at some future point, most likely once the sanctions on Iraq had been lifted and UN weapons inspectors withdrawn. On these points there was relatively little controversy. Even the administration's harshest critics shared its belief that Saddam would never give up his quest for WMDs, especially nuclear weapons and ballistic missiles to carry them.[52]

What Saddam dreamed of and what Iraq could accomplish, however, were separate issues. UN weapons inspectors had been withdrawn from Iraq in December 1998 and not allowed to return until November 2002. Within the Bush administration, this was interpreted as an Iraqi window of opportunity during which Iraq would surely attempt to reconstitute its nuclear program. "When [the] inspectors were allowed to return in November 2002, they found that the combination of sanctions and UN inspections had crippled a nuclear program that senior U.S. officials erroneously claimed had been reconstituted."[53] Hence the real issues here were, How long could containment have continued to thwart Iraqi aspirations for WMDs? What costs and risks might the United States have to accept to thwart Saddam's WMD schemes? Could containment work more or less indefinitely against Saddam's Iraq, or could it work only for a limited

7

period? There are in this regard at least three reasons for believing not only that containment had worked well against Saddam Hussein's Iraq in the past but also that it would continue to do so until Saddam himself was removed from power, by either assassination or a coup staged by his enemies, or by natural causes (he turned sixty-six in 2003).

First, as Kenneth Pollack wrote in *Foreign Affairs* roughly a year before the invasion of Iraq, the "central goal of containment over the past decade has been to prevent Saddam—a serial aggressor—from rebuilding Iraq's military power, including its weapons of mass destruction."[54] That goal—rebuilding Iraq's military power—was to a large extent achieved. On the other hand, Iraq never completely recovered from the crushing defeat inflicted upon it during the first Persian Gulf War in 1991. "By early March 1991," Pollack points out, "the Iraqi armed forces had been reduced to a shadow of their former selves."[55] During Operation Desert Storm, the Iraqi Army lost thousands of tanks, artillery, and other armored vehicles, which Saddam's regime was unable to replace because of UN sanctions limiting what Iraq could buy in the aftermath of the first Gulf War. The Iraqi Army in 2003 was about half the size it had been during the invasion of Kuwait in 1990. Its equipment was aging and no match for US and British armor and airpower. The other Iraqi services fared even worse than did the army. During Desert Storm, Iraqi Air Force planes were either destroyed on the ground or flown to Iran (where they were interned).[56] The handful of ships that made up the Iraqi Navy were either sunk at sea or captured in port. Within Iraq, the Kurdish-populated provinces in the north and the Shiite-majority provinces in the south were largely outside Saddam's control. In 1990 Saddam's writ had extended to every corner of Iraq. In 2003, he controlled less than half the country—chiefly the Sunni-majority provinces in western Iraq and the mixed Sunni-Shiite areas around Baghdad.

Second, Saddam's ambitions notwithstanding, Iraq was never able to reconstitute its nuclear weapons programs in the aftermath of the first Gulf War.[57] Even the George W. Bush administration "concluded by the end of 2004 that Iraq had ended all its nuclear, chemical, and biological programs between 1991 and 1995 and did not have stockpiles of these weapons."[58] Why was Iraq unable to reconstitute its WMD programs? Joseph Cirincione points to "an intrusive inspection regime [that] was showing results. . . . UN sanctions and inspectors . . . had been more effective than most realized in disarming Iraq after the 1991 war."[59] Hans Blix likewise claims that "rigorous inspections during the 1990s succeeded, against the expectations of many, in disarming Saddam Hussein's WMD programs." Saddam tried hard—indeed, very hard—to outlast the sanctions regime, by retaining the scientists and documents necessary to restart his WMD programs once the sanctions had been lifted and UN inspectors withdrawn. The UN inspectors were withdrawn in December 1998, but Iraq made almost no progress toward reconstituting its WMD programs between then and December

2002, when the inspectors were allowed to return. Viewed with the wisdom that hindsight provides, the evidence assembled by various postinvasion study groups suggests that it was the sanctions-and-inspections regime that was outlasting Saddam, and not the other way around.[60]

Third, the Bush administration's depiction of containment as passive, lethargic, and thus doomed to fail was very misleading, to say the least. In 2002 and 2003, the choice facing the United States was not between doing nothing and waging all-out preventive war. It was instead between continuing an activist version of containment and invading a sovereign state.[61] Prior to the invasion of Iraq in March 2003, US and British warplanes were striking Iraqi targets several times per week, as part of their enforcement of the no-fly zones over northern and southern Iraq.[62] Iraqi air defenses were completely ineffective, even though in 2001 Saddam ordered an increase in the number of missile attacks on US and British planes enforcing the southern no-fly zone. In response, US and British planes launched air strikes against Iraqi command-and-control facilities in the suburbs of Baghdad, outside the no-fly zone.[63] Iraq was not in a strong position to resist these air strikes, in no small part because Iraqi ground crews learned early on that turning on their air defense radars was likely to attract a swarm of antiradiation missiles that worked very well against Iraqi targets. As Iraqi air defenses were subjected to this relentless attrition, the targets of the US and British air strikes shifted to include any and all Iraqi military targets, and not just those found within or near the no-fly zones. These air strikes, in turn, were chewing up Iraqi ground forces and air defenses at a time when both were greatly reduced compared to a decade earlier and Saddam's control over much of Iraq was tenuous to say the least.

In effect, containment, as it was practiced against Iraq in 2002 and 2003, included multiple activities intended to thwart Saddam's schemes to reconstitute Iraq's WMD programs. On the ground, UN inspectors were combing through Iraqi documents, consulting with Western intelligence services in search of leads to possible Iraqi WMD activities, and staging short-warning and no-warning inspections of suspected WMD sites. Other UN officials controlled much of Iraq's oil revenues, limiting what Iraq could import. At sea, the US and other Western navies were attempting to track and if possible interdict traffic in WMDs and the ballistic missiles that might carry them. In the skies above, US and British warplanes were pummeling Iraqi forces several times per week, in part to render Saddam's control over Iraq even more tenuous, in part to convey the message that there was worse to come if Saddam's regime did not become more compliant with the demands being made of it. In this case, moreover, the threat of worse to come was likely very credible. In 2001, US armed forces had toppled the Taliban regime in Afghanistan and driven its leaders, along with Osama bin Laden and al-Qaeda, out of their Afghan bases and into caves and other hideouts in the mountains along the border with Pakistan. Even a notorious risk taker like Saddam should have realized that what the US had done to Mullah Omar and the Taliban could also be done to Saddam and the Ba'ath Party.

Seen this way, it was not the United States that faced an unpalatable choice between preventive war now and a heightened risk of catastrophe later (the mushroom cloud as smoking gun). It was instead Saddam for whom the future looked increasingly bleak. If he did not come clean about his WMD programs, the Americans and the British would likely continue to shred the armed forces and security services that shielded him from the fury that his own people might unleash, if only they could get their hands upon him. And if he did come clean about the WMD programs, the carefully contrived illusion of invulnerability that he had managed to sustain all these years would likely come crashing down around him, with potentially catastrophic consequences for himself, his family, and his regime.

As this review suggests, containment is not synonymous with inactivity or passivity.[64] Containment may be passive, but it need not be; it can and often does involve a great deal of activity on the part of both the state attempting to thwart a rival's schemes and the target state. Seen this way, containment is best understood as a game of thrust and parry, move and countermove. The target state will likely have strong incentives to attempt to break out of the constraints imposed upon it; hence it will look for ways to challenge or erode the containment regime. The state engaging in containment will strive to block or thwart many if not all of these new challenges. Precisely because both the containing state and the target state will be making multiple moves to uphold or to challenge the status quo more or less simultaneously, the contest between them will likely make a containment policy seem disjointed, reactive, overtaken by events, and so on. It may well appear as if the containing state lacks priorities, is responding to new challenges on an ad hoc basis, or (worst of all) is being jerked around or outwitted by the target state. Appearances, however, can be deceiving, and they often are, especially if a superpower is involved.

Superpowers are well suited to engage in this kind of game with a smaller state. Precisely because its resources are so vast, a superpower can afford to take on the challenge of blocking or thwarting a miscreant's initiatives. Containment works, Matthew Kroenig points out, because superpowers can find many ways to pursue it, such as widening the scope of containment to include influencing the behavior of third parties. Argentina, for example, "conceded to U.S. pressure and canceled a proposed sale of plutonium reprocessing technology to Libya in 1985."[65] Alternatively, a superpower can confidently expect to outlast a smaller challenger. Regimes based largely on terror, like that of Saddam Hussein's Iraq, rarely outlast the tyrant who created them.[66] And when Saddam and his sons finally did meet their end, the United States was still there, ready to pick up the pieces and reassemble whatever was left into a new Iraq.

Conversely, containment can be and often is selective in its application, in the sense of not trying to solve every problem between a pair of states once and for all.[67] Over the short term, containment is fundamentally defensive in nature; it seeks to block or thwart the target state's attempts to change the status quo. Over the long term, containment seeks to buy time that can be used to resolve disagreements, lessen tensions, and even promote reconciliation. Policy makers intent on containing a foe are more likely to be concerned with shoring up defenses than jumping through windows of opportunity, which is probably a good thing. A containment policy, artfully designed and executed, can be a very good generator of options. By freezing the status quo, so to speak, a containment policy provides time to rethink the current mix of threats, sanctions, and military actions, and to invent new options for consideration by policy makers.[68] Invading the target state, on the other hand, is likely to close off options rather than provide new ones. History can't be rewound and replayed; once an invasion force crosses a border, it is impossible to go back to the status quo ante.

2. WAS DETERRENCE WEAKENING?

During the Cold War, Joseph Stalin, Mao Zedong, and Nikita Khrushchev were all considered, at one time or another, to be "unbalanced dictators with weapons of mass destruction," yet the combination of deterrence and containment worked remarkably well against them.[69] Indeed, "deterrence proved more robust than many expected during the Cold War, as the superpowers proved to be largely reluctant to risk nuclear or even major conventional war with each other."[70] To make the case that deterrence and containment were not enough, President Bush in his January 2002 State of the Union address described Iraq, Iran, and North Korea as an "axis of evil," against which traditional notions of deterrence would not work. "The phrase," John Lewis Gaddis points out, "confused more than it clarified." This was especially so since "Saddam Hussein, the Iranian mullahs, and Kim Jong Il are hardly the only tyrants around, nor are their ties to one another evident. Nor was it clear why containment and deterrence would not work against these tyrants, since they were all more into survival than suicide. Their lifestyles tend more toward palaces than caves."[71]

North Korea and Iraq did strike their neighbors in 1950 (Korean War), 1980 (the Iraq-Iran War), and 1990 (the first Persian Gulf War), but these, as Richard Betts points out, were all cases in which "the United States failed to deter them. Indeed, Washington gave them a green light in all three cases. . . . When the United States has posed deterrent threats against Iraq and North Korea, they have worked."[72] Saddam in particular was rash and reckless, but he never did anything that "Washington told him would be suicidal."[73]

3. TIME IS ON WHOSE SIDE?

Particularly in the United States, a foreign policy aimed at buying time has often been derided as weak and wimpy, unmuscular and unmanly, and therefore un-American. There are, however, at least three reasons why playing for time sometimes makes great good sense.

First, in an anarchic world, time can be a valuable commodity, and buying more of it can be a wise use of scarce resources. As Richard Betts points out, within a few years of calls for preventive war against the Soviet Union in 1949 and 1950, "Stalin was dead," and his successors were much less fearsome. In the 1960s "Mao was considered as fanatically aggressive and crazy as Saddam is today." Within a few years, however, the United States and the People's Republic of China had not only reconciled but "had become tacit allies against the Soviet Union."[74]

Second, nuclear reversal—namely, abandoning programs aimed at production and deployment of nuclear weapons—occurs more often than is generally realized. Writing in 2007, Joseph Cirincione and Carl Robichaud pointed out that "more countries have abandoned nuclear weapons programs over the past fifteen years than have tried to acquire them. These were not easy cases: Argentina, Brazil, South Africa, Ukraine, Belarus, Kazakhstan, Iraq, and most recently Libya all abandoned programs and, in four cases, weapons. No country has commenced a nuclear weapons program since the end of the Cold War."[75] Nuclear reversal can take many forms, ranging from dismantling existing weapons (South Africa) and termination of ongoing research programs (Argentina, Brazil) to modest steps sideways or backward in response to external pressures.[76] The latter may seem inconsequential, but there is often more here than first meets the eye. Every step sideways or backward means a delay of months or even years prior to acquisition of an actual nuclear weapon, and while these delays play themselves out, the leaders who set these programs in motion grow older, their health often takes a turn for the worse, their weapons programs grow moribund, their scientists retire or move elsewhere.

Third, buying time provides the leaders of an aspiring nuclear power an opportunity to change their minds, reorder their priorities, and set new goals for themselves and their state. Libya, as Cirincione points out, "clearly gained prestige by its 2003 decision to abandon its nuclear weapons program." Libya's leader, Muammar al-Qaddafi, was once widely known as the "mad dog of the Middle East." In 2003, however, the second President Bush called Qaddafi "a model" that other leaders should strive to emulate, while Tony Blair put his stamp of approval on what Qaddafi had done by visiting Libya in March 2004.[77]

4. IS ACTING ALWAYS BETTER THAN WAITING?

One reason for questioning whether acting is indeed preferable to waiting is that "it is almost never possible, however, to know that war is inevitable. The most bitter conflicts sometimes cool with time, sometimes even turning enemies into allies. . . . Preventive war is almost always a bad choice."[78]

Second, acting too soon or in haste carries with it its own set of costs and risks. The George W. Bush administration's first *National Security Strategy* (2002) defined rogue states as those that (1) "brutalize their own people and squander their national resources for the personal gain of the rulers"; (2) "display no regard for international law, threaten their neighbors, and callously violate international treaties to which they are party"; (3) are determined to acquire WMDs; (4) sponsor terrorism around the globe; and (5) reject basic human values and hate the United States and everything for which it stands.[79] The 2002 strategy document, however, mentioned only two such rogue states: Iraq and North Korea. Those two, along with Iran, were mentioned in President Bush's January 2002 State of the Union address as composing an "axis of evil" that was hostile to the West and especially to the United States. Iran, however, was not mentioned in the September 2002 strategy paper, and a senior Bush administration official told journalists that Iran was not considered a rogue state. Efforts to disarm North Korea, the official continued, were then focused on the diplomatic track.[80] "We are not making the case that we'll just go around pre-empting every threat we see," the official continued. "It's a pretty special category, a pretty limited category."[81] Limiting the number of preemptive targets to just one—Iraq—would indeed make that a "pretty special category," but it's also hard to see how this could be a truly activist foreign policy and a true break from the past if other miscreants were just ignored or rationalized away.

Third, the Bush administration's reluctance to apply its new doctrine against North Korea and Iran, both of which in 2002–3 were arguably greater threats than Saddam Hussein's Iraq, suggests that implementation of a preemptive attack strategy was likely to be difficult in practice, making the doctrine "appear somewhat hollow."[82] In this regard, it was especially difficult for the Bush administration to explain in public why North Korea "proved too dangerous a target for U.S. preemption, and Iraq did not."[83] North Korea already had one or a few nuclear warheads, and it was working on an ICBM to carry them. In effect, the same President Bush who argued forcefully and repeatedly that the United States could not allow unbalanced dictators to acquire WMDs seemed content to tolerate precisely that in the case of North Korea. In effect, the same Bush administration that argued repeatedly in public that deterrence aimed at Iraq was bound to fail nonetheless managed to suggest through its actions that deterrence was working very well, at least for North Korea.

Fourth and finally, the contrast between the way the George W. Bush administration dealt with Iraq on one hand and Iran and North Korea on the other suggests that the United States invaded Iraq in 2003 not because Iraq was strong and thus an imminent danger, but rather because Iraq was weak and thus an easy target relative to Iran and North Korea. The reason for invading Iraq in 2003 was not so much to neutralize an imminent threat from Iraq as it was to prevent Iraq from becoming the kind of threat that North Korea had already become. Vice President Richard Cheney used precisely this rationale in remarks before the Veterans of Foreign Wars in 2002: the United States had to deal with Saddam Hussein now rather than later, because the United States could not afford to "let him get stronger before we do anything about it."[84] Dealing with enemies in a selective fashion is not unreasonable in an anarchic world, but the Bush Doctrine was stated in universal terms. The contrast between what the Bush administration said it would do and what it actually did was a classic case of ending up with the worst of both worlds. The Bush doctrine was stated in such universal and bellicose terms that it frightened away potential allies in Europe who might otherwise have contributed a lot to a strategy based on containment and deterrence. Meanwhile the exceptions and hesitations suggested to potential targets in Iran and North Korea that they could indeed defy the United States and get away with it, despite the invasion of Iraq in 2003.

5. IS OFFENSE ALWAYS BETTER THAN DEFENSE?

During the Cold War, containment took many forms, one of which was not well-known but very effective nonetheless. This version of containment is what Thomas Schelling calls "relinquishing the initiative," which occurs when a state practicing containment is able to shift responsibility for initiating hostilities from itself to the target state.[85] Seizing the initiative and going on the offensive are often hailed as the hallmarks of a vigorous and therefore a successful policy.[86] In this context, seizing the initiative means taking the fight to the enemy, and fighting on our terms rather than theirs. An important problem with this approach, however, is that a more creative mind-set might well raise the question of whether there is any need to fight at all. A superpower like the United States is well-situated to get its way without fighting. "U.S. military power," as Karl Mueller and his colleagues quite rightly point out, "gives Washington unrivaled ability to launch anticipatory attacks, but it also reduces the need for them. The more powerful a state is, the more likely it will be able to deter or defend itself against the threats it faces. . . . The world is full of political actors that could attack the

United States, but that are extremely unlikely to dare to do so, and which U.S. armed forces could easily deal with if they did."[87]

During the Cold War "relinquishing the initiative" worked well as a way of blocking or parrying Soviet initiatives. During the Soviet-imposed Berlin Blockade (1948–49), the United States and Britain responded with an airlift of supplies to Berlin. The Americans and the British were so closely identified with the airlift and its accomplishments that stopping short of a return to the status quo ante would have made them appear so weak and irresolute that they could hardly be counted on to protect themselves, much less other vulnerable countries in western Europe. On the other hand, once the Americans and the British had proved that they could sustain the airlift indefinitely, all that they had to do to avoid defeat was to keep on doing what they had already been doing, that is, sustain the airlift until the Soviets grew frustrated and quit.

The Soviet situation was even worse. In launching and then sustaining the airlift, the Americans and the British managed to shift to the Soviets the onus for deciding whether to allow the airlift to continue, and every plane that landed in Berlin was silent testimony that the Soviets had seriously misjudged what they might be able to get away with. Alternatively, the Soviets could settle for an ignominious withdrawal. The longer the airlift continued, the greater the likelihood that Soviet options would continue to narrow: either allow the airlift to continue more or less indefinitely with all the drawbacks listed above, or resort to force—a fearsome prospect considering that the United States had a de facto monopoly on nuclear weapons and was not at all reluctant to remind the world that it did so. Stopping the airlift by resorting to force would have required the Soviets to shoot down one or more US or British aircraft—an act of war for sure, and with consequences that likely would have been catastrophic for the Soviet Union. Conversely, keeping the airlift going required of the Americans and the British only that they keep doing what they already were doing.

During the Cuban Missile Crisis, the US naval blockade of Cuba likewise "put the onus on Soviet policy-makers to avoid war."[88] If the Soviet challenge was to be successful, the Soviets would have to sneak their missiles into Cuba before the Americans found out what they were up to. The Americans, however, did indeed discover what the Soviets were doing in Cuba, which put the Soviets in a very difficult position. The Americans could surely sustain the quarantine of Cuba (a blockade in everything but name) indefinitely, and they had powerful incentives to do so, rather than run the risk of being humiliated by an opponent that had already outmaneuvered and outthought them.[89] Once the US blockade was in place, each new day was a reminder that the Soviets' options were essentially two: try to run the blockade, firing at any US naval vessel that sought to thwart Soviet naval access to Cuba, or slink away, taking their missiles with them. Once again the Americans had successfully transferred to the Soviets the responsibility for choosing to retreat (an unpalatable choice) or fight (a worse choice).

6. DOES PREVENTIVE ACTION WORK RELIABLY?

Surely it must rank as one of the great paradoxes of the post-1945 era that perhaps the only outcome worse than a failed preventive war would be a successful one. During the early Cold War years, "none of the advocates of preventive war had an answer for the question of what to do with the Soviet Union after the conflict."[90] Similarly, none of the advocates of the Bush Doctrine knew what to do with Iraq in the aftermath of the invasion that toppled Saddam Hussein's regime. And none of the advocates of a preventive strike on Iran have been able to provide a convincing forecast of what would happen once such an attack had been carried out.

Others May Help

In addition to making the case that containment was hopelessly outdated and outclassed by rogue states and ruthless nonstate actors, the George W. Bush administration sought to line up the widest possible coalition of democracies that could provide political cover for war against Iraq and contribute to the war effort by fighting effectively if needed. The Bush administration was at times openly contemptuous of containment, which it saw as incapable of pursuing the theory of victory it was creating to replace the previous version based on containment and deterrence. The new version was also expected to guide US efforts during the second war with Iraq and beyond.

Regardless of whether containment was succeeding or failing, we should expect to witness some behavioral consequences either way. If containment really was widely perceived to be a political and military failure, then we would expect to find one or more of the small Persian Gulf sheikhdoms bandwagoning with either Iran or Iraq, depending on which of those two ambitious regional powers posed the greater immediate danger for the small states involved. Middle powers like Britain or France would likely prefer to pass the buck to the United States. Buck-passing would enable them to transfer responsibility from themselves to the United States, on the grounds that US forces had far more power projection capability and thus were much better suited to take on the responsibility for containing and deterring Iraq or Iran. If the United States were to refuse to accept the buck, middle powers (Britain, France, and so on) might turn to chain-ganging, even though this would run the risk of entanglement in a war they would prefer to avoid, in view of their belief that containment was already dead or dying.[91]

Conversely, if containment was widely perceived to be working, then the various Arab sheikhdoms—states that might otherwise have kept their distance from the United States—would be more willing to align openly with the United States in the hope that the Americans would accept them as partners and not deadbeats.

The Strengths of Democracies

Containment, the preceding sections suggest, is particularly well-suited for a prolonged struggle between a state intent on upholding the status quo and a state determined to change it. Democracies, especially the United States, are particularly well-suited to wage such a struggle, for two reasons.

First, in democracies, the never-ending competition for higher office (both elective and appointive) puts a premium on new ideas that can enhance a candidate's attractiveness. Stanley Renshon, for example, cites the George W. Bush administration's "drying up bank access to North Korea" as a "highly inventive, non-lethal and successful move."[92] It was a clever move for sure, but the larger point here is that clever people with clever ideas are always pushing themselves and their ideas forward in a democracy. Democracies may not always be able to outfight their opponents, but they can usually outthink them.[93]

Second, in the United States, as Samuel Huntington and Kenneth Waltz both pointed out as far back as the 1960s, the division of power between the executive and legislative branches and the diffusion of power within these two branches mean that many people must sign off on a new policy before anything can be done about it.[94] There are many points within the US government at which action can be blocked or vetoed, and neither is there anyone—not even the president—who can simply dictate what a political outcome will be. Presidential power in the United States, in Richard Neustadt's famous phrase, is the "power to persuade."[95] Would-be political innovators must persuade others whose policy preferences may run along different tracks. New ideas are thus subjected to intense scrutiny, which only the best are likely to survive. At any given time, the public debate over what to do next and how to do it may seem messy and disorderly, but this is actually an essential filtering mechanism, accepting the better ideas and rejecting the rest.

The Plan of This Book

In fairness to the George W. Bush administration, some of its most senior members did speak favorably of containment and deterrence. Secretary of State Colin Powell, for example, told the Senate Foreign Relations Committee on July 9, 2002, "[it is not] as if all other strategies and doctrines have gone away and suddenly preemption is the only strategy doctrine. That's just not the case." Similarly, Condoleezza Rice told journalists on October 1, 2002, "The National Security Strategy does not overturn five decades of doctrine and jettison either containment or deterrence. These strategic concepts are and will continue to be employed where appropriate."[96]

But just when and where would containment and deterrence be more appropriate than preemption and prevention? The Clinton administration, for example, took it as a given that "once the oil starts flowing again, Washington must assume that Saddam will renege on long-term monitoring and begin rebuilding his WMD programs." But instead of using this as a pretext for war, the Clinton administration suggested that sanctions should be maintained during "a long period of testing of the permanent monitoring system."[97] The Clinton administration expected a lengthy period of rivalry with Iraq (but not open warfare); the George W. Bush administration believed it imperative to strike Iraq, and better sooner than later. The Clinton administration believed that it had "forged a realistic and sustainable policy," and that it was "still very much within our power to prevail."[98] The Bush administration believed that hesitation and delay would only make things worse.

The foregoing suggests that one final, and considerable, advantage of a containment policy is that there are many different ways that containment can be pursued. A containment policy is bounded only by the imaginations and the resourcefulness of those who set it in motion and then carry it out. There is, to be sure, a downside here—the implementers may lose patience and flit from one approach to another. Impending elections may put pressure on the implementers to do something, anything, to produce at least the appearance of getting results. The desire for consensus within democracies may hinder the containing state's freedom of action, resulting in lowest-common-denominator policies or even contradictory policies aimed at maintaining public support, at least until the next election.[99]

In the rest of this book, I develop an alternative to the theory of victory offered by the Bush Doctrine. Whereas the Bush Doctrine called for being quick to resort to force, I offer containment, with its willingness to accept a long-term rivalry, as a plausible alternative. Whereas the Bush Doctrine advocated seizing the initiative, I offer relinquishing the initiative. Whereas the Bush Doctrine emphasized unilateral action against a rogue state like Iran, I explore whether and when other states will help the United States. Whereas the Bush Doctrine lamented the weaknesses of democracies, I argue that democracies are more innovative and tenacious than generally realized.

In the next five chapters, I argue further that a containment strategy is easier to create and sustain than is generally realized. I base this argument on three subordinate claims. First, I argue that relinquishing the initiative is often an effective way of thwarting an opponent's plots and schemes. Second, states that are far from the United States but geographically close to aspiring regional hegemons, such as Saddam's Iraq or an Iran ruled by clerics, will feel threatened by these aggressive states and will thus sign on to help the United States thwart or block whatever these ambitious regional powers might do. Third, democracies are well-suited to blocking the rise of would-be hegemons, because they have great inventiveness and staying power.

In the rest of this book, I test these claims against the five case studies presented in chapters 2 through 6. The more that the participants in these cases exhibit the behaviors discussed above (relinquishing the initiative, attracting allies among nearby states, and displaying inventiveness and tenacity), the better suited these states will be to sustain a long-term containment policy. If, however, the participants in these case studies do not exhibit the behaviors predicted by proponents of containment, then the Bush Doctrine will likely be called on to fill the gap that containment has proved unable to plug on its own.

Containing Qaddafi's Libya

On December 19, 2003, Libya announced that it was giving up all its programs aimed at acquiring WMDs. As part of the agreement, all of Libya's WMD facilities were to be destroyed and Libya's nuclear equipment was to be sent to the United States.[1] This announcement was hailed by many in the United States as proof that the policies espoused by the George W. Bush administration were succeeding, in the sense of making the world a safer place.[2] Nonetheless, as Etel Solingen points out, Libya's renunciation of its WMD programs occurred only after roughly thirty years of Libyan defiance of the nonproliferation regime, during which Libya repeatedly tried but failed to bring its WMD programs to fruition.[3] What happened during those thirty years? Did something akin to containment serve to block Libya's path toward acquiring WMDs? Was containment even tried? If so, how well did it work, and why?

In retrospect, the case of Colonel Qaddafi's Libya should have posed a very demanding test for a containment policy. Qaddafi had virtually unchallengeable access to Libya's oil wealth, which he used to finance his various plots and schemes. Qaddafi was also known to be greatly resentful of the United States, in no small part because America—with its high-tech military, its global reach, its endlessly inventive economy—stood for everything that he hoped the Arab world, or at least Libya, might someday become. There were also terrorist gangs and splinter groups ready to do the bidding of an ambitious dictator who sought to inflict harm on the United States and the American people. Qaddafi, in other words, posed a clear and present danger. He had the *means*, he had a *motive*, and he had multiple *opportunities* that he could exploit should he decide to strike at the United States. But while hindsight suggests that Colonel Qaddafi's Libya should have posed a demanding challenge for the United States, for the most part it did not, and it is instructive to explore the reasons why.

The United States, for its part, never formally announced that its policy was to contain Libya during the thirty-plus years of mutual antagonism between them. Even so, virtually everything that five US administrations—those of Jimmy Carter, Ronald Reagan, George H. W. Bush (Bush 41), Bill Clinton, and George W. Bush (Bush 43)—said and did regarding Libya during their more than thirty years in office strongly suggests that containment, in the sense of thwarting, preventing, or defeating Colonel Qaddafi's numerous plots and schemes, was indeed the goal of US policy toward Libya. Chester Crocker, assistant secretary of state for Africa, said early in Ronald Reagan's first term as president that the United States was "deeply concerned about Libyan interventionism in Africa and in particular the presence of Libyan troops in Chad."[4] Nearly five years later, Vice President George II. W. Bush told a press conference on April 1, 1986, "Qaddafi has not changed his spots and it doesn't look to me like he's going to change them." Lest there be any doubt, Vice President Bush also said he was ready to tell anyone who asked "how strongly we feel about Qaddafi, what a menace he is."[5]

On the other hand, Libya was not Grenada. A military operation aimed at ousting Qaddafi by force, Pentagon sources estimated, could require as many as six divisions, or about ninety thousand soldiers.[6] If Qaddafi couldn't or wouldn't change, and military action was deemed infeasible, then all that was left was containment—in other words, keep Qaddafi bottled up, thwart his ambitions, defeat his schemes, and so on. For a superpower like the United States, this was a very reachable goal. Libya did indeed sit on top of billions of barrels of an especially valuable kind of crude oil, the kind that could easily be refined into valuable products like gasoline and aviation fuel. But oil was about all that Qaddafi's Libya had going for it. On just about every other measure of national capability, it came up short—indeed, far short—of being a state whose opinion mattered. Qaddafi's Libya had a population of only about three million during the 1980s, a failing economy, severe food shortages, virtually nothing to sell or trade except oil, and an army judged to be "one of the most inept on earth."[7] In view of these well-known limits on Libya's ability to get its way with other states, what did Qaddafi do that necessitated a containment policy by the United States? What was it about him that so annoyed and energized US policy makers?

Why Contain Libya?

Muammar al-Qaddafi came to power in Libya on September 1, 1969, when he was an army captain.[8] Qaddafi, along with other army officers, staged a bloodless coup that ousted the regime of King Idris, which was both corrupt and incompetent.[9] Once in power, he positioned himself as an opponent of just about everything the United States said and did in its foreign policy. Seen from Washington, what made Qaddafi both distinctive and worrisome was not that he was a dictator with a grudge against the United States—the world already had lots of those people when Qaddafi took control in Libya. It was instead the way in which he hatched and then pursued his myriad schemes that made Qaddafi's Libya different from other, run-of-the-mill authoritarian regimes. During his first decade in power, he had the "rare distinction of fighting with or meddling in the internal affairs of every one of Libya's neighbors."[10] He almost always had multiple schemes under way, so that if one door was slammed in his face, there would be others that he could try instead.[11] Plus he had a knack for making a nuisance of himself, and for doing things in ways that were almost guaranteed to antagonize the United States. Regardless of what was thought and said about him, he was able to earn a place for himself and for Libya on the global stage that was much more prominent than if he had been just another egomaniac using his country's oil wealth to buy some friends and stave off his enemies.[12] Qaddafi never ceased being an irritant to US officials, at least not until 2003. Democrats and Republicans, liberals and conservatives, activists and isolationists—it didn't matter who was running the show in Washington. Colonel Qaddafi, "the quintessential troublemaker," somehow managed to antagonize them all.[13]

The Americans had multiple reasons of their own to feel outraged about and even threatened by Qaddafi's regime in Libya. Qaddafi's determination to obstruct whatever the United States was trying to accomplish was as predictable as tomorrow's sunrise and about as subtle as a terrorist massacre of innocent—indeed, apolitical—civilians.[14] The trouble with Qaddafi, the former secretary of state George Shultz wrote in his memoir, was that every time he was put "back in his box," where US officials thought he belonged, "he didn't stay there."[15] Precisely because he was relentlessly ambitious and endlessly provocative, Qaddafi was a dictator who simply could not be left to his own devices.

Despite all this, invading Libya was judged out of the question, as was assassination. Libya was about one-fifth the size of the continental United States, and 97 percent of that was desert. Invading Libya would have required much more than just a hastily cobbled together invasion force to seize and secure the entire country.[16] Assassination was ruled out in part for the precedent it would set and in part because of the damage it would do to the United States' standing in the rest of the world. Nonetheless, US officials let it be known that Qaddafi was one of the targets of the US bombing raid on Tripoli and Benghazi on April 14, 1986. "We hoped we would get him," one US official involved in planning the raid said, "but nobody was sure where he would be that night." If Qaddafi's behavior was judged intolerable, if he could not or would not change, and if invasion and assassination were ruled out for military or political reasons, then all that was left to US policy makers was to keep him contained, block his schemes, thwart his ambitions, and wait for the day when his enemies or old age caught up with him.[17]

This is not to suggest that containing Qaddafi would be easy to achieve and sustain. Qaddafi's refusal to "stay in his box" was well-known. So too were his ingenuity and notoriety when it came to judging how far he could go when challenging the status quo, without bringing down on himself either an invasion or an attempted assassination. Qaddafi's fine-tuned political instincts were an important part of the explanation why a state as militarily feeble and resource poor[18] as Libya could nonetheless stir up so much trouble that it became the target of a containment policy led by the United States that ultimately lasted for decades. This, however, is only part of the story regarding Libya. There were other reasons why the Carter, Reagan, Bush 41, Clinton, and Bush 43 administrations deemed Qaddafi's Libya to be enough of a threat that it required a determined effort by the United States and its allies to contain Qaddafi's schemes and thwart his ambitions to overthrow the status quo.

First, Qaddafi was an inveterate troublemaker, always on the lookout for opportunities to meddle in the internal affairs of nearby states. Qaddafi was not naive; he understood that a small state like Libya had to pick its spots carefully for its armed forces to be effective. But he was also a dreamer, yearning for situations in which the use of force by Libya might bring to power new rulers who would be more amenable to Qaddafi's schemes to reunite the Arab nation. There were, of course, important limitations on what Qaddafi could hope to accomplish in this regard. Libya was hardly a military juggernaut. What Qaddafi really wanted was a share of the spoils of war, but without having to fight for them. When Qaddafi did commit Libyan forces to battle, they almost always lost due to poor training and leadership. Qaddafi himself "used less sophisticated cryptographic equipment and codes, so the NSA [National Security Agency] broke them consistently. . . . Qaddafi's operatives were sloppy, they left trails."[19] To square this circle, Qaddafi often sought to intimidate neighboring states into believing that they had little choice but to play along with whatever scheme he was hawking. Libya's armed forces were few in number and not very capable, so Qaddafi sought to make them *appear* more formidable by buying billions of dollars' worth of Soviet military equipment—fighter jets, tanks, surface-to-air missiles—in numbers far beyond what Libya's relatively small armed forces could absorb. Libyan purchases in this regard were so great that half or more of what they bought from the Soviets was left in storage on Libyan military bases, prompting speculation in the West that those purchases were precursors to the creation of a Soviet rapid deployment force.[20] The personnel who made up this force would arrive in Libya by air, where they would join up with the Soviet equipment that was waiting for them, thereby creating an instant expeditionary force.[21] As long as Libya was flush with cash from oil exports, the Soviets were willing sellers. But as the price of oil (and Libya's cash reserves) dwindled during the 1980s, even the Soviets became more cautious about getting too deeply entangled with Qaddafi, whose schemes involved more risk than they cared to take on.[22] Even so, all that new weaponry just waiting to be unpacked provided Qaddafi both with a lure that he could dream of dangling in front of the Soviets at some opportune moment in the future (or, alternatively, some moment of desperation, when he might need a protector) and with a tool that Qaddafi could use to intimidate Libya's neighbors.[23]

Second, Qaddafi fancied himself to be a great political thinker whose writings and speeches put him in the same group as Karl Marx and Mao Zedong. His track record, however, suggests an opportunistic streak in his thinking, in the sense that he was always looking for ways to score some points at the expense of the United States, or even pile on when things were going badly for the Americans, as they were for the Carter administration during November and December 1979. In November, the US embassy in Tehran was seized by an Iranian mob and the embassy staff held hostage, except for a lucky few who were able to find refuge at the Canadian embassy. This was followed by the seizure of Islam's holiest site, the Grand Mosque in Mecca, Saudi Arabia, and then by an attack on the American embassy in Islamabad, Pakistan, which was burned to the ground by a mob incited by rumors that the United States had been the mastermind behind the seizure, earlier in November, of the Grand Mosque. Qaddafi's response to these events came on December 2, 1979, when the Libyan police and security services actively encouraged—indeed, gave directions to—a mob that torched the US embassy in Tripoli, Libya.[24] On December 10, a little more than one week after the attack on the US embassy in Tripoli, Qaddafi had the nerve to tell a journalist that he, Qaddafi, had personally assured President Carter "that we can and will protect the embassies in our country."[25]

After the casual way in which Qaddafi had shrugged off the destruction of the US embassy in Tripoli, it may have seemed as if things could hardly get any worse between the United States and Libya, but they did indeed get worse, and sooner rather than later. In January 1980, Qaddafi threatened President Carter with an oil embargo if Carter did not "radically change American policy in the Middle East" during what Qaddafi evidently expected would be President Carter's second term. This was, Qaddafi threatened, the United States' "last chance" to avoid an embargo.[26] In April 1980, Libya launched a campaign of intimidation, harassment, and even assassination directed against Libyan students and political exiles in Europe and the United States, aimed at compelling Libyans living abroad to return home. The Carter administration responded by expelling two Libyan diplomats posted to the United States, who had been distributing among Libyan students in the United States documents calling for the assassination of

Qaddafi's opponents.[27] In May 1980, the United States expelled four more Libyan diplomats on the grounds that they had been sent abroad to intimidate and even kill opponents of Qaddafi who were living in exile in London, Rome, and Washington.[28]

Third, Qaddafi's claim that Libya could and would protect foreign embassies, made just nine days after the US embassy in Tripoli had been ransacked by a mob, suggested to the Carter administration, and even more so to the future US president Ronald Reagan, that Qaddafi was an inveterate liar. "I don't think he's capable of telling the truth about these things," President Reagan said about Qaddafi at a press conference in January 1986, referring to the presence of terrorist training camps in Libya.[29] Three years later, President Reagan was saying the same things about Qaddafi: "I haven't believed anything he has said in a long time."[30] Qaddafi, for his part, contributed to his habitual liar persona through his repeated claims that he had no formal office in the Libyan government and thus was not involved in the day-to-day workings of the Libyan government, when it was obvious to anyone who took a moment or two to look that almost nothing happened in Libya without Qaddafi's approval. Qaddafi, meanwhile, went out of his way to meddle in the affairs of neighboring states, all the while insisting that he had nothing to do with what was going on there (more lies). During his reign, Qaddafi was rarely credited with being a patient man, but he could be patient if his schemes required it. His schemes on occasion took years to hatch and then play themselves out. Thwarting those schemes would require similar patience and diligence, two qualities that a containment policy, properly conceived, should have in abundance.

Fourth, as seen especially by the Reagan administration, Qaddafi and his regime were not content merely to hurl insults and accusations at their enemies, both real and imagined. Instead, Qaddafi's regime was engaged in a dizzying variety of plots and schemes that, taken as a whole, suggested Libyan-led attempts to topple governments all across northern Africa, especially those that were friendly to the United States.[31] Qaddafi, in the words of Alexander Haig, President Reagan's first secretary of state, was "arming an international conspiracy of leftist cutthroats with Soviet weapons and explosives, and he was threatening Chad and Sudan with conventional military power."[32] Qaddafi, Haig continued, had "turned his country into a nest of terrorists," who then established themselves in "every moderate Arab country."[33] Even more galling to Haig and the rest of Reagan's national security team was the discovery that Qaddafi was meddling in Western Hemisphere affairs.[34] Qaddafi gave the Sandinistas in Nicaragua three hundred million dollars with which to buy Soviet weapons, which they then used to fight the Contras as part of the Nicaraguan civil war.[35] Qaddafi's incendiary effect on US policy makers, especially those in the Reagan administration, is readily apparent in Haig's comment that he wanted to "bloody Qaddafi's nose" and "increase the flow of pine boxes [from Chad] back to Libya."[36]

A fifth and final reason why Washington was deeply concerned about the rivalry with Qaddafi can be traced to the way Qaddafi practically flaunted his apparent successes at redrawing the map of northern Africa. Despite Libya's obvious weaknesses, Qaddafi's blend of charisma, daring, and determination, plus the sheer number of plots that he was supporting, led some observers to conclude that he might actually be winning the contest with the United States, or at least that he was "on a roll," in the sense of holding his own against a superpower.[37] A good example in this regard would be the blatantly obvious way in which Libyan forces had crossed the border into Chad in October 1980, followed by Libya's annexing a strip of Chadian territory along the border with Libya. The Libyans made no effort to conceal or legitimize what they were doing, which suggested to many observers that Qaddafi and Libya must be doing very well indeed in their attempts to destabilize northern Africa. More important, Libyan meddling in Chad was inextricably tied to the issue of a Libyan atomic bomb. As seen by observers who followed the proliferation issue, the road to a Libyan atomic bomb ran through Chad and Niger, both of which were uranium rich and cash poor.[38]

Alternatively, Qaddafi's apparent belief that a militarily weak state like Libya could nonetheless hold its own in a decades-long struggle against the United States suggested to some that he must surely be less than rational. "There is an irrationality in Qaddafi's make-up," a British analyst claimed, "that defies explanation and makes it virtually impossible to correctly assess his policies by any normal yardstick."[39] Qaddafi, an influential American pundit wrote on the *New York Times* op-ed page, was an "irrational, militarist dictator."[40] Even President Reagan could not resist taking an occasional shot at Qaddafi, saying at a press conference in January 1986, "I find he's not only a barbarian, but he's flaky."[41]

Qaddafi may have been unpredictable, but he was not a "madman." "He comes across as cool, self-confident, and shrewd," Strobe Talbott wrote regarding his two interviews with the Libyan dictator. "He radiates authority, confidence, and self control."[42] "Nobody should think the colonel is mad," a European diplomat suggested. "He is not mad at all. He doesn't know Europe or America or the world, but he knows how to play with the United States."[43] An Israeli analyst agreed: "The key is that Qaddafi isn't crazy. He wants to survive, personally, and he wants his regime to survive."[44]

Indeed, Qaddafi's behavior suggests that he is much better understood as a resilient survivor who, at roughly the midpoint of his reign, had already overcome multiple plots and attempted coups aimed directly at him, including attempts on his life.[45] Unlike the vision of an irrational egomaniac that Americans often projected onto Qaddafi, his record suggests that his moves were always carefully hedged, in the sense of having fallback positions in place that he could turn to if he needed them, such as his threats to seek admission to the Warsaw Pact whenever the United States seemed to be moving in the direction of more forceful action against Libya.[46] His record also suggests that he took care to strike a balance between meddling in the affairs of his neighbors and periodic charm offensives that occasionally culminated in vaguely worded treaties of union between Libya and other African states. Those treaties, however, had a very short shelf life, remaining in place for maybe a year or two before being discarded as outdated and thus an impediment to whatever new schemes Qaddafi was by then pursuing.[47] He was also careful to nurture his relations with foreign oil companies operating in Libya. Even after the United States and Libya clashed militarily over the Gulf of Sidra in 1981, "none of the 2,000 U.S. oil company workers in the country were molested or abused."[48] In retrospect, it's hard to see how Qaddafi could have survived, much less maintain near total control over Libya for more than forty years, without having outstanding political instincts capable of weighing risks and opportunities.[49]

At roughly the same time that these events were being played out, observers of the US-Libyan relationship were for the most part fixated on how quickly those relations had degenerated, during President Reagan's first year in office, "to the level of open venom."[50] Yet what stands out even more so to an observer blessed with decades of hindsight is the relative ease with which a superpower like the United States could thwart the plots and schemes of a small state like Libya. And the United States could do this not just once but again and again. Contrary to the conventional wisdom that Qaddafi's Libya was a hard target, Qaddafi and Libya were actually easy targets for the United States to take on. Hindsight suggests that there were at least five reasons why this was so.

Why Libya Was an Easy Target

In retrospect, the same stratagems and maneuvers that allowed Qaddafi to cling to power for more than four decades were also the actions that rendered him vulnerable to a US-led containment policy. First, Qaddafi meddled constantly with Libya's armed forces, especially the army, which he considered the principal threat to his continued rule.[51] To hedge against a coup, Qaddafi deliberately kept Libya's armed forces disorganized and ill-prepared for war, so that they could not be used against him the way he and other army officers had used the armed forces to carry out their coup against the Libyan monarchy. He did this in part by repeated purges of the officer corps and by "moving officers from post to post to prevent them from establishing positions of strength."[52] In Qaddafi's Libya, officers were "forbidden in barracks after 3 p.m.," and troops received "a minimum of ammunition."[53] Qaddafi stayed in power, not because he was immensely popular, but because his East German and North Korean military advisers were there when he needed them. Even so, in August 1980, a brigade-sized unit of the Libyan Army mutinied, apparently hoping that they could and would receive help from the Egyptian Army.[54] In 1984 it was the garrison in Benghazi that mutinied. This latter incident was not put down until the Libyan Air Force bombed the barracks that the mutineers were occupying.[55] Writing in the mid-1980s, Lisa Anderson estimated that in the years since 1980, there had been "over a dozen serious attempts to spark [Qaddafi's] overthrow, ranging from military mutinies to assassination attempts."[56]

Second, Qaddafi may have been skilled at manipulating his countrymen, but as a political and military strategist, he appears not to have been especially competent. As part of his effort to convince the world to pay more attention to Libya, Qaddafi repeatedly claimed the Gulf of Sidra, part of the Mediterranean Sea, to be part of Libya's territorial waters and thus solely under Libyan control. To anyone familiar with the US Navy's determination to assert the right of free passage on waterways across the globe, this was practically a written invitation to the Americans to challenge Libya's claim, which they did by periodically announcing that the US Navy would soon be conducting air and naval exercises above and within the Gulf of Sidra. These periodic exercises were actually a clever response by the Americans, because holding these exercises effectively shifted to Libya the responsibility for choosing between resisting this encroachment by the Americans and tacitly accepting the Americans' claim that the Gulf of Sidra was international waters, open to all. If and when the Libyans chose the former, they invariably lost aircraft, ships, and surface-to-air missile ground stations to the technologically superior US forces. If they chose to walk away without challenging what the Americans were doing there in the gulf, they made a mockery of the colonel's extravagant rhetoric.[57]

Third, Qaddafi and the other officers who made up the Revolutionary Command Council—the ruling group in Libya after the overthrow of the monarchy—inherited an impoverished country when they ousted King Idris in 1969. By the mid-1980s, despite having earned billions of dollars in oil sales, the Libyan economy was not much healthier than it had been when the military came to power in 1969. On Qaddafi's watch, Libya did not get militarily stronger. If anything, Libya's position as of the end of the 1980s was weaker than it had been in 1980, when Qaddafi had threatened President Carter with an oil embargo, whereas the US position was incomparably stronger. A perceptive journalist captured Qaddafi's predicament quite neatly: "Libyan leader Muammar Qaddafi, his economy weakened, his foreign adventures faltering and his alliances showing signs of strain, now faces increasingly coordinated pressure from his

North African neighbors. . . . Qaddafi finds himself more vulnerable and isolated than he has been in years."[58]

Fourth, if and when Qaddafi considered the time opportune to pose a challenge of some kind to the United States, the Libyan side almost always found itself in unfavorable circumstances due to the wide range of options that a superpower like the United States could draw on when dealing with a minor power like Libya. For every Libyan move, there was always at least one and often several countermoves open to the United States. In September and October 1980, for example, the Libyans provoked a war of nerves by sending jet fighters to check out US aircraft flying through airspace above the Mediterranean that was claimed by Libya. In response, the United States introduced a new and more advanced aircraft (the RC-135, the military version of the Boeing 707) with performance characteristics that the Libyans could not match (at least not right away). When the Libyans, after receiving better Soviet-made fighters that could keep up with the Americans, threatened the US aircraft with attack—for example, by "locking on" their fire control radars or flying within two hundred yards of the American reconnaissance aircraft, the United States responded by sending carrier-based fighters to intercept and shoo away the Libyan forces.[59] In 1983 the Libyans moved some of their fighter aircraft to bases close to Sudan, apparently intending to topple the government there, beginning with an air raid on Khartoum. In response, the United States (which was monitoring events along the Libya-Sudan border) sent three Airborne Warning and Control System (AWACS) aircraft to Egypt and moved a carrier and its escorts closer to Libya and Egypt.[60] There was no Libyan attack on Sudan, not then and not ever.

Finally, Libya was not a particularly imaginative opponent. In 1979, as was explained earlier, the US embassy in Tripoli was attacked by a mob proclaiming solidarity with oppressed peoples like the Iranians in their struggle with the United States. The Libyans got away with it that time, but they would not be so lucky the second time around. In April 1992, the United Nations Security Council voted to impose an air and arms embargo on Libya. Qaddafi's regime retaliated by sending mobs to attack the embassies of states that had voted for the resolution, as they had done in 1979 to the US embassy in Tripoli. In 1992, however, the protests were carried out in a lackadaisical manner that would likely have come across as comic if the dangers inherent in what the Libyans were doing had not been so apparent. In one such instance, firefighters asking, "Where's the fire?" arrived at the Venezuelan embassy *before* the mob that had been sent to torch the building. There were four Libyan policemen at the door to the Venezuelan embassy, but despite warnings from the Venezuelan ambassador, the police just stood there, watching, while the mob burned down the embassy. "Diplomats said whatever lingering good will toward Libya that existed among the non-aligned countries in the wake of [the

Security Council's vote] could be seriously compromised by the attacks [on foreign embassies]."[61]

Background

During President Reagan's first term in office, it was widely believed within his administration that "Qaddafi was on a roll, enthused by the weakness shown by Western countries . . . and their failure to do much about Qaddafi's actions."[62] High-level officials, such as White House Chief of Staff Donald Regan and Secretary of State George Shultz, put Libya at the top of their list of "terrorist states." Shultz repeatedly told his staff, "We have to put Qaddafi in a box and close the lid."[63] Toward this end, the Reagan administration was especially interested in identifying options that would be more forceful than the seemingly timid responses offered by the Carter administration.[64] The Reagan administration wanted to do something about its Qaddafi problem quickly, before the colonel could spring any more unpleasant surprises on the United States and its allies.

Why did the Reagan administration attach such importance to acting quickly and forcefully? Background and context are important here, because they help us understand why the Reagan administration acted as it did. The United States had been flying aerial reconnaissance missions off the Libyan coastline since 1972, in part as a way of keeping tabs on the flow of weapons from the Soviet Union to Libya, and in part as a way of keeping tabs on Libya's neighbors too. In March 1973, the Libyans responded to these reconnaissance flights by sending two fighter aircraft to intercept and fire upon a US Air Force C-130 that the Libyans claimed was violating their airspace—a claim that the United States did not recognize. In this instance, the American plane escaped unharmed. Thereafter, the Libyans would occasionally send fighters to intercept these reconnaissance aircraft, but there was little that they could do about them, because the US side was flying more modern aircraft, specifically the air force's RC-135, against which Libya's (not very capable) fighter aircraft and (poorly trained) pilots were not a good match.[65]

Beginning in 1979, however, the Libyans began sending newer and better fighter planes piloted by Syrians and North Koreans, among others, to intercept these American RC-135s, sometimes approaching to within five miles of their target.[66] During the summer of 1979, the pace of these intercepts picked up again. US Air Force reconnaissance aircraft drew an increasing number of intercepts by Libyan fighters, some of which "locked on" their fire control radars, thereby simulating an attack on the US aircraft. Other Libyan fighters approached to within two hundred yards of the US planes. Also during 1980, Syrian pilots flying Libyan MiGs challenged and nearly clashed with carrier-based US Navy reconnaissance aircraft and their fighter escorts from the US Sixth Fleet in the Mediterranean.[67]

In effect, during 1979 and 1980, the United States and Libya were already waging a war of nerves that seemed to be steadily intensifying. President Carter's actions suggest that he had been willing to engage in such a war with Libya, at least until the seizure of the US embassy in Iran in November 1979. The hostage crisis, in turn, made plain that there were limits to President Carter's willingness to confront the Libyans, especially while the hostage crisis was still unsolved. The US Navy's Sixth Fleet was scheduled to stage missile-firing exercises in the Mediterranean during September 1980, some of which were planned to take place over the Gulf of Sidra, which Libya continued to claim as its territorial waters. After extensive deliberations, Carter allowed the missile-firing exercises to go forward, provided that the US military aircraft and naval vessels involved in the exercises refrained from deliberately antagonizing the Libyans by sailing across or flying over the Gulf of Sidra. Carter imposed these limits because he did not want to provoke a crisis with Libya at the same time that his administration was facing a seemingly intractable crisis over the seizure of the US embassy in Tehran and the fate of the American diplomats who were being held hostage in Iran. Carter's administration was also very preoccupied with how to respond to the Soviet invasion of Afghanistan, which was another reason not to get too deeply involved with the Libyans.[68]

Carter may well have wished to avoid a confrontation over a less-than-cosmic issue like access to the Gulf of Sidra, but the Libyans acted as if they were eager to take on the Americans. On September 16, 1980, and again on September 21, US Air Force RC-135s flying over international waters, but also parallel to what the Libyans claimed was their restricted airspace, encountered Libyan fighter planes on an intercept course. During the incident on September 16, two Libyan MiGs were ordered by their ground controllers to each fire an air-to-air missile at the RC-135 flying over international waters in the Mediterranean. No one on the American side actually saw these missiles being fired, and the only evidence that a missile had been launched took the form of a radio command to do so that was intercepted by the RC-135.[69] The RC-135 took evasive action and landed safely in Greece. Five days later, on September 21, another RC-135 flying the same route encountered eight Libyan fighter aircraft. As the Libyan pilots maneuvered to intercept the US plane, they encountered several US Navy F-14s from the aircraft carrier USS *John F. Kennedy*. This time, the Syrian pilots who were flying the Libyan aircraft broke off the contact without firing any missiles at all.[70]

Why was the US Navy (and the air force too) so eager to continue sailing across and flying above the Gulf of Sidra? Part of the answer—the lesser part, in my judgment—is that the navy had been staging these missile-firing exercises on an annual basis ever since 1973, and like any good organization facing a challenge to its autonomy, it did not want to give up the right to continue doing what it was already doing. The Gulf of Sidra, navy officers explained, was especially well-suited for the missile-firing exercises the navy wanted to hold because the area was "generally free of commercial air and sea traffic" and had "no appreciable commercial fishing activity."[71] The air and naval exercises that the navy wanted to stage in 1980 and 1981 would have been the eighth and ninth, respectively, since the navy had begun holding these exercises in 1977.[72]

By far the larger part of the reason why the navy was so eager to assert the right of free passage above and across the Gulf of Sidra had to do with the precedents that might be set if the exercises had been cancelled. President Carter had been willing to allow air force and navy aircraft to fly parallel to the boundary claimed by Libya, but he was unwilling to authorize overflights of the Gulf of Sidra, at least until the Iran hostage crisis had been resolved. Even though President Carter had accepted the navy's request to stage another round of missile-firing exercises in 1980, navy officers feared that an important precedent was being set, whereby access to the gulf would be taken away and future missile-firing exercises would be limited to waters adjacent to the Gulf of Sidra but not within the gulf itself.[73] And it wasn't just the absence of commercial air and sea traffic that made the Gulf of Sidra a desirable location for the navy to hold these missile-firing exercises. It was proximity to Libya that made the gulf a valuable asset. Any time the United States wished to get Qaddafi's attention or send a message to the colonel, ignoring the boundary claimed by the Libyans offered an easy and convenient way to do so. This is why navy officers, concerned that President Carter's restriction on what the navy and the air force could do might become permanent, requested permission early in President Reagan's first term to overfly the Gulf of Sidra in order to show that the United States did not recognize Libya's claim to these waters.[74] Planning for a new round of missile firing exercises, which the navy expected would be held in August or September of 1981, thus began in February 1981, giving the Reagan administration months in which to plan how the next round of military exercises might be used to bring Qaddafi down a notch or two in the eyes of his own people and the world too.[75]

In the meantime, the Iranians had one last act of revenge to inflict on Jimmy Carter. The Americans held hostage in Iran were released and flown to Algiers on January 21, 1981, the same day that Ronald Reagan was inaugurated as president of the United States. The plane carrying the hostages landed only after President Reagan had taken the oath of office, thereby denying Carter any possibility of claiming that the hostages had been freed on his watch. With the hostages no longer in danger, President Reagan decided that this was an opportune moment to reassert freedom of the seas, ordering that naval and air exercises should be held in that part of the Gulf of Sidra claimed by Libya but not recognized by the United States.[76]

Relinquishing the Initiative

Perhaps the most interesting aspect of the strategy used by the Reagan administration to take Qaddafi down a notch was its revival of an idea invented by Thomas Schelling at a time when the Cold War seemed very intense and very dangerous. Schelling called his idea "relinquishing the initiative," and he used it to draw a striking contrast between his approach and traditional military strategizing.[77]

For decades prior to Schelling's work on tacit and explicit bargaining during wartime, traditional military strategy proclaimed that a state already at or near the brink of war should focus its efforts on seizing the initiative rather than waiting passively to see what its opponent(s) might do. Seizing the initiative was especially attractive to pre-1945 strategists because of the military advantages that were expected to accrue to whichever side struck first, because the ensuing war would likely be fought mostly on the other side's territory, and because it just seemed intuitively obvious that it was better to be the one calling the shots than the one reacting to an enemy's choices.[78]

In the nuclear age, Schelling wrote, having the initiative was good if it involved "imaginativeness, boldness, [and] new ideas." On the other hand, deterrence of just about any hostile act short of an attack on the United States itself "often depends on getting into a position where the initiative is up to the enemy," leaving the latter "to make the awful decision to proceed to a clash."[79] It was one of Schelling's strengths as a strategist—and he was one of the best—that where others saw threats and dangers, he saw clever gambits. Relinquishing the initiative was one such gambit.[80] As presented by Schelling, "relinquishing the initiative . . . consists of maneuvering one's self into a position in which one no longer has any effective choice over how he shall behave or respond. The purpose of these tactics is to get rid of an embarrassing initiative, making the outcome depend solely on the other party's choice."[81] Why would a state engaged in coercion or deterrence *want* to rid itself of an initiative of this kind? What would be accomplished by maneuvering in this fashion?

During the Cold War, the rivalry between the United States and the Soviet Union often took the form of deploying or maneuvering their armed forces for the sake of some political or military advantage.[82] "In strategy," Schelling wrote, "when both sides abhor collision the advantage often goes to the one who arranges the status quo in his favor and leaves to the other the 'last clear chance' to stop or turn aside."[83] During the Cold War, arranging the status quo and relinquishing the initiative were techniques used by the United States and the Soviet Union to jockey for advantage over each other. As explained by Schelling, the idea behind relinquishing the initiative was to manipulate an opponent, in effect making *it* the party that would have to choose between further risk-taking and walking away.

Since the consequences of a war between the two superpowers were expected to be inestimably worse than tolerating the new status quo, it was expected by Schelling and most post-1945 strategists that, if a state like the United States could "arrange the status quo" in a way that relinquished the initiative to its opponent, then the opponent (the Soviet Union) would likely have little or no choice but to learn to live with whatever political-military arrangement the United States had cobbled together prior to relinquishing the initiative to the Soviets.[84] Learning to live with those political-military arrangements might not have appeared (to the Soviets) as an attractive option, but no matter how distasteful the consequences of walking away or fashioning some kind of compromise might be, choosing anything that heightened the risk of nuclear war would almost always be worse—indeed, incomparably worse—than a political outcome fashioned in this way. Put differently, arranging the status quo and relinquishing the initiative were strategies intended to wage politically a struggle that was too dangerous to be waged militarily.

The Reagan administration never did refer explicitly to "relinquishing the initiative" when planning for and participating in various confrontations with Libya, and administration officials dismissed as "preposterous" claims that the United States had provoked any of the military engagements between US and Libyan forces that occurred during President Reagan's first year in office.[85] Even so, much of what Reagan administration officials said and did during their initial confrontations with Qaddafi's Libya suggests that their policies were almost instinctively aimed at relinquishing the initiative to the Libyans, by maneuvering them into situations in which it would be Qaddafi, and not the United States, who would have to choose between firing the first shot, thereby initiating hostilities that Libya's armed forces would surely lose, and backing away from whatever challenge the Americans were posing, with all the unfavorable consequences that withdrawal would entail, both for Qaddafi personally and for his standing within Libya and on the global stage.

If relinquishing the initiative is a strategy for maneuvering an opponent into situations that are politically untenable, how does such a strategy differ from provoking a conflict? *Provocation* involves an either-or choice for the state being provoked: either accept the challenge posed by the provocateur (fight) or decline (walk away). *Relinquishing the initiative,* on the other hand, aims to create situations in which the state issuing the challenge *cannot* walk away without incurring substantial costs, especially reputation and audience costs. In effect, relinquishing the initiative is an attempt to lay a trap for the target state, and the state laying the trap tries to make it unavoidable by issuing challenges that the target state might prefer to avoid but which it cannot now avoid without incurring serious reputation and audience costs of its own.

Armed with hindsight, we can see that, on at least three occasions during Ronald Reagan's presidency, his administration sought to set a trap for Qaddafi. In each case the colonel walked right into it, thereby suggesting that he did not learn from past mistakes. To illustrate these claims, consider the following three incidents in which the Reagan administration confronted and outmaneuvered Qaddafi and his regime, thereby placing on the Libyans the onus for choosing between starting a military confrontation with the United States and avoiding hostilities with the US planes and ships that were repeatedly flying over and sailing across the Gulf of Sidra, in effect daring the Libyans to do something about it.

1. CONFRONTATION OVER THE GULF OF SIDRA (AUGUST 1981)

In October 1980, Qaddafi wrote to both President Carter and the Republican presidential candidate Ronald Reagan, demanding that the United States "keep its naval and air forces away from the Libyan Arab borders in the Mediterranean." Otherwise, Qaddafi continued, "confrontation and the outbreak of an armed war, in the legal term, would regretfully be a possibility within view at any moment." Libya would not be at fault. "Should war break out," Qaddafi warned, "it will be a war forced upon us by America."[86]

The Reagan administration was indeed eager for a showdown with Qaddafi, but only a showdown and certainly not a war. The Reagan administration's strategy during its encounters with Libya by and large followed Schelling by arranging the status quo so that it strongly favored the United States. In practical terms, this meant positioning US forces where they could easily challenge Libya's claims that the Gulf of Sidra was its territorial waters. The goal was to narrow the choices available to the Libyans to two (and only two) distasteful alternatives—being called on to back their words with deeds (in effect, initiating hostilities, which would mean almost certain defeat for Libya), or walking away from a fight with the Americans, which would make it plain for all the world to see that Qaddafi could not back up his grandiose rhetoric with actual deeds.[87]

How do we know what the parties to this conflict were thinking as they maneuvered for advantage and the confrontation played itself out? An important clue in this regard is the number of sorties flown by Libyan Air Force fighters attempting to penetrate the restricted zone within which the Americans were carrying out their missile-firing exercises.[88] Between the start of these exercises on Tuesday, August 18, 1981, and the aerial dog fight early Wednesday morning, August 19, the Libyan Air Force made multiple attempts to get closer to the US aircraft carriers USS *Nimitz* and USS *Forrestal*. Estimates of how active the Libyans were vary considerably. *Newsweek* credits the Libyans with seventy-two sorties, plus eight more after the aerial clash that resulted in the loss of two Libyan aircraft. *Time* cites "about 40" sorties, plus eight more on the second day of the US naval exercises. Secretary of the Navy John Lehman was more circumspect, saying only that the Libyans had launched "a considerable number of . . . sorties."[89] The commander of the navy's Sixth Fleet, Vice Admiral William Rowden, offered a different but still useful number, telling journalists that US fighter aircraft had made forty-five intercepts of Libyan aircraft during the missile-firing exercises, but also that they had held fire until two Libyan Su-22s finally launched air-to-air missiles at two US Navy F-14s on the second day of the exercises.[90] These numbers are important because they suggest that both sides were trying hard to lure the other into firing first.

Why did the Libyans launch so many sorties to check on what the Americans were doing? And why did hostilities break out only after the Libyans had flown dozens of sorties in the direction of the US fleet? There are two plausible answers to these questions. First, the Libyans were hoping to spring a trap of their own for the US Navy's carriers and carrier-based aircraft. If the Libyans could somehow entice the Americans into firing first, then the Libyans could play the role of victim while making the United States appear the villain. World opinion might be so appalled that the Americans would cease (at least temporarily) their efforts to undermine Libya's claim to the Gulf of Sidra. This suggests that the reason for all those sorties was to present the Americans with lucrative targets that they (the Americans) could not ignore. Provided the Americans could be enticed into firing the first air-to-air missile, the Libyans could plausibly claim that the American superpower was picking on plucky little Libya. Plus, the Libyans had already bought so many fighter jets from the Soviets that they could easily absorb the loss of a few planes if in return they could humiliate the Americans.

Second, the Libyans may have sent so many aircraft in the direction of the US fleet in the hope that a shoot-out over the gulf might offer the Libyans an opportunity to reassert Libya's claim to control over the Gulf of Sidra in its entirety. With so many Libyan planes in the air, the Americans might lose their nerve and fire the first missile, and in the ensuing air engagement there would be enough Libyan aircraft nearby that the Libyans might actually shoot down one or a few US aircraft. A variant on this last scenario would be one in which Libyan planes were able to penetrate the US defenses and engage one of the US Navy's surface ships or maybe even one of the two carriers. If the Libyans could down one or more of the American fighter jets or damage one of the navy's surface ships, they would have additional opportunities to portray themselves worldwide as the victims of a US attack who had then held their own in an aerial engagement against the US Navy's vaunted carrier strike forces. Alternatively, the Libyans could portray themselves as vigilant defenders of Libya's territorial waters in the Gulf of Sidra.

Shifting our perspective to the United States, a first cut at the evidence available suggests that the United States was itself attempting to manipulate the Libyans into shooting first, and that the Reagan administration was much better situated than were the Libyans to arrange the status quo in its favor, leaving Libya "the 'last clear chance' to stop or turn aside."[91] What exactly does it mean to say that the Americans were in a stronger position than the Libyans when it came to rearranging the status quo to their liking?

The United States posted its warnings to airmen and mariners on August 12 and August 14, respectively, announcing that military exercises were scheduled for August 18 and 19 and that part of the exercise area would extend into the Gulf of Sidra (claimed by Libya). Next, the US fleet was deployed to positions from which it could quickly and easily cross Qaddafi's "line of death" if ordered to do so. Once the air and naval warnings had been posted and the fleet deployed, the Reagan administration for all practical purposes had burned its bridges and would have exposed itself to a loss of credibility and even ridicule if it had cancelled the planned exercises or limited them to areas outside the Gulf of Sidra. In addition, US military planners had been working on the exercises scheduled for August 1981 ever since the previous February. If those exercises had been suddenly changed in response to demands or warnings from the Libyans, those changes almost certainly would have leaked to Congress and the press. Once the leaks had started to flow, it likely would have been at most a few days or even a few hours before the news made the front page of newspapers across the country. Even worse, unfavorable comparisons between Presidents Reagan and Carter would almost certainly be widespread on editorial and op-ed pages, not to mention television news broadcasts, nationwide. Carter, after all, had placed restrictions on what the navy could and could not do during what proved to be the last few months of his presidency, and look what had happened to him. President Reagan and his senior advisers were so concerned that they not adopt any policy that smacked of Carter's weakness and indecision that they almost instinctively opted for whatever was the opposite of what Jimmy Carter likely would have done.[92]

In effect, by August 1981 US naval forces were deployed in locations that they could easily maintain more or less indefinitely while they waited to see what the Libyans would do. More important, there would have been substantial costs charged to the Reagan administration's account if it did not do what it said it would do—namely, cross Qaddafi's so-called line of death but not open fire unless the Libyans fired first. In this situation, a disinterested observer would likely conclude that the Reagan administration had successfully relinquished the initiative, thereby shifting to the Libyans the onus of choosing between backing their words with deeds and returning to their home ports and airfields.

How did the Libyans respond? Once the Reagan administration had positioned two navy carrier task forces around and close to the Gulf of Sidra, about all that the administration had to do to claim "victory" over the Libyans was to keep those naval task forces in place until the Libyans grew weary and ordered their forces to return to their home bases for maintenance and crew change. The Libyans had no plausible plan for compelling the navy to give up the positions it had staked out near the Gulf of Sidra. Indeed, once the Reagan administration had successfully relinquished the initiative to Tripoli, probably the best option for the Libyans would have been to relinquish it back by toning down very considerably their role in this episode and by managing expectations in Libya and worldwide regarding what a small state could plausibly hope to accomplish when matched up against a superpower. The Libyans could have avoided some of the risk and potential embarrassment simply by not trying very hard to penetrate the area where the US Navy's exercises were being held and above all by not firing on the Americans. The Libyans had taken advantage of the missile-firing exercises to launch dozens of fighter aircraft sorties in the direction of the US Navy's carrier groups. Having done so, they should have announced that they had made their point (proclaimed victory) and then recalled their aircraft back to their home bases. Instead, the Libyans ended up with perhaps the worst possible outcome: two Libyan aircraft fired the first shots, resulting in the loss of both of them. Qaddafi may have dreamed of a world in which Libya's armed forces (lavishly equipped by the Soviets and others) could hold their own with the Americans, but that was not to be, at least not now. Instead, Libya's armed forces were shown to be inept, and the Americans were left to make a mockery of Libya's claim to all of the Gulf of Sidra.

Alternatively, the Libyans might have tried staging some military exercises of their own, although once the Americans had posted their warnings and deployed their carrier task forces, the Libyans found themselves in a decidedly inferior position vis-à-vis the Americans. The Libyans could have argued, semi-plausibly, that they needed to continue launching airplanes to keep an eye on what the Americans were doing. The Libyans could also argue, again semi-plausibly, that they were merely doing what the United States was also doing, in effect claiming the status of de facto peer of the United States. On the other hand, once the Libyans had fired first, the arguments that they could plausibly make to justify their role in this episode diminished quickly. Firing first had the effect of revealing, for the whole world to see, just how weak and inept Libya's armed forces really were. Firing first had also ruined the Libyans' chances of playing the role of victim. There was nothing glamorous or heroic about using the Libyan Air Force to attack the US Navy's vastly superior F-14s. The Libyans' performance in this case was so dismal that even *Newsweek* magazine couldn't resist volunteering a comment: "For now,

[Qaddafi] seems stymied. Despite his overstocked war machine, he holds no realistic military option."[93]

2. CONFRONTATION OVER THE GULF OF SIDRA (MARCH 1986)

The second of these three episodes occurred in March 1986, when the US Navy was once again conducting exercises in the Mediterranean that involved flying over and sailing across the Gulf of Sidra. Once the navy had announced that it would be conducting air and naval exercises in the vicinity of the Gulf of Sidra and that the fleet had been deployed, the Reagan administration had once again arranged the status quo in its favor—in effect confronting Qaddafi with the need to choose between standing up to the Americans or developing a sudden case of amnesia regarding the Gulf of Sidra. The Reagan administration could not cancel or change its plans for military exercises near the Gulf of Sidra without seeming weak and indecisive. On the other hand, once the navy had taken up positions close to the Gulf of Sidra, it could hold those positions more or less indefinitely even as the continued presence of the navy's ships and aircraft was practically daring the Libyans to do something about it.

Once again, then, the Reagan administration had successfully relinquished the initiative to the Libyans. There is no reason to believe that Libya's military options were any better in 1986 than they had been in 1981. More important, in 1986 "senior U.S. officials seemed eager to provoke Qaddafi into a military response. Said one Pentagon official, 'If they don't react, we've exposed them as a paper tiger.'"[94] The issue came to a head on March 20, 1986, when the Reagan administration announced that US naval vessels would soon cross the border—also known as Qaddafi's "line of death"—but this would lead to shooting only if Libya fired first.[95]

Faced with a choice between challenging the US presence around and over the Gulf of Sidra and acquiescing to a US air and naval presence there, Qaddafi's best option once again was to avoid military action against the US fleet, while periodically announcing that he was using the Libyan military to keep tabs on the US planes and ships flying over and sailing across the Gulf of Sidra. There would have been an element of pretense here—namely, that Libya's planes and pilots were up to the challenge of keeping tabs on their US Navy counterparts. On the other hand, even pretense was better than a military confrontation that the Libyans surely would lose. Qaddafi, however, opted for challenging the Americans rather than acquiescing to their presence. Unlike the other confrontations between the United States and Libya in 1981 and 1989, which were limited to fighter aircraft only, this time Qaddafi opted for sending Libyan naval patrol boats in the general direction of the Sixth Fleet's warships. Libya's forces also fired long-range Soviet surface-to-air missiles (SA-5s) in the general direction of

US Navy aircraft flying over the Gulf of Sidra. In response, US Navy war-planes and the cruiser USS *Yorktown* sank two Libyan patrol boats and damaged three others. US Navy aircraft fired antiradar missiles that struck, and temporarily disabled, the radar dishes that were identifying targets for Libya's SA-5s. Everything the Libyans launched against the Americans proved to be a failure, while everything the Americans targeted was destroyed.[96]

In this case, Qaddafi not only made bad strategic choices but also com-pounded his problems with the United States by invoking bombastic lan-guage that highlighted Libya's status as an object for derision in the eyes of the rest of the world. On January 9, 1986, roughly two months before this latest confrontation over and around the Gulf of Sidra, Qaddafi told a meeting in Tripoli of ambassadors from European states that, if Libya were attacked by the United States from bases in Europe, the Libyans would "close our eyes and ears and hit indiscriminately." If war did come, Qad-dafi told the European ambassadors, he would "drag Europe into it."[97] Within about three months of these remarks, Libya would be on the losing side of the March 1986 naval battle in the Gulf of Sidra. On April 14, Tripoli and Benghazi were both struck by US naval and air forces, including air strikes by US aircraft based in Britain, but none of Qaddafi's threats was acted upon.[98]

In similar fashion, on April 9, 1986, Qaddafi told a news conference that Libya's plans for a military confrontation with the United States were complete, and that a US attack would trigger retaliation against targets associated with the United States around the world. "It is axiomatic that America will be defeated militarily," Qaddafi said. "It is axiomatic that if aggression is staged against us, then we shall escalate the violence, civilian and non-civilian, throughout the world."[99] These remarks were followed on April 14 by the US nighttime raid on Tripoli and Benghazi—a raid that included strikes on Qaddafi's headquarters and living quarters in an obvious attempt to kill or wound him. Despite what Qaddafi had said at his news conference of April 9, there were no strikes against US targets throughout the world. As Edward Schumacher says, "Power commands respect in the Arab world, and the American bombing showed that Qad-dafi's power was limited. If the Libyan military was discredited inside the government by its failure to protect Libya, so was Qaddafi among the public."[100]

3. CHEMICAL WEAPONS FACTORIES AND CONFLICT OVER THE GULF OF SIDRA (JANUARY 1989)

By the end of the 1980s, a growing body of evidence suggested that Libya was pursuing the facilities and the expertise needed for large-scale produc-tion of chemical weapons (CWs).[101] Ultimately, the Libyan program took the form of four facilities devoted to large-scale production of CWs: a factory near Rabta, southwest of Tripoli, which the Americans repeatedly described as the largest chemical weapons site that the US intelligence community had ever found in the Third World; a second factory at Sebha, about 650 miles south of Tripoli and reportedly almost identical to the Rabta factory; a third factory at Tarhuna, southeast of Tripoli; and a fourth plant near Benghazi in northeastern Libya, which was intended to produce the precursor chemicals needed to operate the Tarhuna facility. Once the Rabta facility had been unmasked by the Americans, the Libyans tried to salvage some of their investment by claiming that the factory had been built strictly for peaceful purposes, such as producing pharmaceuticals and fertilizer,[102] and then by faking a fire and claiming that the Rabta facility had been rendered unusable, temporarily at least. Faking the fire was such an amateurish ploy that nobody, except maybe the Libyans themselves, believed Libya's claims about the Rabta facility: that it was meant for peaceful purposes and besides, it wasn't working anyway. In any event, once the Rabta facility had been exposed, the attention of the parties concerned shifted to the Tarhuna facility, because whatever happened there would likely determine whether Libya would have a CW program or not.[103]

In this case, it was the Libyans who attempted to relinquish the initiative to the Americans, albeit not very successfully. The Libyans tried to do this by speeding up the pace of construction at their CW factories, surrounding their factory sites with extensive anti-air defenses, and shifting to the Americans the choice between taking military action now (which US allies and even President Reagan all strongly opposed) and waiting to see what diplomacy might produce. These tactics proved to be much more effective when employed by the Americans against the Libyans than vice versa. The Americans had already pummeled the Libyans on more than one occasion. In this situation, US threats were both persuasive and inherently credible. No one doubted that US Navy carriers and their escorts would be back again if the Libyans continued to claim the Gulf of Sidra as territorial waters. Indeed, the United States was in a strong position to play its own version of relinquishing the initiative. The principal instrument available to the United States was its aircraft carrier battle groups, which could be moved into or out of the Gulf of Sidra, whenever the US political leadership requested. The US position was so strong that it could relinquish the initiative to the Libyans and ratchet the pressures on the Libyans up or down simply by ordering the navy's carriers to position themselves here or there.

On the Libyan side, because Libya's CW facilities were built on a very large scale, the Libyans had no realistic option to relocate any of these facilities, and even if they attempted covertly to transfer some of the machinery within them, US reconnaissance satellites would almost certainly detect and track any such move by the Libyans. More important, because Libya had multiple CW facilities, any air attack would likely have to be on a large scale and very destructive; otherwise the Libyans might hope to ride out the storm by shifting personnel and technology from one location to another. Because it was the Americans attempting to relinquish the initiative to the Libyans, the US side could afford to wait, pondering (and occasionally sharing) the satellite imagery and the other kinds of intercepts that the US intelligence community was producing about Libya's CWs. US actions in this regard were at first intended to identify the parties that were suspected of helping the Libyans to construct the Rabta plant. Mostly these were private firms in US allies, most prominently Japan, West Germany, France, and Italy.[104] Identifying these firms was a prerequisite to persuading them to break off their ties to Libya and cease whatever role they might have been playing in the construction process.

Identifying Libya's helpers was a crucial first step, but it wasn't the only step open to the Americans. The Libyans had tried to play the relinquishing-the-initiative card against the Americans, but the United States was and is a superpower, and a superpower will almost always have additional cards that it can play against a small state like Libya—cards that the Libyan side could only wish it had too. For example, the United States organized a diplomatic conference, scheduled for January 7–11, 1989, the purpose of which was to discuss ways of enforcing the 1925 Geneva Convention outlawing CWs. Since Libya was at the time the most prominent seeker after CWs, the conference was essentially a device for increasing the pressure on Libya to give up its CW program. At the same time, the United States could use the conference as a convenient venue for discussing with its allies the possibility of taking military action against the Libyan CW program and the facilities at Rabta and Tarhuna. The US military advantage relative to Libya was so great that the mere act of discussing military action against Libya constituted an existential threat to the Libyan CW program. In effect, it was the Libyans who had to take into account how far they could go in pursuit of a CW capability, but without so antagonizing the United States and its allies that they would agree to take military action against Libya.[105] *How much* the Libyans would take into account US willingness to use force against the Rabta facility is hard to say. President Reagan had let it be known, during the waning weeks of his presidency, that he did not favor military action against the Libyan CW program. With force seemingly ruled out, an alternative would have to be found. Secretary of State Shultz characterized US policy as attempting to make the Libyans "feel uncomfortable" about continuing with their CW program.[106] How might this be done, given that President Reagan was not in favor of an air strike at Libya, at least not right then? There are at least two ways in which the United States could have continued to pressure the Libyans to give up their CW program without taking military action against one or more of Libya's CW factories.

First, there was the January 1989 conference on chemical weapons in Paris, although the conference was hardly an unqualified success for the Americans. Many of the conferees, especially among the Arab states, were critical of US policy, which tacitly accepted a nuclear-armed Israel while threatening sanctions and air strikes to prevent Libya from acquiring even a modest CW arsenal. Even so, such criticism of the United States would be small comfort to the Libyans, especially if the United States succeeded with its "campaign to orchestrate the widest possible international criticism" of what officials claimed was "the world's largest poison gas factory."[107] The problem for the Libyans was that the Americans could be very persuasive when it came to mobilizing other states to join a worldwide anti-Libya coalition, especially when they came bearing offers of increased military and economic assistance. Conversely, Qaddafi had alienated many of the leaders whose support he now needed. All those insults Qaddafi had hurled at other leaders, all those secessionist movements he had supported, all those terrorist groups he had funded and armed and supported—all his past transgressions were now coming back to haunt him. The danger to Qaddafi and his regime would be acute if the Americans could persuade the conferees to consider issuing a harsh condemnation of possession of CWs—a condemnation that everyone knew was aimed at one state and one state only, Libya. Libya would be isolated internationally, and this at a time when the US side would likely be talking with its allies regarding possible military action. If this was indeed the way events were moving, the result might well be that Libya's CW program could come to serve as a kind of political and military lightning rod, drawing a US military strike on Libya.[108]

Second, on January 4, 1989, two US F-14s based on the carrier *John F. Kennedy* shot down two Libyan MiG-23s after the latter two aircraft had persistently followed an intercept course that gave the appearance of lining up for a clean shot at the F-14s.[109] During the waning days of the Reagan presidency, Libyan spokesmen had said that they expected that Libya would be attacked by the United States, as in the case of the April 14, 1986, raid on Tripoli and Benghazi.[110] "Apparently because they expected to be attacked, the continuing controversy over the Libyan [CW facilities] has made Libyan pilots increasingly active in recent days, resulting in closer Libyan surveillance of American aircraft operations in the Mediterranean."[111]

This is not to say that a clash was inevitable. Speaking in the aftermath of the aerial clash and attempting to justify what the United States had done, Dan Howard (Secretary of Defense Frank Carlucci's chief spokesman) pointed out, "In every previous case, when MiGs had been 'painted' [by an F-14 search radar] while headed toward a carrier, the Floggers [MiG-23s] have reported this lock-on back to the tower [in Libya] and the tower has told them to go home. And the closest approach we record within the past several years was 30 miles away from our aircraft. They've always gone home. In this case," Howard continued, "something peculiar happened. And that is why the MiG-23s did not report [the F-14 search radars] to their tower." The tower apparently did not order the MiGs back home, so the Libyan pilots proceeded out to sea and started tangling with the F-14s more than forty miles from the coast.[112]

Was it inevitable that this incident should turn into another aerial dogfight? The F-14s were warned about the approaching MiGs by a US E-2C command-and-control aircraft. The F-14s took five different evasive maneuvers to avoid the MiGs, but the latter matched these maneuvers and continued to close on the F-14s. According to Secretary of Defense Carlucci, each time the F-14s took evasive action, "the Libyan aircraft sought to put their nose on our aircraft." In light of this behavior, Carlucci argued, "hostile intent" seemed "fairly clear."[113] There was also a second indicator of hostile intent on the part of the Libyans. According to navy sources, the MiGs illuminated the F-14s with their fire-control radars, suggesting that the MiGs were about to fire at the US aircraft.[114] In this case, with the MiGs pursuing the F-14s and matching the latter's evasive maneuvers, turning on the MiGs' fire-control radars appeared to the US side to be a hostile act that required an immediate response.

There is, however, an obvious problem with this explanation. We know from earlier cases discussed in this chapter that, as part of the war of nerves between the United States and Libya in 1980 and 1981, Libyan aircraft had at times approached to within two hundred yards of US reconnaissance flights. Libyan aircraft also occasionally turned on their fire-control radars to illuminate a US aircraft, without bringing a hail of missiles in their direction. Also relevant here is that US naval forces had been conducting training operations in the same general area off the Libyan coast about a dozen times in the past year.[115]

If such aerial challenges were "normal," as the US secretary of defense put it, then why did this challenge turn violent? One explanation points to heightened Libyan nervousness that the Rabta site was about to be struck, much like the United States had struck Tripoli and Benghazi in April 1986. "Pentagon officials said that the controversy over the Libyan [CW] facility has made Libyan pilots increasingly active in recent days, resulting in closer Libyan surveillance of American aircraft operations in the Mediterranean."[116] In previous US attacks on Libyan air and naval forces, the United States acted only after massing naval forces close to where any fighting would likely occur. There were at least two aircraft carriers and their escorts in the Mediterranean during the August 1981 clash over the Gulf of Sidra, and three carriers and their escorts during the naval battle in March 1986 and then the raid on Tripoli and Benghazi in April 1986. In January 1989, in contrast, there was just a single carrier (the *Kennedy*) operating in the eastern Mediterranean. In the March 1986 and April 1986 clashes between US and Libyan armed forces, the navy launched dozens of sorties that then struck multiple targets on the ground and in the Gulf of Sidra. In January 1989, the US carrier dispatched two F-14s to investigate and shoo away two Libyan MiGs. Two planes flying combat air patrol (the aerial equivalent of sentry duty) hardly seem like a precursor to another overwhelming aerial attack. Indeed, there didn't have to be any signs that a massive attack was coming. By 1989 Qaddafi's regime was so worn down by a decade's worth of move and countermove that it was looking more and more like a failed state, no longer capable of keeping up with the United States. Who would have thought that, by 1989, the seemingly indefatigable Colonel Qaddafi would manage to transform politics in Libya into a question of who could hold out longer—the colonel, or the coup plotters in his government?

Evaluating Success

Did containment work in the Libyan case? In retrospect, there would seem to be little room for doubting that it did. Qaddafi was one of the leaders of the 1969 coup staged by the Libyan military to overthrow the Libyan monarchy. Qaddafi's Libya was a state that consumed a great deal but produced next to nothing (oil being the obvious exception). The treaties of political union that Qaddafi signed with his neighbors inevitably came to a premature end once his cosigners judged that they had swindled him of all they were likely to get. Qaddafi had access to Libya's cash stockpiles derived from oil sales, which he used to buy weapons and ammunition that were greatly in excess of what Libya could reasonably expect to use on its own against the United States. Libya had no way of maintaining the billions of dollars' worth of Soviet weapons and equipment that it bought under Qaddafi's supervision. And even if the Libyans had known how to keep their weapons and equipment in good working order, there was still the problem of what to do with the mercenary pilots (Syrians and North Koreans) who had been hired to fly Libya's aircraft but who refused even to take off as long as US Navy F-14s were in the vicinity during the March and April 1986 clashes between Libyan and US forces.[117]

All the US-Libyan clashes discussed so far (March 1981, March 1986, April 1986, January 1989) were an embarrassment for Libya, whose forces performed very poorly. Of the four listed here, it was the third—the nighttime raid on Tripoli and Benghazi in April 1986—that had the most lasting impact. "A Raid That Went Right" and "Bombing Gadhafi Worked" were among the many headlines intended to capture the prevailing sentiment in the United States after the April 14, 1986, bombing of Tripoli and Benghazi.[118] The raid on Tripoli and Benghazi was a turning point in this regard. Qaddafi emerged alive and in one piece but also badly shaken by the realization that the raid had been intended, among other things, to injure or even kill him. American and British officials emerged more confident than before that they had Qaddafi's number and that it was only a matter of time before he finally gave up trying to get out of his box. In the aftermath of the Libyan-orchestrated bombings of Pan Am 103 and UTA 772, Libya moved closer and closer to what can only be described as capitulation to US and British demands. "Tired of international isolation and economic sanctions, the Libyans decided in the late 1990s to seek normalized relations with the United States, and held secret discussions with Clinton administration officials to convey that message."[119] Libya announced in December 2003 that it would abandon decades of work on nuclear and chemical weapons and missile programs. Containment, Joseph Cirincione wrote some years later, "was an unqualified triumph" for the United States.[120] On June 30, 2006, Secretary of State Condoleezza Rice rescinded the US designation of Libya as a supporter of terrorism, which had first been put in place on December 29, 1979, during the Carter administration. This was also the first time the United States had rescinded a terrorism designation without a change of government.[121]

Lally Weymouth, in contrast, takes a more skeptical view of Libya's unilateral disarmament, pointing out that Qaddafi did not stop supporting terrorism in the aftermath of the April 14, 1986, bombing raid that had targeted (among other things) his office and living quarters. Instead, Qaddafi continued supporting terrorists, albeit more discreetly and with greater care and caution.[122] Others have pointed out that, in the year after the 1986 raid that attempted to assassinate him, Qaddafi made substantial progress toward restoring his already frayed relationships with the leaders of other Arab states.[123]

Is there a way to reconcile these conflicting views of containment as they were applied to Qaddafi's Libya? What role did the United States play in bringing a change of policy in Libya? There are several lines of inquiry we might follow regarding whether and how containment "worked" against Qaddafi and Libya.

First, what does it mean to say that containment "worked"? Earlier in this chapter, I argued that containment at its core is an argument about policy change. An ambitious challenger sponsors insurgencies or terrorist groups that aim to remake the status quo by overthrowing the governments of nearby states and replacing them with governments that the challenger finds more to its liking. Status quo powers, in contrast, attempt to thwart, block, or at least hamper what their opponents are doing, and to do so long enough for a change of government or policy to occur in the challenger. Seen this way, containment can be said to have "worked" when there is evidence—preferably lots of evidence—that the target state's support for terrorist or other military operations has ended or has been greatly scaled back. As described by Deputy Secretary of State John Whitehead in connection with the 1986 bombing raid on Tripoli and Benghazi, the goal of US threats and military moves was "to get Qaddafi to change his conduct" by making clear "the kind of dangers" that would result from his "continuing to conduct these horrible terrorist actions all over the world."[124] Put differently, containment "works" when the target state (in this case, Libya) changes its behavior to escape whatever punishments or other constraints are being imposed upon it in the form of military actions, economic sanctions, and isolation from the global economy.

Second, containment is not static; it is instead a bargaining contest between opponents and supporters of the status quo, each of which has its own distinctive set of assets and liabilities, as it competes for leverage and support against its foes. More important, the participants in this bargaining contest can change the terms of the contest by introducing new capabilities into the contest (what I earlier called move and countermove) and by bringing in new actors with new assets at their disposal (others will help). What conclusions does this evidence point toward about the efficacy of these moves as they were incorporated into US policy toward Libya? Did US military actions and economic sanctions contribute to thwarting Qaddafi's schemes? Did US actions compel Qaddafi to abandon many, or at least some, of the schemes he had been pursuing? Would Qaddafi's regime still have given up Libya's WMD programs if there had been no concerted effort by the Americans and the British to thwart what the Libyans were up to? We'll never know what the leading figures on both sides were thinking during the years and then decades when the United States was practicing containment against Libya, but the very extensive press coverage of the US-Libyan relationship makes it possible for us to observe in considerable detail what those leading figures were saying and doing in public. And if containment was indeed at work in the Libyan case, there ought to be evidence of its presence, often but not exclusively in the form of policy changes and reversals on the part of the target state (Libya).

Third, what policy outcomes were the US and Libya able to achieve during Colonel Qaddafi's tenure as the leader of Libya? What do these policy outcomes tell us about Qaddafi's ability to outwit his enemies and the United States' ability to thwart Qaddafi's schemes? Jonathan Schwartz points out, quite rightly, that there was nothing inevitable about the way in which the Libya case turned out.[125] US officials used numerous policy tools during the thirty-some years that they were striving to keep Qaddafi contained. These included air strikes, sanctions, criminal prosecutions, UN resolutions, and direct diplomacy. "U.S. officials, both in the executive branch and in Congress, had to make difficult judgments, weighing the prospects for success of each option, its likely reception by international and American audiences, and its collateral effects on other U.S. foreign policy objectives."[126] Containing Qaddafi took decades of hard work and some serious risk-taking too, but it appears nonetheless to have turned out remarkably well. Libya renounced its support for terrorists like the Abu Nidal group that had caused so much pain and suffering during the Cold War. It accepted responsibility for the bombing of Pan Am flight 103 as well as the bombing of a French airliner, UTA flight 772. Libya also paid compensation to the victims' families. Finally, Libya gave up its WMD stockpiles unconditionally and in their entirety. Libya's programs aimed at producing WMDs were likewise turned over to the United States and Britain, once again unconditionally and in their entirety.[127]

More important, Qaddafi's regime took all these steps to placate the Americans and the British even though a strong case can be made that giving up Libya's WMDs increased Qaddafi's vulnerability to coups, mutinies, and even cross-border invasions. Surrendering the WMDs also meant consorting with the same "colonial" states—the United States and Britain—that Qaddafi had demonized for more than thirty years. The United States and Britain were once considered Libya's most vicious foes; now they were Libya's new best friends. Giving up the WMDs was not only politically risky; it also served as a constant reminder to the Libyan people that these programs had "failed to reward Libya with anything of substance in return." The terms laid down by the Americans and the British, and accepted by Qaddafi and his regime in their entirety, meant that Libya surrendered its WMDs to a policy that was all sticks and no carrots.[128]

A Revolution That Failed

Consider first the question, What outcomes did Qaddafi achieve during his forty-plus years in charge of Libyan foreign policy (1969 to 2011)? What steps did he take to secure his hold on power, and how did those steps affect his ability to compete with the United States?

1. WHY QADDAFI WAS NOT AS DANGEROUS AS HE APPEARED AT THE TIME

Hindsight suggests that Qaddafi was less dangerous than he appeared at the time. He was not a rising challenger; he was more the neighborhood nuisance than anything else. In an opinion piece that appeared in the *Washington Post* two days before the April 1986 US bombing raid on Tripoli and Benghazi, Lisa Anderson offered a harsh but also very insightful view of Qaddafi's role seventeen years into the revolution that Qaddafi himself had claimed would transform Libyan society. "Qaddafi," she wrote, "symbolizes a revolution that failed. His radical program for transforming Libya has gone sour. . . . Since the beginning of the 1980s, there have been over a

dozen serious attempts to spark his overthrow, ranging from military mutinies to assassination attempts."[129]

Qaddafi himself appears to have been aware that discontent within his
regime was growing, particularly within the army. In January 1989, Qaddafi used a press conference to blame all Libya's troubles on the Americans:
"America must understand that the policy of force, threats, terrorism, aircraft carriers and siege has failed miserably."[130] Really? By the time Qaddafi
made this statement, he had been in power in Libya for roughly twenty
years and had little to show for his tenure, besides a ruined economy, mul-
tibillion dollar debts incurred to the Soviet Union and other weapons sup-
pliers, poorly trained and largely ineffective armed forces, and a populace
that lived off government handouts.[131] Colonel Qaddafi, as one diplomat
put it in an interview with an American journalist, "tried to organize disor-
ganization to keep himself alive, so nobody could oppose him." But while
Qaddafi himself survived (until 2011), his undermining of Libya's profes-
sional military "may have worsened problems of maintenance and training
and made Qaddafi even more dependent on foreign advisers—especially
the Soviets, the Czechoslovaks, and East Germans—to keep his arsenal
functioning."[132]

Qaddafi's relations with the Soviets were especially strained. "Gorbachev
had refused to promise aid in the event of a U.S. attack. And when the U.S.
did attack, while the Soviet technical personnel and their commanders
picked up early warning signs, they took care of their own vulnerability by
evacuating their positions at Libyan air defense installations. But they
didn't bother to warn Qaddafi."[133]

Qaddafi did manage to keep Libya's armed forces functioning, but not
very well. During the March 1986 naval and air battle over and on the Gulf
of Sidra, US ships and planes eavesdropped on radio conversations by
Syrian pilots assigned to Libyan Air Force planes. In this case, Qaddafi
asked for more than the Syrians were willing to provide—namely, that
they engage the US Navy's carrier-based aircraft that were then shooting
up the Libyan Navy. The Syrians repeatedly refused to take off as long as
US Navy F-14s were in the area.[134] The same thing happened again during
the US bombing raid on Tripoli and Benghazi on April 14, 1986. No Libyan
fighters launched to meet the US attack. "Pilots at an air base near Surt on
the Gulf of Sidra, in fact, ignored direct orders to respond to the [US]
attack."[135]

Libyan foreign policy was another area largely devoid of any accomplishments. Libya's support for Palestinian terrorists like Abu Nidal was an
"insurmountable obstacle" to Qaddafi's attempts to forge a better relationship with the United States. Algeria and Tunisia both signed treaties of
friendship or union with Libya, but then jilted the Libyans before either
could lead to something serious.[136] In 1984 an American journalist

published an especially stinging indictment of Qaddafi's Libya at what would prove to be roughly the halfway point of his rule: "Oil revenues are down almost to half what they were four years ago. [Libya's] involvement in Chad, where an estimated 5,000 Libyan troops are based, has proven costly and . . . unpopular. And Colonel Qaddafi's gain in notoriety does not appear to have been accompanied by an increase in influence." A "western specialist on Libya" offered an even harsher judgment: "When there's an incident . . . , he attracts attention, but in the major matters of international affairs, he counts for nothing."[137]

By 1989, the US policy of containing Libya had blocked or thwarted many of Qaddafi's plots and schemes, so he reversed course and pursued reconciliation with the United States.[138] Even so, the animus built up over the previous twenty years toward Libya, especially but not exclusively because of Libya's long track record of supporting foreign terrorists, meant that about all Qaddafi could do in this regard was to express hope that the president-elect George H. W. Bush would prove easier to deal with than Ronald Reagan.

2. HOW DID QADDAFI SURVIVE FOR SO LONG?

In 1981 a "State Department analyst" told a journalist, "He [Qaddafi] looks as if he will be around for a long time."[139] The prediction was both timely and accurate—Qaddafi would continue clinging to power in Libya for another three decades, until he was swept away in 2011 by the political tidal wave known as the Arab Spring. Even so, the key word here is that Qaddafi *clung* to power in Libya. What exactly did he accomplish by hanging on, year after year after year?

In this regard, a strong case can be made that the very steps that Qaddafi took to maintain his place in Libya's political hierarchy undermined Libya's ability to compete with a superpower like the United States. Qaddafi's relationship with his own armed forces was like a security dilemma in reverse. Qaddafi feared Libya's armed forces, especially the army, as the most likely source of the coup that might sweep him out of office, so he meddled incessantly with the armed forces, transferring officers to new posts and assigning new tasks to army units, so that they never became proficient at whatever tasks they were supposed to be learning. These moves may have protected Qaddafi from coups and mutinies launched from within the Libyan armed forces, but they also hampered the armed forces' ability to perform well in encounters with the Americans. So Qaddafi tried to narrow the gap between Libyan and American forces by buying newer, more sophisticated weaponry, such as Soviet-made surface-to-air missiles or expensive multi-role jet fighters. The new weapons, however, consumed funds that might otherwise have been spent on economic development, which might have shored up Qaddafi's standing within the civilian population.[140] All that new weaponry raised new fears that it might be used against Qaddafi, so he had to meddle even more in the armed forces' internal affairs, with predictable results.

3. A LIBYA COUNTERFACTUAL

The discussion to this point has focused by and large on the search for evidence that Qaddafi, his policies, and Libya all changed in response to adoption by the United States of a containment strategy. Evidence of change by and within Libya is one way of concluding that containment "worked." There is, however, an alternative approach that complements the search for evidence of change, which is to pose some counterfactual questions: How would the Libyan case likely have turned out if the United States had held itself aloof from events in Libya? What if there had been no containment policy? What, if anything, would have changed in response?

To anyone with even a modest knowledge of the colonel's track record, these questions practically answer themselves. In retrospect, it seems most unlikely—inconceivable, even—that an inveterate troublemaker like Qaddafi would have scaled back his ambitions if the United States had done less too. The evidence considered thus far makes an overwhelming case that Qaddafi would likely have done even more if the United States had not stood in his path and threatened him with dire consequences if he did not do less. And if there had been no debilitating conflict with the United States, what incentive would there have been for Qaddafi to scale back his activities at all? In the absence of conflict with the United States, Qaddafi would likely have had even more money that he could devote to crushing (or bribing) his internal opposition, fending off coups, buying Soviet weapons (and the Eastern bloc advisers and technicians needed to operate them), and launching military invasions or insurgencies in countries other than Chad.

4. MOVE AND COUNTERMOVE

Qaddafi was not the only actor on stage as the United States pursued the goal of containing Qaddafi for years and then decades. Democracies, and especially the United States, are often said to be fickle creatures that quickly lose interest in tedious and costly foreign ventures, such as containing some crackpot foreign dictator who expects us to buy his oil and overlook his various foreign transgressions. Contrary to the conventional wisdom, eight US administrations spanning more than thirty years (those of Richard Nixon, Gerald Ford, Jimmy Carter, Ronald Reagan, George H. W. Bush, Bill Clinton, George W. Bush, and Barack Obama) consistently and even tenaciously pursued the goal of thwarting Qaddafi's schemes. How they did it is a subject worth investigating, and in this regard our Libya case study suggests that there are at least three aspects of current thinking about the relationship between democracies and containment that are in need of some revision.

First, the United States proved to be a more formidable and clever competitor than the conventional wisdom about democracies might seem to suggest. In each of the military engagements in 1981, 1986 (twice), and 1989, the United States managed to maneuver itself and the Libyans into positions in which the onus for choosing whether or not to shoot first was squarely on the Libyan side. In this way the United States was able to inflict considerable damage on the Libyan armed forces but without the opprobrium that would have come with being the one who struck first.

Second, Geoffrey Kemp is quite right when he points out that each of the options open to the United States for striking Libya carried with it serious risks.[141] Attacking Tripoli, Benghazi, or some other heavily defended site carried with it the risk of losing planes and pilots, while attacking Libyan air defenses like the Soviet-built SA-5 missile batteries that the Soviets sold to Libya risked injuring or even killing some of the Soviet military advisers who were operating these missiles on behalf of the Libyans.

Third, pundits and cartoonists of all political preferences have earned their living by poking fun at a muscle-bound Uncle Sam unable to cope with a pipsqueak threat like Libya's Qaddafi. Often lost sight of in this regard is that only a superpower like the United States will have the resources needed to assemble a wide range of options to choose from, and the Libyans knew that the United States had these capabilities. Put differently, the Libyans would have to be prepared to deter or, if necessary, defend against a wide range of possible attacks. The United States, in contrast, only had to do enough to keep the Libyans consistently off balance or uncertain about what else the United States might do. As a superpower, the United States can effectively "win" such a confrontation by keeping the target state paralyzed by doubts and fears of potential US actions. When practicing containment, the superpower effectively wins if its smaller rival is intimidated by the superpower's range of options.

5. OTHERS HELPED

Containment is not always as difficult as it might seem, because local actors will often work together or with the United States to thwart an adversary whose schemes are in need of containment. In 1980 and 1981, for example, "Egypt and Sudan . . . locked arms and pledged to help each other fend off Libyan incursions."[142] In 1983 the United States and Egypt learned independently of a Libyan plot to overthrow the government of Sudan. The United States sent an AWACS aircraft to Cairo West airfield, while the navy's USS *Nimitz* and its escorts were ordered to move closer to Egypt. The plan, according to US officials, was to relinquish the initiative by luring Libya into a situation in which Libya's choices were between striking first, in which case the United States and Egypt planned to destroy the Libyan Air Force, and slinking back to their bases. Execution of the plan went awry, however, in part because of misstatements by President Reagan and other White House officials.[143]

Contrary to claims that Qaddafi was "on a roll," by the mid-1980s a very different Qaddafi was appearing in the press: his economy weakened, his foreign adventures faltering, and his alliances showing signs of strain. Qaddafi himself was said to be facing increasingly coordinated pressure from his North African neighbors.[144] In 1992 Belgium, Denmark, France, Germany, Italy, Japan, Sweden, Switzerland, Algeria, Pakistan, and Egypt joined the United States and Britain to pass a United Nations Security Council resolution cutting air links to Libya, in retaliation for Libya's refusing to surrender for trial two intelligence agents wanted in the West in connection with the destruction of Pan Am 103. There were states on a roll during the 1990s, but Libya wasn't one of them. The 1990s were a decade when many states posted exceptionally strong economic growth rates.[145] About the best that could be said about Libya was said by Robert Litwak, who describes Libya as "successfully contained and deterred since the U.S. bombing of Tripoli in [April] 1986."[146]

A second reason why containment is not as difficult as critics have often claimed is that the state that is the target of a containment policy has often irritated multiple other states, and not just the United States. This means that the United States does not need to do everything by itself. Other states will likely have grievances that motivate them to act too. Libya's intervention into Chad's civil war "set all of Northern Africa atremble." In addition, the *Economist* noted, "Chad's old protectors, the French, were incensed by the very suggestion that they had looked the other way because Libya had just awarded a handsome contract for oil exploration to a state-owned French company. The deal was put on ice and the French fleet was put on alert."[147]

This is not to say that other states will always help or that other states will do exactly what is asked of them. It is only to say that the United States has a lengthy list of allies who can often be prevailed upon to help in a conflict like the one with Libya. Also it is useful to remind ourselves that the United States has a wide range of capabilities that can be used against other states, and not just military action. In the case involving Egypt and Sudan mentioned above, one US contribution took the form of increased aid to Libya's neighbors.[148]

In retrospect, perhaps the most significant lesson to be derived from the Libya case is that, for every move taken by the Libyans, there was always a countermove available to the United States. Statesmen who kept their attention fixed firmly on what their next move might be might not have had an opportunity to realize where this particular conflict spiral was leading, but it was indeed heading toward a resolution. Qaddafi himself may not have changed as much as the newspaper headlines suggested, as evidenced by his alleged involvement in an amateurish scheme to assassinate the Saudi crown prince in 2003. Even so, Qaddafi was willing to jettison policies he had been pursuing for decades. And because Qaddafi changed, Libya changed too. These policy changes, by Qaddafi and by Libya, are the principal reasons why we can say that, in this case at least, containment worked.

Dual Containment of Iraq and Iran

During their heydays, Iraq's Saddam Hussein and Iran's Ayatollah Ruhollah Khomeini were both widely believed to be difficult targets for a containment policy, even one designed and implemented by a superpower like the United States.[1] Why was this so? What was it about these two that made them seem such difficult cases? Five points come readily to mind.

First, consider the ways in which Saddam Hussein and Ayatollah Khomeini used the various instruments of state power (Saddam Hussein) and religious fervor (Ayatollah Khomeini) that were available to them as they pursued their respective foreign policy goals. Saddam Hussein qualifies for the short list of difficult targets because of the murderous ruthlessness that he relied on as he clawed his way to the pinnacle of power within the Iraqi state, the Iraqi Ba'ath Party, and the Iraqi armed forces.[2] Ayatollah Khomeini qualifies on the grounds that he personified certain qualities such as religious zeal, political acumen, and sheer revolutionary will—qualities that served him well during prolonged conflicts with the shah of Iran (over who would rule Iran), the Americans (the hostage crisis), and the Iraqis (the Iraq-Iran War).[3] All three of these conflicts were frequently cited as personal triumphs for the ayatollah, giving him the kind of hold on the loyalties of the Iranian people that many rulers aspire to but few achieve. Ayatollah Khomeini was a religious fanatic, but he was also an Iranian fanatic, and his nationalism allowed him to embrace wholeheartedly just about anything and everything that empowered Iran or the Shiite branch of Islam that he represented.[4]

Second, Saddam Hussein and Ayatollah Khomeini were often portrayed as very different political actors because of the contrast between Saddam's secularism and the ayatollah's religious fervor, but they were also similar in a few key ways. In Saddam Hussein's world, anyone and everyone who posed a threat to Saddam or his family was likely to make the acquaintanceship of the Iraqi security services, especially the torturers and assassins that Saddam kept on his payroll. In Ayatollah Khomeini's world, people who did not embrace the Shiite version of Islam that the ayatollah personified were obviously against Islam and thus infidels to be used and then discarded once they had outlived their usefulness. This insistence by Saddam and the ayatollah on ridding Iraq and Iran of anyone who told them something they did not want to hear made them seem very difficult to coerce.

Third, Iraq and Iran were thought to be difficult targets for a policy of dual containment in part because of the war that they waged against each other between 1980 and 1988. The Iraq-Iran War began in September 1980, when Iraq invaded Iran, seizing much of Iran's Khuzestan province, which sits atop Iran's largest and most productive oil fields.[5] Prior to the start of the Iraq-Iran War, the Carter administration for the most part shared the conventional wisdom that the Iraqi armed forces would slice through Iran's armed forces like a warm knife encountering a stick of butter.[6] A crushing Iraqi victory, it was expected, would confront Carter's administration with a choice it would have preferred not to make: either back Iran, or allow a regional imbalance in Iraq's favor to take hold.

What actually happened, however, proved to be quite different from what the Carter administration and, indeed, much of the rest of the world was expecting. The ayatollah rallied his people, and Iran did not collapse. By May 1982 "the Iranians had driven Iraqi forces [out of Iran and] back onto their own territory, and the [Iraq-Iran] war had grown into a titanic struggle in which the Islamic but non-Arab Shiite regime of Ayatollah Khomeini was pounding hard on Iraq, thereby threatening the wealth, the religious legitimacy, and perhaps even the existence of the Gulf Arab states."[7] These events left the Carter administration and subsequently the Reagan administration with what they each saw as an unwelcome choice, which they would likely have to face again and again for as long as Iraq and Iran were at war. To support Iraq against Iran, with the latter ruled by the same regime that had held American diplomats as hostages for more than a year, might be emotionally satisfying, but it might also encourage more Iraqi attacks on neighboring states. Opposing Iraq would mean siding with the ayatollah's regime in Iran—a regime that many Americans detested more than any other.[8] There was also the issue of what the United States might be buying if it were to align more openly with either Iraq or Iran. States locked in a life-or-death struggle are unlikely to do something just because the United States asks them to do it. The Carter administration had already been unpleasantly surprised more than once regarding the efficacy of using force against Iran. After studying the record amassed by its predecessor, the Reagan administration chose not to use force against Iran, at least not right away. President Reagan's newly installed administration could hardly be blamed for wanting to avoid any unpleasant surprises of its own.

Fourth, particularly as seen by Washington during the 1980s, Iraq and Iran had certain national qualities that made them appear to be especially difficult targets for a US-led policy of dual containment. Consider, in this regard, Iran's placement within the Persian Gulf region: too big to invade, too rich to bribe, and too angry and resentful to conciliate. Worse still, in Ayatollah Khomeini's view, "cooperation with the United States" would be "inconsistent with adherence to Islam. Muslim nations must choose."[9] Turning to the Iraqi side of the conflict, during the 1980s, Iraq built not only the largest but also the best-equipped army in the Arab world. The Iraq-Iran War would not go on forever. When it finally came to an end, what would Iraq do with the army it had built to defeat Iran? Might Iraq use that army to intimidate or even invade one of its smaller neighbors? A similar question could be asked about Iran. Once the Iranians had driven the Iraqis out of Iran and back to Iraqi territory, the Iranians had tried hard to stay on the offensive against Iraq. What would happen to Iran's armed forces once the war had ended? What role might they play in the various rivalries that had sprung up during and after the Iraq-Iran War?

Fifth, once the war was finally over, how might the United States reestablish some leverage over Iraq, Iran, and the other gulf states? Compared to Iraq and Iran, with their mass armies and multiple police and security services, the US tool kit looked positively barren. In retrospect, the US tool kit looked barren because it *was* barren. Once the shah had fled Iran, as he did in 1979, the Iranian government and armed forces had been torn apart and then stitched back together by supporters of Ayatollah Khomeini, thereby depriving the Carter and Reagan administrations of prospective agents that the United States could have used to reassert its influence there. As described by Graham Fuller, the CIA's national intelligence officer for the Near East and South Asia, the United States had "almost no cards to play" in Iran, and the Soviets had "many." Worse still, this situation seemed likely to persist for some time. "Nobody," Fuller continued, had "any brilliant ideas about how to get us back into Tehran."[10]

Background

Much has been written about "dual containment" as a way of coping with two ambitious middle powers more or less simultaneously.[11] Indeed, so much has been written that perhaps the most important point about dual containment has often been overlooked. For more than twenty years—from the first year of Ronald Reagan's presidency (1981) to the midpoint of George W. Bush's presidency (2004)—"dual containment" figured prominently in US foreign policy toward a strategically vital part of the world. Democracies in general and the United States in particular are often criticized for their allegedly short attention spans when faced by vexing problems such as containing Iraq and Iran.[12] In this case, at least, the custodians of dual containment of Iraq and Iran, namely, the Reagan, Bush 41, and

Clinton administrations, exhibited great care and determination as they pursued the goal of containing both Iraq and Iran at the same time. How this came to be is a story worth telling.

In retrospect, Iraq and Iran do indeed appear as difficult targets for a containment policy intended to block or thwart their ability to cause trouble throughout the Persian Gulf region and the Middle East, or at least this was the prevailing view within the Reagan, Bush 41, and Clinton administrations.[13] Iraq and Iran, moreover, were such reviled states[14] that there was an all-too-real possibility that one or more of these US administrations, with the backing of the American people, would succumb to the temptation "to stand by and watch this dictatorial and threatening pair of countries pound each other to pulp."[15] Tempting it may have been, but there were at least four reasons why not even a superpower like the United States had the luxury of standing on the sideline while lesser states aligned and fought and then aligned and fought some more, until one or more of them could fight no more.

First, Iraq and Iran were natural rivals.[16] They shared a contested border (the Shatt al Arab waterway), they both aspired to be the dominant power in the Persian Gulf region, and they both were more interested in overturning the status quo than supporting it. Iran searched tirelessly for ways to export its Shiite-led revolution to other Persian Gulf states, even while waging war against Iraq.[17] Iraq invaded Iran in 1980 and Kuwait in 1990. The Khomeini regime in Iran made no attempt to conceal its hostility toward the West in general and the United States in particular. Seen this way, dual containment was both a moderate and a sensible response by the Reagan, Bush 41, and Clinton administrations to the emergence of Iraq and Iran as middle powers that aspired to dominate their corner of the world. Iraq and Iran were both anti-Western and anti-American. How could these administrations be so certain of Iraq's and Iran's animus toward them? Like Libya under Colonel Qaddafi, Iraq and Iran each had the *means* (the armed forces that they had mobilized to fight each other), a *motive* (a long list of grievances that they blamed on the United States and the West), and the *opportunity* to cause trouble (they shared the Persian Gulf region with smaller states that were very wealthy but also practically defenseless). There was a lot of evidence that either Iraq or Iran could and very likely would cause trouble internationally if it emerged as the victor in the Iraq-Iran War. The more decisive one side's victory over the other might be, the greater the likelihood that the winner would go on to cause serious trouble in the postwar world. Dual containment was more than just one more item on a checklist intended to ensure that neither side would win a decisive victory over the other. Dual containment was instead a way of practicing realpolitik against two states with a history of causing trouble for the West.

Second, during the 1980s and 1990s, Iraq and Iran were both following policies inimical to US interests. "In between Iranian challenges came Iraqi feints at territorial acquisition as well as attempts to gain influence in decision making on Gulf and wider Arab political, economic, and strategic affairs."[18]

Third, those Arab states that bordered the Persian Gulf (Saudi Arabia, Kuwait, the United Arab Emirates, and Bahrain) were all acutely aware of the power disparities between them and both Iraq and Iran, and during the 1980s they moved discreetly but also purposefully to line up outsiders to be prepared to come to their assistance—in the form of protection, support, military aid—should the need arise. Kuwait in particular tried to play off the Americans and the Soviets by broaching the idea that one or both of the superpowers' navies could help Kuwait to break the naval blockade that the Iranians had imposed on the shipping lanes through the gulf as a way of pressuring Kuwait to end its support for Iraq. The Kuwaitis raised this issue with the Soviets as well as with the Americans, knowing that the Americans were very much opposed to any international arrangement that would allow the Soviets to gain a foothold near the Persian Gulf. And while the Americans were annoyed with the Kuwaitis, they had good reason to move quickly once the Kuwaitis had put the issue of superpower involvement in play.[19] If the Soviets had accepted the Kuwaiti invitation, the Kuwaitis could hardly reverse course just because they were hoping the Americans would at last come round to their point of view.

Fourth, the United States had important goals of its own at stake in the gulf.[20] Oil prices had roughly quadrupled in 1973–74 in response to the Yom Kippur War, the Arab states' embargo on oil shipments to the United States and the Netherlands, and the Saudi cutback of their own oil production. Oil prices roughly doubled once again in 1979 and 1980, in response to the Iranian revolution, the overthrow of the shah of Iran, the Soviet invasion of Afghanistan, the Iraqi invasion of Iran, and a general feeling that the world was on the brink of some foreign policy catastrophe, and maybe even war.[21] Higher oil prices meant more revenue for oil producers, such as Iraq and Iran, which they could and did use to buy weapons with which to intimidate and even invade neighboring states. The United States was not itself much dependent on Persian Gulf oil, but western Europe and Japan were very dependent on oil from the gulf. Carter's administration wasn't looking for a fight, and neither was Ronald Reagan's. Even so, anything that jeopardized the free flow of oil from the Persian Gulf to Europe and Japan was an existential threat to their economies, and anyone or anything that threatened Europe and Japan was an existential threat to the United States as well. In effect, the United States needed a policy that made it possible to warn off both Iraq and Iran without seeming to risk the infrastructure that made possible the continued and steady flow of Persian Gulf oil to Europe and Japan.

Seen this way, there was no question that the United States would be involved almost from the start in any future conflict in the Persian Gulf or Middle East. What was not foreordained was that the Reagan, Bush 41, and Clinton administrations would choose dual containment of Iraq and Iran as the foundation for their strategy toward the region, and that they would stick to dual containment for nearly two decades. These outcomes are especially surprising because they occurred at a time when the United States was already containing a third regional power (Libya) and deterring a fourth (North Korea). Neither the Reagan nor the Bush 41 administration used the term "dual containment" to describe its policies toward Iraq and Iran, but their actions suggest an almost instinctive urge to thwart whatever schemes those two might be concocting, and above all "to ensure that both Iran and Iraq [would] remain equally weak for an indefinite period."[22] "Decisive victory or decisive defeat of Iran in the war," Milton Viorst wrote in a contemporary article about Iraq at war, "could cause chaos in the region. Either would create very serious problems for the United States."[23] The Clinton administration formally adopted dual containment in May 1993, but the origins of the policy could be traced back to months or even years before the Clinton administration took control of US foreign policy.[24]

In the decade between the first Persian Gulf War (when Iraq invaded Kuwait) and the September 11, 2001, attacks on the World Trade Center and the Pentagon, "the strategy of dual containment of Iraq and Iran was a key driver of U.S. military training and force posture for the region."[25] If neither side could be allowed a decisive victory over the other, then the only solution left would be dual containment of both Iraq and Iran, until one or (preferably) both had exhausted themselves, thereby bringing the war between them to a halt and setting the stage for a prolonged peace. Iran, because of its larger population and resource base, may have preferred to fight on in pursuit of a more conclusive outcome, but this could not be allowed to happen. Dual containment was intended to forestall this by making more fighting prohibitively costly.

Dual containment was the parties' default option, chosen because neither Iraq nor Iran was deemed a suitable candidate to ally with the United States against the other. Both were eager to overturn the international status quo. If left to their own devices, who knows what sort of trouble they might cause? Neither could the United States align with one of them against the other. Iran was detested in the United States all through the 1980s and into the 1990s for its mistreatment of the US embassy staff in Tehran. Iraq was ruled by a murderous psychopath who seemed likely to use any further help from the United States to launch another war against some other Persian Gulf state, such as Kuwait or even Saudi Arabia. Kuwait and Saudi Arabia were not a military threat to anyone, but that only made them more tempting to Saddam and his henchmen.[26]

Twin Pillars

During the 1950s and the 1960s, the West in general and the United States in particular relied on Britain to play the role of stabilizer in the Persian Gulf region. For roughly a quarter century after the Second World War, Britain's protective role in the gulf "paid great dividends." Britain "deterred outside powers from establishing a major presence or from pursuing direct competition in the region. It had contained or froze territorial disputes" and it accommodated social pressures.[27] Britain's Persian Gulf security blanket, however, ultimately proved unsustainable. During the late 1960s and the early 1970s, Britain's responsibilities "east of Suez" were handed off to Iran (then a monarchy ruled by the shah) and Saudi Arabia (also a monarchy). This transfer of responsibilities was endorsed by the Nixon administration, which viewed Iran and Saudi Arabia as twin pillars that could oversee and support a new regional order, backed by "faith in both the stability and the political reliability of these regimes."[28] The twin pillars notion was an American creation through and through, although the Nixon administration was content to leave the precise nature of the relationship between the pillars and the United States ambiguous—not quite formal allies like western Europe or Japan, but more than merely friends.[29] This kind of ambiguity, as practiced by the Nixon administration, was a way of shifting burdens away from the United States and onto regional actors, but without seeming to weaken whatever commitments the United States might have extended to Saudi Arabia or Iran during the shah's rule. Burden shifting was an important consideration for every US administration since Harry S. Truman's, because they feared that the American people might not accept the obligations of global leadership unless there were some foreign policy successes along the way that could offset the bad taste left by the way the United States departed South Vietnam in 1975.[30]

While the British were carrying out their planned withdrawals from the gulf region, which they did during the late 1960s and early 1970s, Iran, Iraq, and Saudi Arabia competed with one another to create a political order for the Persian Gulf that was more to their liking. Iraq tried to radicalize its neighbors, Iran helped Oman (also a monarchy, ruled by a sultan) suppress an insurgency based in Oman's southern province, and Saudi Arabia used its oil wealth to promote norms such as moderation and nonintervention among Persian Gulf states.[31] The United States tried multiple approaches, such as relying on the "twin pillars" of Iran and Saudi Arabia during the 1970s, "tilting" toward Iraq during the 1980s, and pursuing "dual containment" of Iraq and Iran during the 1990s. None of these approaches worked very well, in no small part because of what Kenneth Pollack has very astutely labeled the "paradox of Iraqi power." As Pollack puts it, "[an] Iraq that is strong enough to balance and contain Iran will inevitably be capable of overrunning Kuwait and Saudi Arabia."[32]

In the United States, meanwhile, during the first three years of Jimmy Carter's presidency, Iraq and Iran received relatively little attention from the upper reaches of the Carter administration, at least when compared to Carter's major accomplishments—the Panama Canal Treaty, the Camp David Accords (Israel and Egypt), and a second Strategic Arms Limitation Treaty with the Soviets. The seizure of the US embassy in Tehran in November 1979, followed by attacks on the US embassies in Pakistan and Libya, and then by the Soviet invasion of Afghanistan, suddenly crowded out just about every issue that did not have something to do with Iran or Afghanistan, particularly after September 1980, when Iraq suddenly and unexpectedly invaded Iran. On those previous occasions when the Carter administration had worried about the rivalry between Iraq and Iran, it had accepted, more or less unquestioningly, the conventional wisdom of 1979–80, which was that a war between Iraq and Iran would lead to a crushing defeat for Iran. Iran's expected defeat would be in large part due to the purge of the Iranian officer corps that had been carried out by Khomeini's revolutionary zealots, thereby depriving the Iranian armed forces of their most experienced and capable leaders. Iran was also expected to be greatly hampered by its inability to buy replacement weapons and spare parts for its armed forces, most of which would have to come from the United States, which had been Iran's principal source for weaponry and equipment during the reign of the shah.

Carter's Reversal

In retrospect, neither Iran nor Saudi Arabia proved to be much of a pillar. Indeed, the "twin pillars were exposed as hollow even before an external threat was confronted."[33] The shah's regime collapsed in the face of Ayatollah Khomeini's Islamic revolution in 1978 and 1979, just a few years after the shah had accepted the role of regional pillar and special friend of the United States. The Saudis preferred to play the game their own way—by appeasing or bribing regional threats rather than confronting them.[34] As the twin pillars' weakness and timidity became more apparent, the Carter administration and even more so its successor, the Reagan administration, turned their attention to new policies more appropriate for the 1980s than the 1970s.

This was not an easy thing to do. In January 1977, when Jimmy Carter succeeded Gerald Ford as president, the United States had no permanent military presence on or near the Indian Ocean. There were occasional visits by US Navy task forces, but there was no unified, dedicated military command to supervise any US forces that might be deployed to the Indian Ocean and the area around it. Instead, US defense policy toward the Persian Gulf and Indian Ocean regions was largely improvised and ad hoc. Pre-1980, the United States was simply not "prepared to conduct major military operations in Southwest Asia and the broader Middle East."[35] Post-1980, the US military position was much stronger, due in no small part to two seemingly modest steps taken during Jimmy Carter's presidency.

First, in August 1977, President Carter signed Presidential Directive 18 (PD-18). This document was important because it stipulated, among other things, that the priority given to projecting US military power into the Persian Gulf region should be just as high as in the case of reinforcing US forces in Korea. To make this goal a reality, PD-18 ordered the Defense Department to create a Rapid Deployment Force (RDF) for use in the Persian Gulf region.[36]

Second, Carter's administration set in motion the bureaucratic wheels that would culminate during the 1980s in the creation of the US Central Command, also known as CENTCOM. As explained by William Odom, CENTCOM's origins are to be found in Jimmy Carter's one term as president (1977–81). "The basic foundations of CENTCOM were created at this time."[37]

Signing PD-18, ordering the armed services to create an RDF, and laying the foundation for CENTCOM were the easy parts. The hard part was convincing the services and their civilian counterparts to work together in reasonably harmonious fashion. Once PD-18 had been signed, Odom writes, "the Pentagon essentially ignored the directive to set up an RDF, and the State Department showed no interest in making it acceptable to U.S. friends in the region."[38] These responses to what the White House hoped would be one of President Carter's signature accomplishments in defense policy meant that if President Carter wanted an RDF and CENTCOM too, he would have to invest more of his own energy and attentiveness during what proved to be the last two years of his one-term presidency. These were political imperatives that President Carter had hoped to avoid, for two reasons.

First, the State Department, the Defense Department, the intelligence community and the uniformed services all had their reasons for opposing creation of an RDF. The differences between them and the National Security Council staff took years to resolve, in no small part because President Carter thought there were better uses of his time than mediating disputes sparked by petty bureaucratic rivalries. Jimmy Carter as president aspired to shift the global agenda away from weapons, arms races, and nuclear proliferation, and to replace it with a new agenda built around limits on conventional arms sales, nuclear nonproliferation, human rights, and economic development.[39] If Carter had intervened sooner, more often, and more insistently in these disputes over how best to project US military power into the Indian Ocean and nearby territories, he might have been able to use his presidential "power to persuade"[40] to push some of them to an earlier resolution.[41] Instead, Carter acted as if he had time—indeed, lots of time—to deal with issues like the RDF, but time was something that he did not have in abundance, especially after the attacks on the US embassies in Iran, Pakistan, and Libya and the Soviet invasion of Afghanistan. Viewed in retrospect, those events were especially important because they sparked a sudden awareness that the United States was facing multiple imminent threats to its interests in the gulf region, rather than something that could be deferred until a second term.

Second, the slow pace of progress toward creating an RDF was glaringly apparent in the mostly empty military cupboard that the Carter administration inherited from its immediate predecessor, the Ford administration. To Jimmy Carter's credit, at least some of these bureaucratic hurdles were resolved by the time Ronald Reagan was elected president. The Reagan administration proved to be both cautious and careful in its approach to Persian Gulf security issues, just like Carter's administration had been. The principal difference between them was that Reagan inherited armed forces that were better prepared to intervene in the gulf, thanks to modest increases in the defense budget during Carter's years in office and larger increases during President Reagan's first term.[42]

This too was hard work, and it was also an accomplishment for which Carter and his administration received little credit at the time. And there was indeed credit that could be handed out. Odom estimates that, if the planning and organizational activity that was carried out during Carter's presidency had not been done, the US-led multinational effort to eject the Iraqis from Kuwait in 1990 and 1991 would likely have been more difficult and taken much longer.[43] CENTCOM, in Odom's judgment, was crucial to the success of Operations Desert Shield and Desert Storm in 1990 and 1991, to the toppling of the Taliban and al-Qaeda in Afghanistan in 2001, to the US invasion of Iraq in 2003, and to many smaller operations in the 1980s and 1990s.[44]

In effect, Jimmy Carter presided over the rebirth of the military and political arrangements that proved to be crucial to the success of US policy toward the Middle East and Persian Gulf in the 1980s, 1990s, and beyond. But because the payoffs for these endeavors came mostly during the 1980s and beyond—years after Carter had left the White House—Carter's presidency was and still is remembered as a time when the United States talked big but acted small. Much like the case of Qaddafi and Libya, these perceptions of US weakness would have a powerful impact on the Reagan administration, which was understandably eager to distance itself from any tie-in or connection to what Carter had accomplished.

Accentuating the differences between Carter and Reagan was, again, easier said than done, in no small part because the RDF, to be militarily effective, would require access to ports and airfields outside but close to the Persian Gulf region. As Carter found out during his last year in office, many prospective negotiating partners were by and large content with the status quo and thus reluctant to embark on a long and difficult path without a good idea of how all this might end.

Making matters worse, at least in the Reagan administration's view, Carter's administration had no stomach to confront a Soviet Union that seemed to be flaunting its geopolitical inroads in states such as Ethiopia, South Yemen, Angola, and so on. "The Soviet military undertook massive air- and sea-lifts . . . of Cuban troops plus large quantities of tanks, armored fighting vehicles, and artillery to reinforce the Ethiopian army in its Ogaden war against Somalia. Soviet military transport aircraft overflew Turkey, Syria, and other states en route to Ethiopia without asking permission. Not a single county openly protested, and the United States also stood by quietly, making no protest to Moscow."[45]

Reagan's Revival

It was precisely this sort of pusillanimous response to the growth in Soviet power that the Reagan administration wanted to get away from. The Reagan administration "took office [in 1981] with a singular purpose in the foreign policy area: to restore and revitalize a strategy of global containment of the Soviet Union."[46] Global containment was required, Reagan and his appointees argued, because the United States was facing a range of threats that were both global and regional in nature. As seen by the Reagan administration, the Soviets were forming a global coalition against the United States that included Cuba, East Germany, Libya, North Korea, Ethiopia, and Nicaragua. Global containment was the Reagan administration's preferred choice to thwart these Soviet schemes, because it offered a kind of diplomatic two-for-one: anything that weakened a Soviet proxy also weakened the Soviet position globally. Conversely, weakening the Soviet Union would likely weaken some Soviet proxies too, because of the latters' continued demands on their Soviet patrons to supply more weapons, money, oil, advisers, and so on. At the very least, global containment was attractive to the Reagan administration because it was a way of denying the Soviets any illusions that they might actually be able to subvert or browbeat vulnerable pro-Western governments until they could be overthrown or intimidated into accepting Soviet hegemony.

The Reagan administration's attempted revival of global containment, however, met with only limited success. This was due in part to Congress's refusal to appropriate all the funds that the Reagan administration had requested in order to put into practice its expansive (and expensive) thinking regarding how much was enough, and in part because the American people were willing to support only to a limited degree the use of US proxies like the Contras in Nicaragua and UNITA in Angola, neither of which was a paragon of liberal democracy. If there was only limited support for global containment, why stick with it? Why not try for a strategy that might be more in line with the preferences of Congress and the American people?[47]

As seen by the Reagan administration, especially during its first term, global containment should have been a relatively easy sell to the Congress, to the American people, and to US friends and allies worldwide, for several reasons. First, global containment was seen by the Reagan administration as another means of waging a vigorous Cold War against the Soviets, by threatening to do to them the same things that they were attempting to do to us (e.g., line up clients, pay for proxy wars, and so on). Second, global containment appealed to the Reagan administration because they thought it would work and, indeed, work quite well against the Soviets. President Reagan's view of the world was fundamentally optimistic—the United States, he believed, could win the Cold War.[48] Winning the Cold War within a reasonable period of time would require the United States and its allies to do more now, but this condition should have been relatively easy to satisfy. In the Reagan administration's view, the most important requirement for a strategy of global containment was to stop dithering and start acting, making full use of the range of the capabilities available to the United States, including a substantial increase in military and economic assistance to US friends and allies worldwide, reliance on US proxies as appropriate, and the occasional commitment of US forces, as in Grenada (1983), the Persian Gulf (1987), and Panama (1989).

In addition to global containment there were also regional threats that cried out for some kind of response from the United States. In Iran, for example, the revolution led by Ayatollah Khomeini had effectively wrecked the twin-pillar scheme that American policy makers had found so appealing for the Persian Gulf region during the 1970s. Instead of being a partner the United States could rely on, the Iranian regime—dominated by clerics—sought to maintain its revolutionary zeal by promoting Iran-style revolutions in other Persian Gulf states.[49] It was precisely this mix of zealotry and asceticism that was Iran's greatest weakness as well as its greatest strength.

In this regard, an obvious problem for Khomeini and his successors was that the ayatollah would not live forever. As long as Khomeini was a living, breathing, charismatic leader, political communities both within and around Iran found it to their advantage to deal with him. Once Khomeini was no longer around, however, the same peoples and regimes that found it politic to deal with him as de facto ruler of Iran would likely grow weary of the restrictions and constraints that Khomeini's ultra-austere version of Islam would entail. Seen from Washington, it wouldn't be necessary for the United States to occupy or liberate Iran from Khomeini's grand schemes for spreading Islam to nonbelievers. All that was necessary for the United States was to shore up Khomeini's targets and let old age catch up to him, all the while leaving open the option of closer ties to the West for those in Iran who preferred a less austere life style.[50] Indeed, the last US ambassador to Iran, William Sullivan, argued in his dispatches to the State Department that propping up the shah's regime was a lost cause, that the United States should not oppose Khomeini's takeover, and that the United States should instead treat Khomeini's revolution as a progressive step on the path to increased democratization and political participation.[51]

Meanwhile, on the Iraqi side of dual containment, American policy makers had by and large convinced themselves that Iraq under Saddam Hussein would be mostly quiescent during the 1990s and beyond, in part because of the enormous debts that Iraq had taken on during its war with Iran, and in part because of casualties and the enormous destruction that war with Iran had inflicted on Iraq. Postwar Iraq was so burdened by debt that the Reagan and Bush 41 administrations took it almost as a given that Iraq was the lesser danger relative to Iran and thus a relatively easy target for a policy based on dual containment.[52] "After eight years of brutal fighting with Iran," the former secretary of state James A. Baker III wrote in his memoir of the first Bush presidency, "Saddam Hussein [presided] over a battered and demoralized nation. Iraq's industry was wrecked and its cities were pockmarked by the damage inflicted by hundreds of Iranian SCUD missiles. Iraq, a nation of only eighteen million, had suffered more than half a million deaths." As Baker recalled, "None of us would have guessed that this country America had sought to engage could muster the capacity to set the world on a course for war in August 1990."[53]

In retrospect, these expectations proved to be very misleading. More important, the greater the difficulties involved in persuading Congress and the American people of the merits of global containment, the more appealing dual containment became to the Reagan administration. Left to its own devices, the Reagan administration almost certainly would have preferred global containment to dual containment, on the grounds that the Soviet Union was the greatest danger facing the United States, and thus global containment should have had first claim on American resources. On the other hand, the Reagan administration, like President Reagan himself, was nothing if not pragmatic when it came to judging what the American people would be willing to support. In this sense, dual containment was attractive to the Reagan administration because it asked less of the United States than did global containment, making it something that Congress and the American people would be more willing to accept. Dual containment promised less than global containment, but it also asked less and thus seemed easier to sustain.[54]

In sum, dual containment was attractive to the Reagan administration because it filled the role of containment-lite better than any of the alternatives. The Reagan administration did indeed pressure reluctant allies and neutrals to join in forging a "strategic consensus" that would include actual or prospective Middle East partners such as Egypt, Israel, Jordan, Saudi Arabia, and the smaller but also more moderate Arab oil producers. But when even the lite version of global containment proved to be beyond the administration's grasp, the Reagan administration had no difficulty switching gears. Dual containment ultimately aimed to ensure that no Middle East state, with the exception of Israel, might become so powerful relative to the other Middle East states that an ambitious, would-be regional hegemon might come to see war as a plausible alternative to the status quo.

Back in the United States, meanwhile, the Reagan administration may have longed for a more clear-cut division of the world into pro-Soviet and anti-Soviet forces, but events in the Middle East and Southwest Asia made it increasingly difficult to see the world this way. Compounding matters, as William Odom explained, were the Iraq-Iran War, the tenacity with which the combatants had fought each other and the Iranians' success at recovering all the territory that had been lost to Iraq during the first weeks of the war.[55]

These events, in Odom's view, "turned Iran into a serious concern for CENTCOM."[56] If Iran were to conquer Iraq, it would be in a strong position to impose its brand of militant Islam on the smaller Persian Gulf states, which collectively exported to the West several million barrels of oil per day. If for whatever reason a large amount of this oil were to be suddenly removed from global supply, the result would likely be ruinous economic failures both for the oil sheikhdoms and for their customers in the West. Conversely, if Iraq won the war against Iran and bit off some of Iran as payment for years of suffering and hardships both before and during the war with Iran, Saddam's ill-concealed ambitions to acquire WMDs would not bode well for the West either.[57] The only thing worse than not having a clear winner in the Iraq-Iran War would be to have such a victor that could then use its talents to cause trouble all through the Persian Gulf region. Hence US policy turned in the direction of taking limited steps intended to prevent either of the combatants from scoring a decisive victory over the other.[58]

This was the context for the expansion of the US role in the Persian Gulf region that took place discreetly but also determinedly during the 1980s. CENTCOM's involvement in July 1987 originated in a military operation code-named Earnest Will, which was tasked with preventing the Iranians from interfering in the movement of oil tankers from Kuwait and then through the Persian Gulf en route to ports in the West or in Japan. The Reagan administration had already made up its collective mind that an Iranian victory in the war against Iraq would be unacceptable. To thwart such an outcome, the Reagan administration tacitly accepted a set of policies aimed at helping the Iraqis (clearly the weaker party to the conflict) to stave off defeat. These took the form of intelligence sharing, turning a blind eye to Iraq's purchase of Soviet weapons, and allowing those weapons to move across Saudi Arabia and Jordan from Red Sea ports.

Implementation

Dual containment of Iraq and Iran, as practiced by the Reagan, Bush 41, and Clinton administrations, took as its starting point the judgment that Iraq and Iran were both hostile to the United States and unlikely to shed their hostility anytime soon. Left to their own devices, Iraq and Iran would almost certainly act in ways that threatened US interests, both during and after the war between them.[59] Building up one to counter the other was a plausible solution to this problem, except for one obvious flaw, which was that the weapons Iraq and Iran were using against each other could be turned against the United States or its allies in the region, like the two French-made, Iraqi-launched Exocet missiles that nearly sank the US Navy's USS *Stark* on May 17, 1987. In response, the Reagan administration used a mixture of words and deeds to obtain and hold the Iraqis' attention. At the suggestion of President Reagan's second secretary of state, George Shultz, the Reagan administration threatened that US forces would shoot down any plane that moved in a potentially threatening way toward any US naval vessels in and around the Persian Gulf or moving toward it. This was a threat that was very credible considering that it came after the United States had sunk or damaged five Libyan naval patrol boats in March 1986, raided Libya's two largest cities (Tripoli and Benghazi) in April 1986, and shot down two Libyan fighter aircraft in 1981.[60]

Because Iraq and Iran were both considered to be hostile to the United States and therefore likely to pursue policies inimical to US interests, the Clinton administration took as its starting point that "building up one to counter the other" should be "rejected in favor of 'dual containment.'"[61] In practical terms, this meant that "the basic strategic principle in the Persian Gulf region" was "to establish a favorable balance of power" that would "protect critical American interests in the security of our friends and in the free flow of oil at stable prices."[62]

That was all obvious enough, although Anthony Lake, President Clinton's first national security adviser, was studiously vague when asked who might align with whom for whatever period of time. More important, the available precedents suggested that this kind of balancing was easy to talk about but hard to do in practice. Lake, for example, was very critical of the Nixon administration's attempts to build up the shah of Iran as a regional pillar. He was also very critical of the Reagan administration's efforts to tilt toward Iraq during its war with Iran. Both of these maneuvers, Lake claimed, "proved disastrous" for the United States, because they effectively left the issue of who would align with and against whom largely unsettled.[63]

Despite these imperfections, dual containment was nonetheless a welcome development for the United States, which was still looking, albeit not very successfully, to devolve some of the burdens of containment onto its allies. Dual containment was widely believed to be more feasible during Clinton's presidency than it had been in the recent past, because the Clinton administration was the beneficiary of important changes that had not been available to previous administrations. As described by Anthony Lake, four changes had recently occurred that suggested to the Clinton administration that dual containment could be sustained for years and maybe even longer.[64]

First, the end of the Cold War meant that the United States no longer had to fear Soviet attempts to establish a foothold in the Persian Gulf region. The Soviet Union's resources were sufficient that it could, during the Cold War at least, realistically aspire to compete with the United States for influence in the Persian Gulf. But as the Cold War ended and the Russian economy imploded, the notion that Russia could continue to serve as a peer competitor of the United States seemed more and more fanciful. Second, both Iraq and Iran had much less military capability when the Iraq-Iran War ended in 1988 than they did when the war started in 1980. With Iraq and Iran greatly diminished as potential regional threats, dual containment might well be sustained for years, even with a smaller contribution by the United States. Third, the first Persian Gulf War (1990–91) made the smaller Arab Persian Gulf states less reluctant to work closely with the United States to provide new arrangements for regional security and for pre-positioning military equipment that could be used to deter or if necessary defeat any future regional conflicts caused by either Iraq or Iran. Fourth and finally, trends within the Persian Gulf region were both positive and favorable to the United States. In the Clinton administration's view, the United States was facing a favorable situation that likely could be sustained for years to come.[65]

What exactly did the Clinton administration see that its predecessors had not been able to visualize? As practiced by the United States, dual containment of Iraq and Iran included three strategic imperatives which, taken together, suggested a very favorable strategic situation. First, in the event of another war between Iraq and Iran, the United States and its Arab allies would "tilt" toward whichever side seemed to be losing. The goal here was to prevent a clear-cut victor from emerging. Second, the United States and its allies should keep a low profile, be discreet, and above all not do anything that might embarrass the United States in the eyes of Congress or US allies overseas, which might lead them to conclude that the administration didn't know what it was doing and result in more restrictions and less freedom of action for US forces in the Persian Gulf region. Third, they should be flexible, and if the need arose, be ready to commit US forces to prevent the emergence of a winner and a loser.

Concerning the first of these, dual containment during the Iraq-Iran War was intended by the United States to be applied more or less evenly to both Iraq and Iran. "Dual containment," however, did not mean "duplicate containment." The challenges posed by Iraq and Iran were "distinct and therefore require[d] tailored approaches."[66] Each of these two "backlash states" was pursuing an agenda that was hostile to the United States, which meant that neither of them could be allowed to win the war that they would be waging against each other. Neither could be allowed to win that war because of the risk that the winner's ambitions might expand in ways that increased rather than decreased the likelihood of another war, only this time with the United States included. Alternatively, the side that was losing might direct its hostility toward the United States and the West, for the sake of revenge if nothing else. Finally, either or both sides might use the bloated military establishments that they had created to fight each other during the Iraq-Iran War to extort money from one or more of the Persian Gulf sheikhdoms that could then be used to pay off debts, buy more weapons, or even to threaten conquest of the smaller and vulnerable Arab states.

How was the "tilt" to be done in practice? Prior to the Iraq-Iran War, it was widely believed within the Carter administration that Iraq posed a threat to Iran but not to the United States. Iran, on the other hand, was a threat to US interests throughout the Persian Gulf region. "Washington's first serious overture [to Iraq] came on the eve of the seizure of the U.S. Embassy in Tehran." In 1979, "after a dozen years of only icy contacts, Washington decided to step up its involvement with Iraq," just as "Iran's revolution began emitting ominous waves."[67] Once the Iraq-Iran War had begun, Washington announced that its policy would be one of strict neutrality. Shortly thereafter, however, regular meetings began between high-ranking US and Iraqi officials. In 1982, the Reagan administration gave the first overt signs of a tilt toward Iraq by extending credits (which ultimately reached $750 million) to buy US agricultural products.[68] "From 1982 to early 1990, American leaders had viewed Iraq as a quasi-ally."[69]

The US tilt toward Iraq thus took two forms, at least at first: a warmer political climate and agricultural credits that Iraq could use to buy food in the United States with which to feed the Iraqi people. The aid that the United States gave to Iraq served two purposes. First, continued progress toward a warmer bilateral relationship, symbolized by gestures such as the restoration of diplomatic ties between the United States and Iraq, was intended to bolster Iraqi morale and thereby encourage the Iraqis to fight harder. Second, the military aid that the United States offered was intended to bolster Iraq's armed forces, so that the Iraqis could keep up the fight by shifting Iraqi Army units to whichever part of the Iraqi front seemed to be most imperiled by Iran's latest attempt to achieve a breakthrough.

As the war between Iraq and Iran waxed and waned, depending on the availability of conscripts and weaponry, the Reagan administration tilted toward Baghdad on more than one occasion, as George H. W. Bush and Brent Scowcroft put it, "not out of preference for one of two reprehensible regimes, but because we wanted neither to win the war and were worried that Iraq would prove to be the weaker."[70] By early 1984, to cite one example, Iran's position had improved to the point that the Reagan administration feared that it might be able to launch multiple attacks along an eight-hundred-mile front. These might be more than Iraq, with a population one-third that of Iran, would be able to repel. "In this situation, a tilt toward Iraq was warranted to prevent Iranian dominance of the Persian Gulf and the countries around it."[71]

Armed once again with all the wisdom that hindsight provides, we might see dual containment as practiced by the Reagan administration during the Iraq-Iran War as a problem with an easy solution. The United States was formally neutral, which meant that US officials could maintain a low profile, acting discreetly to bolster Iraq whenever it appeared as if Iran might be getting closer to winning the war outright. The United States was able to thwart these Iranian efforts in no small part because the United States had multiple tools at its disposal, such as looking the other way when other states discreetly increased arms sales to Iraq, increasing the amount of trade credits at Iraq's disposal, and sharing intelligence information showing where the Iranians were concentrating their forces for their next assault on the Iraqi Army.[72]

This is not to suggest that dual containment was easy, or that it worked perfectly. First and foremost, the Reagan administration, to cite one example, exhibited an unhealthy desire to engage Iraq's ruling clique, regardless of whatever games Saddam might be playing on his own initiative. This was a serious problem for a containment strategy because even as the Reagan administration was praising Iraq for its progress toward becoming a normal state, that very same Iraq was preparing to use chemical weapons against Iranian soldiers and Iraq's Kurdish minority. Iraq, George Shultz later wrote, was actually one of Washington's principal foes. Even so, in the latter half of 1983, the US posture changed. Iraqi officials visited Washington and the United States sent two emissaries to Iraq to show concern about the possible defeat of Iraq.[73] "Their message was that the United States did not want to see an Iranian victory."[74]

Second, the US Navy seriously misjudged the burdens and the risks imposed by the US reflagging operation in the Persian Gulf. The navy at first estimated that four ships in the Persian Gulf and five more nearby would be enough to intimidate the Iranians, but this estimate proved to be woefully off the mark. Within a month of the start of Operation Earnest Will, there were about fifty or so US and allied ships in the gulf.[75]

Third, as the Reagan administration's trading of arms for hostages suggests, dual containment required excellent political judgment and a deft touch when it came to adjusting the amount and kind of assistance that the United States gave to Iraq to prevent an Iraqi collapse. This kind of deft touch was not always there when it was needed the most. Claudia Wright, for example, wrote in an article published just before the attack on the US embassy in Tehran by Iranian militants that "Washington has seriously misjudged [Saddam Hussein] and underestimates the capabilities of his government. For better or worse, Iraq does indeed have weight in the Middle East and means to use it."[76]

Fourth, Iraq and Iran were inveterate troublemakers. They were both anti-West and especially anti–United States, and there was plenty of evidence suggesting that both of them would continue to cause trouble internationally if the opportunity should arise once again. Selling arms to Iran, for example, as a way of winning freedom for American and British citizens held hostage by Iranian surrogates in Lebanon almost certainly encouraged the Iranians to seize more hostages who could then be traded for more weapons, which likely had the effect of encouraging the Iranians to fight on rather than accept a cease-fire and an end to the fighting. Once the Iraq-Iran War had finally ended in a stalemate and a cease-fire, the Reagan administration lost interest in maintaining a balance of power in the gulf by tilting toward Iraq. Iraq was not exactly helpful either. Instead of moving away from supporting terrorism, favoring a Middle East peace, and joining the international community of responsible citizens, Iraq was relapsing and becoming once again the kind of local bully that had gotten itself stuck in an unwinnable war.[77]

Fifth, during the Iraq-Iran War the United States proclaimed itself to be formally neutral between Iraq and Iran. It was, however, common knowledge that the United States was secretly helping the Iraqis in a variety of ways, such as grain sales and exchanging intelligence; indeed these actions by the United States sales had to become public knowledge if they were to have the intended effect of bolstering Iraqi morale and discouraging the Iranians. In 1985 and 1986, the United States sold weapons to Iran in an attempt to free American citizens held hostage in Lebanon. This time, the Reagan administration wanted these arms sales to remain secret, but nothing as sensitive as trading arms for hostages remains secret for very long in the sieve-like political culture found in Washington, DC. This was especially true because each hostage released was promptly replaced by another American kidnapped and held for ransom. There was a distinctly amateurish quality to the way the Reagan administration handled the arms-for-hostages affair, which made the administration look less than competent. If the goal of dual containment was to bolster the Iraqis and intimidate the Iranians, the missteps that took place in public over who was responsible for what came to be known as the Iran-Contra Affair did not contribute much toward convincing the Iranians that they should settle now rather than later.[78]

Relinquishing the Initiative

During 1987, the Kuwaitis raised with both the Soviets and the Americans the issue of greater superpower involvement in the war between Iraq and Iran. On March 23, 1987, the Reagan administration offered to extend US military protection to Kuwaiti oil tankers traveling through the Persian Gulf. On April 6, 1987, the Kuwaitis proposed transferring the registry on some of their oil tankers to the United States. This latter move was by far the more important of the two, because, if it were agreed to by the United States and Kuwait, "the U.S. Navy would then have more of an obligation to escort such commercial shipping up and down the Gulf, and the Iranians would have no doubt of U.S. intentions to keep the sea lanes open."[79]

Brave words indeed, but how much substance lay behind them? The US military posture toward the Persian Gulf during the Reagan years was one of "dramatizing the Iranian threat and positioning itself to contain it."[80] Once the navy had been ordered to keep the sea lanes open and assembled a large fleet to do just that, the Reagan administration had finally relinquished the initiative to the Iranians. A retreat under fire (or even at the sufferance of the Iranians) would be worse than humiliating, because it would validate everything the Iranians (and the Iraqis too) had been saying about the decadence of the West in general and the United States in particular. On the other hand, relinquishing the initiative meant that it was up to the Iranians to choose whether and when to attack those vulnerable Kuwaiti tankers and their US escorts. If the Iranians chose to continue their attacks, they faced almost certain defeat inflicted by the US Navy, which clearly outclassed them. If the Iranians refrained from striking first, they would be accepting an outcome that upheld the status quo and offered a clear-cut path to victory for the United States.

Seen this way, relinquishing the initiative was a way of positioning or arranging the status quo so that it was the Iranians who would have to choose between war against the United States and returning to their bases (neither of which had much appeal in Tehran). This form of relinquishing the initiative had worked very well when employed against the Libyans, but against the Iranians the operation got off to a less-than-stellar start. The Reagan administration was at first reluctant to raise the level of US involvement in the gulf, but did eventually do so, because "it was critical that Iran not come to dominate the Gulf and therefore the Arabian Peninsula."[81] On July 22, 1987, "three U.S Navy ships escorted two reflagged Kuwaiti tankers up the Gulf to Kuwait."[82] The navy positioned its ships parallel to the Kuwaiti tankers, in effect daring the Iranians to do something to make them go away. The navy, however, neglected to sweep for mines laid by the Iranians ahead of the first tanker convoy. On the first US Navy–escorted mission through the Persian Gulf, the first tanker in the queue, the *Bridgeton*, struck a mine, thereby calling the navy's competence into question. Cynics said the *Bridgeton* was escorting the navy instead of vice versa. Worse still, in a statement released on July 31, 1987, the British turned down a request from the United States to send minesweepers to the Persian Gulf. The United States was pursuing a "'dead end' policy, the British said, and they wanted no part of it."[83] To get out of a dead end, it's necessary to make at least one U-turn, and within a very short period of time the British and other NATO allies would be eager to own a piece of Operation Earnest Will. To its credit, and the Europeans' too, the navy learned quickly from its initial mistake. Within a month there would be fifty or more US and allied warships in and around the Persian Gulf.[84] Hindsight reminds us that the US Navy wasn't the only organization that changed its collective mind regarding deeper involvement in the Persian Gulf.[85] The British and the French both changed their views on the minesweeper issue, sending some to the Persian Gulf in mid-August 1987, followed by Italy, the Netherlands, and Belgium soon thereafter.

"The U.S. Navy," Secretary Shultz later recalled, "drove the final spike into this affair in late September 1987," sinking an Iranian amphibious landing craft that had been outfitted for mine laying.[86] The Iranians were more daring and more determined than the Libyans, but in both cases the moral of the story was very clear: don't challenge the US Navy unless you're prepared to lose your entire fleet. The US Navy, with its ships hugging the west side of the Persian Gulf, once again positioned its forces in such a way that the Iranians would have to shoot first if they were determined not to let the reflagged Kuwaiti tankers transit through the Persian Gulf to the Indian Ocean. Rather than striking the first blow by attacking the Iranians, the Reagan administration's reflagging operation stands out in retrospect as a case of arranging the status quo to place on the Iranians a choice between an unwelcome option (a retreat back to their bases) and an even worse option—war with the Americans. Some of the Iranians, especially the Islamic Revolutionary Guard Corps, appear to have been ready to take their chances, but revolutionary élan is a poor substitute for the concentrated firepower carried by the world's most modern warships. "The presence of the U.S. Navy and its demonstrated willingness to meet Iranian provocations with both retaliatory and preventive military actions was key to keeping the sea lanes open while the war dragged on."[87]

Others Will Help

I suggest in chapter 1 that if containment really was widely thought of as unreliable or ineffectual, then we should expect to see efforts by one or more of the gulf's lesser powers to align with Iraq or Iran—in effect allying with the strongest regional power rather than with the United States, also known as bandwagoning. Conversely, if containment was believed to be working well, and the danger posed by Iraq or Iran was not imminent,[88] then we would expect the Persian Gulf sheikhdoms to respond by buckpassing—attempting to persuade the United States to do more for the smaller gulf states, which were practically indefensible, so they could put their own resources to other uses (bribery, gifts, loans, and so on). If the threat posed by Iraq, Iran, or both was widely believed to be both menacing and close at hand, we would expect the small Arab states to seek more protection against Iraq and Iran by chaining themselves to the United States, so as not to be ignored or overlooked when it came time to assess who would play what role in a future confrontation. Chain-ganging with the United States in this fashion should have produced greater security for the Arab states, and it could be done at reasonably low cost and risk, thanks once again to the enormous military advantage enjoyed by the United States.

Chain-ganging suggests another possible outcome.[89] During the first and second Persian Gulf Wars, the deepest, most worrisome fear of America's Arab allies was not that the United States would coerce them, invade them, or threaten them with other kinds of forceful military action. Instead, it often seemed as if America's Persian Gulf allies' greatest fear was that the United States would ignore them. The more the Americans sought to keep at arm's length the smaller Arab states and their endless insecurities, the more tightly those smaller states sought to cling to the United States. Of these three (bandwagon with Iraq or Iran, pass the buck to Washington, or chain-gang with the Americans), the evidence available is more supportive of the latter two than of the former. Comparisons between the Cold War and the post–Cold War world offer some interesting insights in this regard.

During the Cold War, for example, the small Arab states often sought to escape any unpleasantness with Iraq or Iran by making themselves as inconspicuous as possible, which they rationalized by means of barely concealed hopes that each would be the last one to be eaten and that their pursuers would by then have developed indigestion. As the Cold War came to an end, those same small Persian Gulf states were less likely to spurn military cooperation with the United States than they had been during the Cold War. With the Soviet Union gone and Iraq and Iran greatly diminished in strength, the smaller Arab states were more secure than ever before and thus more willing to align with the United States (against Iraq and Iran). Greater access to the gulf's air and naval facilities made it easier for the United States to station forces in the region and bring in reinforcements as needed, which made the smaller Arab states more secure and thus more willing to cooperate with the United States. In effect, the smaller Arab states were most willing to accept close ties and US protection when they needed them the least.

There remains the question of whether the smaller Arab states felt more secure because of or despite their growing dependence on the United States. The United States, as Janice Gross Stein writes, had long sought to intensify its military cooperation with the gulf states, and cooperation did increase in the wake of the American naval deployment to the Persian Gulf in 1987. On the other hand, collective action theory also suggests that small states will resist taking on a larger role in any kind of ongoing conflict, preferring to avoid burdens rather than accept them. Collective action theory suggests further that small states will be reluctant to take on any kind of larger role, lest they be asked to do more than their own resources could achieve yet less than what their larger allies could easily accomplish. These fears regarding small states' being asked to take on larger responsibilities, however, appear not to have materialized in the case of dual containment. The United States made many requests for help during the so-called War of the Tankers. Qatar, Bahrain, Kuwait, and Saudi Arabia were all asked to do more by way of cooperation with the United States, and they all agreed to do so.[90] "Qatar provided storage facilities for weapons, lubricants, jet fuel, and medicine; Bahrain provided port-call facilities and the use of naval mooring facilities. The exchange of intelligence information between the United States and Saudi Arabia also increased. . . . European participation in naval operations in the Gulf has [also] been extensive." France, Britain, and Germany—after some hesitation and delay—all redeployed some of their naval forces to protect tanker traffic within and through the Persian Gulf. Belgium, the Netherlands, and Italy dispatched minesweepers to the gulf to avoid any additional embarrassments like the attack on the *Bridgeton*.[91]

If small-to-medium powers are supposedly reluctant to align too closely with a larger state for fear of being dragged into unwanted conflicts, then how do we account for the apparent reversals by Britain and France, and then by Germany, Italy, the Netherlands, and Belgium, at first declining a US request for help and then joining the growing naval flotilla after all? The initial hesitation on the part of the Europeans is not difficult to explain. The US Navy failed to anticipate that the Iranian Navy and the Iranian Revolutionary Guard Corps would sow mines along the western coastline of the Persian Gulf. Because the navy did not anticipate that the Iranians would mount so brazen a challenge, it wasn't looking for mines, which is why it was caught by surprise by the attack on the *Bridgeton*. Also very embarrassing for the United States was Britain's initial response to the US request for greater aid and support. The United States was flogging a "dead-end policy," and the British wanted no part of it.[92] This fueled doubts in Europe about what this naval war was intended to accomplish. To its credit, the navy learned quickly. As George Shultz recalled, "The Iranians tested us again several times, and we struck back." Iran's Ayatollah Khomeini and his entourage were "shocked by our attack; they had never believed the U.S. Navy would ever act against them directly." Instead, the Iranians appear to have believed that the United States would likely pull out and go home after absorbing a few casualties.[93] The navy, however, did indeed act against them, and on more than one occasion. This gave the United States an opportunity to destroy the Iranian Navy, without suffering any losses of its own.[94] Or as Kenneth Pollack subsequently wrote, "Iran's naval threat to Persian Gulf shipping in the 1980s was easy to handle, because [of] the vast preponderance enjoyed by U.S. naval and air forces."[95]

Viewed this way, the choices made by Belgium, the Netherlands, Italy, and Germany are reasonably easy to explain. These countries' armed forces are relatively small and almost completely dedicated to the defense of their home turf. Britain and France, on the other hand, have a long and distinguished history of sending forces to engage in expeditionary campaigns. Why, then, did the British and the French change their minds about helping out in the Persian Gulf?

The answer is that superpower involvement often reduces the inhibitions and reluctance to get involved that can afflict smaller states. Hence, the greater the US Navy's preponderance, the greater the sense of security and confidence that middle powers like Britain and France were likely to feel as they contemplated aligning openly with the United States. If the United States is involved, the chances of success are likely to increase, and middle and small powers will look for ways to become involved, both to further their own interests and to ingratiate themselves with an American administration eager to acquire some political cover by persuading other states to join in too.

Move and Countermove

Iran was a formidable foe, but one with weak spots too. Much like the Libyan case, for every move made by the Iranians, there was a countermove available to the United States. When the Iranians massed their ground forces in an attempt to break through Iraq's defenses, the United States shared satellite intelligence with the Iraqis, so that the Iraqis could move their own reserve forces to plug holes in their lines, which effectively thwarted Iranian ambitions of inflicting a crushing defeat on the Iraqis. When the Iranians attacked Kuwaiti oil tankers attempting to pass through the Strait of Hormuz, the United States responded by reflagging the Kuwaiti ships and by sinking—on October 8—three Iranian gunboats. On October 16 an Iranian Silkworm missile hit the reflagged tanker *Sea Isle City* at its Kuwaiti anchorage. Three days later the US Navy destroyed an Iranian oil rig used as a gunboat base, and President Reagan banned all imports from Iran.[96]

It was no secret during the 1980s that Iraq and Iran were both pursuing nuclear, biological, and chemical weapons, and ballistic missiles that could carry those warheads to targets in other countries. Defense analysts explained in detail how the Iranians had upgraded their armed forces to make them a more formidable threat to the United States as well as to Iraq. But the same analysts devoted less attention to the countermoves available to the United States.[97] Even as Iran was improving its armed forces by acquiring more ballistic missiles, more antiship missiles, and more diesel-electric submarines, the United States was modernizing and upgrading its own forces too, most prominently in the form of "smart weapons"—a product of the "accuracy revolution"—and the United States was doing it faster and better. The Iranians had little choice but to absorb the losses sustained during the "tanker war." Those losses, however, were also a warning of things to come, because they made it plain for everyone except the most committed fanatic that the gap between the Iranian armed forces and the US armed forces was widening, not narrowing.

Assuming that one of the purposes of dual containment as pursued by the United States was to buy time during which Iraq and Iran could mellow, reconcile, and perhaps become law-abiding states, how much time might be required for these outcomes to be achieved? Khomeini's successors were effectively "oblivious to such mundane details as state frontiers or secular authority." This kind of Iran still "poses immense problems for all the states of the Gulf."[98]

By the late 1980s, post-Khomeini Iran was still stirring up trouble for the West wherever and whenever it could. As recalled by George Shultz, as of January 1987, "Iran was mining the [Persian] Gulf, menacing commercial shipping, and threatening to close the Gulf and strangle the states of the Arabian Peninsula, let alone Iraq. Iran sought to position itself to dominate the entire region."[99] With the superpowers hedging and stalling, the Kuwaitis took matters into their own hands by raising with both the Soviets and the Americans the idea of greater superpower involvement in the security of the gulf states. The Kuwaitis, Shultz continued, knew that the Reagan administration did not like this idea, but the Americans liked even less the idea of greater Soviet involvement in Persian Gulf security. The Reagan administration was at first reluctant to raise the level of US involvement in the gulf—for example, by reflagging Kuwaiti tankers as American ships and in that way making them eligible for protection by the US Navy. Once it had done so, however, the Reagan administration quickly found itself engaged in a shooting war with the Iranians, and this was a burden that could not be shirked. It was "critical," as Shultz put it, "that Iran not come to dominate the Gulf and therefore the Arabian Peninsula."[100]

Dual containment of Iraq and Iran during the 1980s was thus a case in which multiple US administrations did not want either side to emerge victorious. While the Soviet Union, China, Britain, France, and even the European Community states likely preferred this outcome too, none of them had the strength and the willpower needed to bring this outcome to fruition. Only the United States could reasonably aspire to bring about this outcome, because of the enormous resources that were at its disposal. As described by George Shultz, even after seven years of fighting and a million or so casualties on both sides combined, Iran was still seeking to position itself to dominate the entire Persian Gulf region. "In January 1987, Iran had launched a major offensive, driving into Iraq just north of Baghdad and south of Basra, near the Persian Gulf."[101]

Perhaps the most important point here is the way the United States, in the face of a stiff challenge from the Iranians, was able to draw on its own enormous resources to thwart the Iranian scheme. "We were at first reluctant," Secretary Shultz subsequently wrote, "to raise the level of our direct involvement in the Gulf by making Kuwaiti ships our direct responsibility, registering them as American vessels."[102] But the Reagan administration greatly preferred taking on the task of protecting Kuwaiti oil tankers over having the Kuwaitis turn to the Soviets instead. Reflagging Kuwaiti vessels, in turn, would require the US Navy to escort commercial shipping up and down the Persian Gulf, and an important payoff would be that the Iranians could have no doubt of US intentions to keep the sea lanes open. If the United States was to make this effort, Shultz continued, "we should be prepared to see it through. . . . I did not want the U.S. to get drawn into the Iraq-Iran war. But it was critical that Iran not come to dominate the Gulf and therefore the Arabian Peninsula."[103]

Critiques of Dual Containment

Dual containment of Iraq and Iran was based on three assumptions that were taken almost as self-evident by the American side. These were, first, that neither Iraq nor Iran could be allowed to win the war between them; second, the best way to deny them victory was to contain each separately; and third, that Iraq was a less imposing foe than Iran.[104] The US side was very confident that it could keep Iraq bottled up more or less indefinitely. The US side was also hugely confident of its ability to stymie whatever tricks and maneuvers that Iraq might undertake. James A. Baker III, George H. W. Bush's first secretary of state, wrote in his memoir that he and others in the first Bush administration thought it "inconceivable" that the United States might one day be at war against Iraq.[105]

"Inconceivable" or not, the United States fought Iraq twice, once in 1991 and again in 2003. Does this mean that dual containment failed? Several respected scholars have reviewed these cases and concluded that the answer to this question is yes. Kenneth Pollack, for example, notes that the "initial American strategy" for Persian Gulf security was offshore balancing. This approach failed "because Iran and Iraq were still quite strong and the United States' over-the-horizon posture was not a sufficient deterrent."[106] The United States tried different ways to uphold Persian Gulf security, such as the "twin pillars" approach during the 1970s, "tilting" toward Iraq during the 1980s, and pursuing "dual containment" of Iraq and Iran during the 1990s. It was Pollack's view that "none of these approaches worked very well," including dual containment.[107] Other scholars have echoed this view. Janice Gross Stein describes the US naval commitment to keep the Persian Gulf shipping lanes open as "the right strategy in the wrong place."[108] As seen by Joseph McMillan, "using sanctions, inspections, and the threat of military retaliation to contain the Iraqi regime" was "a strategy whose time had passed."[109] In Richard Sokolsky's snapshot of gulf security as of 2002, dual containment was "barely alive,"[110] while F. Gregory Gause III judged dual containment to be illogical and therefore ineffective.[111]

On the other hand, there was also considerable evidence that could be cited in support of a qualified yes. William Odom notes that the United States pursued "a coherent overall strategy toward the [Middle East] region during the first few decades of the Cold War." The goal of the strategy was to straddle two regional conflicts—Arab/Israeli and Persian/Arab—in order to "maintain a regional balance of power. By maintaining reasonably good ties with both sides to these conflicts, the U.S. Government was able to rely mainly on diplomacy, supplemented on occasion by military power."[112] The appearance of success notwithstanding, there was never a shortage in the United States of critics of dual containment. Among the more insightful critiques of dual containment were those offered by Joseph McMillan[113] and F. Gregory Gause III.[114]

During the two Clinton administrations, Joseph McMillan points out, Saddam was constantly "testing the limits of obstruction."[115] But what, if anything, did Saddam's actions add up to? Were they evidence that dual containment was working or faltering? McMillan's choice is the latter. During the second half of the 1990s, he argues, "it became apparent that containment exercised through sanctions, inspections, and no-fly zones could not bring about regime change, secure Iraqi compliance with its cease-fire commitments, or provide any degree of certainty that Iraq was not developing WMD." Even worse, Saddam was succeeding in making the United States, rather than his own recalcitrance, appear responsible for the suffering of Iraqis under sanctions.[116]

Saddam, in effect, was doing what ruthless dictators often do—namely, convert a middle power like Iraq or Iran into a rising challenger with regional or even global aspirations. Superpowers, in contrast, have a wider range of options to choose from. In 1998 the Clinton administration concluded that "reacting to Iraqi provocations actually strengthened rather than weakened Saddam's position. Accordingly, it began looking for ways to move Iraq off the front pages and avoid incidents that would require the use of force."[117] In this way, "Saddam's persistence in testing the limits of obstruction eventually convinced the Clinton administration to launch the most robust coalition military action since the [first] Gulf War, the four days of missile and air attacks known as *Desert Fox*."[118] What may have appeared to the outside world as a strategy whose time had passed is better understood as a superpower's ability to recycle old options into something new. Superpowers will by definition have multiple options at their disposal because superpowers will always have a broad pool of resources to draw on.

F. Gregory Gause III's critique of dual containment as practiced by the Clinton administration rests on four main points. First, in Gause's view, the "most serious flaw in the dual containment policy is its unstated assumption that the regional status quo in the gulf can be maintained over the coming years," and that changes and adjustments to dual containment could be "stage-managed" by Washington.[119] In retrospect, there was indeed a lot of stage managing in the post–Cold War world, but it was the Americans who were doing most of it, not someone else.

Second, "it is hard to see," Gause wrote in *Foreign Affairs* in 1994, "how either Iraq or Iran could be contained" without at least the tacit cooperation "of its hostile counterpart."[120] Gause deems this to be the "major logical flaw in dual containment." To contain either Iraq or Iran required that the other be strong, lest it too become a target. Therefore, in Gause's view, to contain Iran, Iraq must be strong; to contain Iraq, Iran must be strong too.[121] Even if we concede Gause's claim, there is no reason to believe that dual containment of two middle powers (Iraq and Iran) would be more difficult than containing the Soviet Union—a superpower that still aspired to join the United States to form a peer group of two. Because the United States was a superpower during the Cold War (bipolarity) and a global hegemon after the Cold War had ended, it almost always had before it multiple lines of policy that could be used to support dual containment. Jimmy Carter's administration was often criticized for an allegedly weak foreign policy, yet it was Carter's administration that created some of the options that Ronald Reagan's administration found very useful, such as increased defense spending; an RDF; diplomatic initiatives in pursuit of access to aid; and naval facilities that could be used to support US naval operations in and around the Indian Ocean, the Red Sea, and the Persian Gulf itself.[122]

Third, Gause argues, the United States' allies in the Persian Gulf region and elsewhere have shown little or no enthusiasm for dual containment, making its implementation "highly problematic," especially since dual containment ties US policy to an inherently unstable regional status quo.[123] There is, however, a second side to this particular coin. The more the United States strives to leave itself free to pursue whatever options it may prefer, the more reluctant regional partners are likely to be about aligning openly with the United States, for fear that it will someday abandon them, leaving them to face the Iraqis or the Iranians (or both) on their own. Conversely, the more firmly the United States commits itself to containing Iraq and Iran—meaning deeds and not just words—the more willing local states are likely to be to jump on the American bandwagon.

Fourth, dual containment assigns to the United States a unilateral role in managing Persian Gulf security at a time when America's capability to influence events in Iran and Iraq is thought to be limited at best.[124] Janice Gross Stein, for example, describes the 1987 commitment of US Navy warships to escort Kuwaiti oil tankers out of and then back into the Persian

Gulf during the Iraq-Iran War as the wrong strategy in the right place. As seen by Stein, the escalation of US military naval commitment was "poorly conceived, ineffective, and dangerous."[125] When Kuwait approached both the Soviet Union and the United States for assistance protecting its shipping through the gulf, the Reagan administration was initially reluctant to take on yet another commitment to act in agreement with the Soviet Union, North Korea, Nicaragua, Libya, Cuba, Angola, and Ethiopia. But the Reagan administration came around, and rather quickly too, seeing this Kuwaiti initiative as an opportunity to extend deterrence, and thus peacefulness and stability, into the gulf region.

Gause, Stein, and McMillan together make a strong case for doubting dual containment. Even so, there are at least three additional reasons for believing that dual containment worked better than is generally believed to be the case. First, Iraq grudgingly accepted a stalemate in 1988 and a crushing defeat in 1991. Boundary lines were not redrawn. In this case at least, there was nothing that Iraq or Iran could point to as a sign that it was victorious or that it had profited from its wars against the other.

Second, US protection of the sea lanes through the Persian Gulf and the Strait of Hormuz eventually caused Iran to drop its threats to attack Kuwaiti shipping and Kuwait to stop looking for ways to bring the Soviets in.[126] Granted, neither of these outcomes was achieved quickly and skillfully. There were multiple encounters between US and Iranian forces, one consequence of which was "further U.S. drift toward Iraq's side in the Iran-Iraq war," as evidenced by the Iraqi attack on the USS *Stark* and the absence of any US move to punish Saddam Hussein, which likely accounts for Saddam's apparent belief that Iraq could count on US assistance against Iran without any reciprocity.[127]

Third, dual containment, as developed by the Clinton administration and applied to "backlash states" such as Iraq and Iran, was neither static nor stationary. Instead, the United States and its allies continually tinkered with the sanctions and other matters that were being used to stifle delusions of conquest in both Iraq and Iran. This is one of several important themes that can and should carry over from chapter 2 to chapter 3—namely, that US wealth and power were so much greater than those of Libya, Iraq, and Iran that the United States could respond in many and varied ways to whatever these states were doing.

Evaluating Success

Dual containment of Iraq and Iran was a formidable task, but not as insuperable as analogies based on, say, US involvement in Vietnam might suggest. As a superpower, the United States had multiple tools that it could use on problems like dual containment. The Reagan administration, for example, shared intelligence with the Iraqis, offered agricultural credits to help feed the Iraqi people, and made use of the US Navy to escort commercial shipping through the Persian Gulf, to keep open the sea lanes to and from Kuwait. The US Navy, in turn, took advantage of the escort mission to destroy much of Iran's conventional naval capabilities, thereby leaving the Iranians to harass shipping with irregular hit-and-run speedboat attacks. The Iranians fought bravely, but they fared no better than the Libyans. It can hardly have escaped notice in Tehran that engaging the US Navy in surface warfare was so one-sided as to be practically suicidal.[128]

If naval warfare in the gulf was so one-sided, how can we know whether dual containment—or any threat-based deterrent strategy, for that matter—is working when employed against states like Iraq and Iran? One way of untangling this puzzle is to focus on the means employed by a superpower like the United States to block or thwart the target state's moves. If and when the United States sets out to hinder or impede another state's unwelcome schemes, it ought to leave behind a trail of evidence that tells us that it was or is here, influencing other states. There should also be a string of minor moves that can be used to demonstrate that the strategy is working or not. In the Iraq-Iran case, there is indeed an evidentiary trail telling us that a superpower and its threats have been involved. Especially prominent here would be the Carter administration's strategy paper PD-18, the creation of the RDF, the creation of CENTCOM (based at MacDill Air Force Base) in Florida, and the creation of the Fifth Fleet, stationed in Bahrain.

Of even greater importance would be what US officials did, as opposed to what they said. In 1977, when Jimmy Carter succeeded Gerald Ford as president, the United States had no permanent military presence in or around the Persian Gulf. In 1981, when Ronald Reagan succeeded Jimmy Carter, the United States was on its way toward creating just such a permanent military presence. In 1977 the United States was ill-prepared to take on just about any kind of military operation in the vicinity of the Persian Gulf. In 1987 the United States was able to commit roughly fifty naval vessels to escorting Kuwaiti oil tankers, temporarily reflagged so that the US Navy could escort them from their home ports along the Persian Gulf to the open waters of the Indian Ocean. In the course of fighting what proved to be an undeclared war with Iran, the US Navy effectively sank the Iranian Navy.[129] The reflagging operation was and is important not just for actions taken and precedents set; it also produced a string of outcomes that showed that the United States was no slouch when it came to playing the move-and-countermove game. As Bruce Jentleson put it, despite or perhaps because of the reflagging controversy, "Kuwait was protected, the sea lanes were kept open, the Soviet Union was kept out, and Iran was contained."[130]

Saddam Hussein was contained too. Saddam, Joseph McMillan writes, was "constantly testing the limits of obstruction," which led the Clinton administration to conclude that reacting to Iraqi provocations actually strengthened rather than weakened Saddam's positions. In 1998 the United States and Britain launched the largest military attack on Iraq since the Persian Gulf War in 1991: the four days of missile and air attacks known as Desert Fox. By that time, however, "it had already become obvious that using sanctions, inspections, and the threat of military retaliation to contain the Iraqi regime" was not working. On this basis, McMillan concludes, "dual containment was a strategy whose time had passed."[131]

Had it really? The key point about using a containment strategy to thwart the dreams and schemes of an aging dictator like Saddam is not that Iraq could absorb the consequences of sanctions, inspections, and frequent military actions, but that the United States had multiple actions at its disposal that it could use to impose even greater consequences for not responding. If US policy was not as effective as desired, the United States could switch to some other policy that could offer better progress toward Saddam's ouster.

An additional way to explore the issue of whether dual containment worked is to pose a counterfactual question: What would have happened if either Iraq or Iran had won a decisive victory over its adversary during the Iraq-Iran War? As described by William Odom in his retrospective account of the formation of CENTCOM, the Iraq-Iran War during the 1980s was a serious concern for CENTCOM. If Iran were to conquer Iraq, it would be in a strong position to impose its brand of anti-Western, militant Islam on the smaller Persian Gulf sheikhdoms, which collectively exported several million barrels of oil per day—enough to cause ruinous economic losses for both the sheikhdoms and their customers in western Europe and Japan. If Iraq had won, Saddam's ill-concealed ambitions to acquire WMD would not have boded well for the West either.[132]

By this time, the Reagan administration had already decided that an Iranian victory in the war with Iraq would be unacceptable to the United States, and so it was that the Reagan administration was tacitly accepting help for the Iraqis (clearly the smaller but also the initiator of this conflict) aimed at helping the Iraqis stave off defeat—for example, intelligence support, and turning a blind eye to Iraq's purchase of Soviet weapons and their movement across Saudi Arabia and Jordan from ports on the Red Sea. The Kuwaitis had first approached the Soviets about escorting Kuwaiti tankers through the gulf, hoping to play off the two superpowers in search of the best deal for Kuwait. "The U.S. responded quickly as Kuwait played it off against the Soviet Union. The mission ended up with CENTCOM."[133]

Like many of the military operations handled by the Reagan administration during the 1980s, the navy's escort service may not have been pretty, but it all worked out very well indeed. Iraq and Iran stumbled across the finish line with no clear-cut winner but two exhausted belligerents, which was the outcome that the Reagan administration wanted all along. The Iran-Contra Affair remains an outstanding example of how easily an ill-conceived venture can nonetheless turn out tolerably well. Stalin, Mao, and Saddam never learned how to admit they had made a mistake. Because they admitted nothing, they never learned how to change, to adapt, to grow. Ronald Reagan, in contrast, was never paralyzed by fear of the consequences of admitting a mistake, which is a large part of the explanation why Ronald Reagan was and still is an amazingly popular president.

Containing Iraq

Iraq's Saddam Hussein, like Libya's Colonel Qaddafi, is a very useful case study of whether, when, and why containment works, and when it does not. This is particularly true for the interval between the first and second Persian Gulf Wars (1991–2003). During that interval, Saddam refused repeated demands by the United States and other states that he should abandon his WMD programs and his aspirations for regional hegemony. He also refused to repay Kuwait for the looting of Kuwaiti assets both during and after the first Persian Gulf War (1990–91). During the half decade or so leading up to the second Persian Gulf War, Saddam seemed to become even more defiant, not less. "Not surprisingly, some observers" began to wonder whether he could "be coerced at all."[1]

Newly released records likewise portray Saddam as a "leader who was extremely hard, occasionally even impossible, to deter, but for reasons that have little to do with irrationality." Containing Saddam was especially difficult because of his tendency to "ignore inconvenient factors and unpleasant information."[2] US officials realized that the effort that the United States had expended during the run-up to the start of the first Gulf War likely would not be enough to impress a brute like Saddam, and they resolved to do better the second time around. And if Congress should decide to withhold authority to use force to expel Iraq from Kuwait, officials resolved to "*contain* him—keep sanctions on and keep forces there" as the United States had "in Germany and Korea."[3]

On the other hand, it does no good to show that "by the logic of deterrence, American threats should be credible. If the target does not see them in this way or is willing to fight in spite of them, then they will not deter."[4] Saddam knew a great deal about bluff and bluster, and about putting on a good show for the benefit of the Iraqi people. As a military strategist, however, his tenure was disastrous for Iraq and for practically everyone who lived there.

Who was Saddam Hussein? Was he another Hitler, "a sociopath who cannot be deterred, who will discount the American military superiority and run unreasonable risks in order to gain even a small chance at domination"?[5] Alternatively, even if Saddam could not be deterred, might he at least have been contained? If the United States could have thwarted or blocked, or somehow neutralized Saddam's plans while they were still taking shape, then his preparations might still have fallen short of what he considered necessary to hatch his plots and schemes and then live long enough to bring them to fruition. For reasons that are examined in this chapter, the US effort to contain Saddam Hussein did indeed falter in 1990–91, just before Iraq invaded Kuwait. From 1991 until the US invasion of Iraq in 2003, however, the United States was able to use the vast range of capabilities at its disposal to thwart Saddam's schemes.

Why Saddam Was Thought to Be a Difficult Target

The former US secretary of state James A. Baker wrote in his memoir of the George H. W. Bush presidency that Iraq had "emerged from the [Iraq-Iran War] in desperate straits. Its economy had virtually collapsed, and many of its cities and much of its infrastructure were in ruins. Saddam needed capital to rebuild his ravaged country, which in turn required friendly relations not only with the rich Arab states of the Gulf, but also with the West."[6] The war with Iran had "sapped [Iraq's] resources and made Iraq dependent on financial and strategic support from Kuwait, Saudi Arabia, and other Arab states. Iraqi sources estimated the economic losses from lower oil revenue and higher arms purchases (excluding war-related destruction) at approximately $208 billion."[7] Damage estimates presented in US dollars give an indication of the hardships inflicted on Iraq by eight years of war with Iran, but they don't capture the deprivation, the demoralization, and the dismay that the war had imposed on Iraq.

Secretary Baker neatly captures the surprise felt by many in the United States when the end of the Iraq-Iran War proved to be more like an intermission than a lasting peace. As seen by Baker, the damage and destruction inflicted on Iraq during the Iraq-Iran War had been so great that, when the first President Bush was inaugurated in January 1989, "it was inconceivable that the United States would soon be at war with Iraq." Such an assumption seemed reasonable, given that "after eight years of brutal fighting with Iran Saddam Hussein presided over a battered and demoralized nation. Iraq's industry was wrecked and its cities were pockmarked by the damage inflicted by hundreds of Iranian Scud missiles. Iraq, a nation of only eighteen million, had suffered more than half a million deaths. None of us would have guessed that this country [that] America had sought to engage could muster the capacity to set the world on a course for war in August 1990."[8]

Inconceivable or not, only two years after the Iraqis and the Iranians had agreed on a cease-fire, Saddam launched another ill-conceived invasion of one of his neighbors—this time, Kuwait. At first the war seemed to go extraordinarily well for the Iraqis, largely because the Kuwaitis put up next to nothing by way of organized resistance. Once the Americans and the British had moved more than five hundred thousand of their own forces to Saudi Arabia and other locations in the Persian Gulf region, however, the outcome was a series of crushing defeats for the Iraqi armed forces during Operation Desert Storm. During six weeks of air strikes on Iraqi targets followed by roughly one hundred hours of ground war, the Iraqi Air Force managed to lose most of its aircraft (either destroyed on the ground or flown to Iran, where they were impounded by the Iranians). The Iraqi Navy lost virtually all its ships, either destroyed in port or lost at sea. The Iraqi Army lost thousands of tanks, artillery, and armored personnel carriers.[9]

Despite the magnitude of the losses inflicted on the Iraqis during Desert Storm, Saddam still had some formidable military assets at his disposal. The Iraqi military demobilization after the Iraq-Iran War had been measured and slow paced. Saddam's regime "preferred to pay soldiers rather than leave them unemployed to create social unrest." From August 1988 to August 1990, only about 250,000 to 350,000 Iraqi soldiers had been released from the armed forces, with over a million still in uniform when Iraq invaded Kuwait in August 1990.[10] Miller and Mylroie offer a similar estimate here. About three hundred thousand soldiers, they estimate—or one-third of the Iraqi armed forces—were demobilized during the eighteen months following the signing of the cease-fire with Iran.[11] Both estimates suggest that Saddam's regime had to tread carefully here, because it feared the consequences if hundreds of thousands of Iraqi war veterans (not to mention the sixty-five thousand Iraqi prisoners of war held by Iran) were suddenly discharged from the armed forces and told to find jobs in the civilian economy. Since it was plain to see that the Iraqi economy was not ready to place tens of thousands of demobilized soldiers into productive economic activities, many Iraqi veterans of the war with Iran were encouraged to stay in the armed forces while Iraq rebuilt and recovered from the war with Iran. During the two years of peace that followed the cease-fire with Iran, the Iraqis maintained very large armed forces, apparently in anticipation of a future conflict, perhaps with Saudi Arabia or Kuwait, or maybe a prolonged and bloody war with the United States. On the other hand, the war with the United States in 1991 ended so abruptly that roughly half of Iraq's armed forces had not been involved in the fighting at all.

What all this meant in practice was that, even after suffering a crushing defeat during Operation Desert Storm, Saddam still had a lot of military assets that he could draw on if he believed that he and his regime could survive another war. Toward that end, Saddam used the Iraqi Army to crush rebellions that broke out among the Iraqi Shiites in southern Iraq and the Iraqi Kurds in northern Iraq. Because Iraq had amassed such large armed forces prior to and during the war with Iran, the Iraqi forces that survived Desert Storm still outclassed the combined armed forces available to Saudi Arabia, the United Arab Emirates, and the other members of the Gulf Cooperation Council. Plus, Saddam had already invaded neighboring states twice (Iran in 1980, Kuwait in 1990). After he regrouped and consolidated his remaining armed forces, who could say for sure whether Saddam would refrain from going for broke a third time? Within the first Bush administration, US officials had become very sensitive to the possibility of renewed war in the Middle East, in no small part because victory in the Cold War, followed by victory against Iraq, coincided with demands from Congress and the public for deep cuts in US defense spending in order to make possible a "peace dividend" that could be used to support entitlement programs or deficit reduction.

The first Bush administration was very much aware that it had taken about six months to transport and then position the forces that had produced such a resounding victory over Iraq. A future opponent might not be as accommodating as Saddam's regime had been to the United States in allowing this process to go unhindered. President Bush 41 and his senior advisers were very much aware that the United States had needed every one of those six months to get ready to launch Operation Desert Storm, which first took the form of an air war and then the US invasion of Iraq. As to who might provoke such a war, in the Bush administration's view, Saddam Hussein was not only the most likely catalyst; he would likely prove to be a very difficult opponent and thus a hard test for a containment policy. "Saddam," as described by the first President Bush and his national security adviser, Brent Scowcroft, "was a tough, ruthless and even paranoid dictator with little exposure to, and deep suspicion of, the West. His regime's human rights record was abysmal."[12]

Saddam was indeed a tough case, but there was more to him than just another dictator looking to liquidate his enemies in one way or another. There were also, as Bush and Scowcroft wrote in typically understated fashion, "a number of security problems which complicated the arrangement." Saddam was widely believed to have chemical and biological weapons—a claim that he did little or nothing to refute. His regime had already used chemical weapons against Iran's armed forces and against Iraqi Kurds as well. Prior to the war with Iran, Saddam's regime had been acquiring ballistic missiles, and was attempting to develop nuclear weapons.[13]

On the other hand, with the exception of Iraq's invasion of Kuwait in 1990, the Iraqi Army performed poorly against any and all foreign opponents, dating back to Iraq's emergence as an independent state in 1932. One critic notes that "the only [Iraqi] army successes have been against tribesmen and defenseless civilians."[14]

Finally, if Saddam was indeed the inveterate troublemaker that many observers of the international scene believed him to be, then why had the United States devoted so much time and effort during the 1980s to improving relations with Iraq? How was it that Saddam Hussein came to be seen in Washington as someone the United States could work with regarding Persian Gulf security? To answer these questions, it's helpful to reconsider how the United States and Iraq changed their views of containment during the 1980s.

Background

Saddam Hussein ascended to absolute power in Iraq in July 1979. A little more than a year later, in September 1980, he launched what proved to be an unwinnable war against Iran, which dragged on until 1988.[15] In August 1990, just two years after the cease-fire that ended the Iraq-Iran War, Iraq was at war again. The first Persian Gulf War was the product of Saddam's decision to invade Kuwait, thereby provoking the formation of an international coalition that ultimately included more than thirty states arrayed against Iraq.

Seen this way, Saddam's management of Iraq's foreign policy was nothing less than a catastrophe for Iraq, and for Iran and Kuwait, too. But if that was the case, why did Saddam provoke these two wars? Nobody forced him to invade Iran and then Kuwait. More important, how did he manage to hold the loyalty of the Iraqi people despite two colossal mistakes?[16] Saddam's policies in this regard appear in retrospect as a combination of paranoia, opportunism, and greed. Put differently, there are several factors lurking in the background here that we need to understand in order to make sense of what Saddam actually did.

If we are to answer the question, Why did Iraq invade Iran in 1980 and Kuwait in 1990? we need to know what had happened during the run-up to each of these two wars that convinced Saddam that Iraq could win them both. During the 1980s, the Reagan administration had pursued dual containment of Iraq and Iran, but Reagan's administration frequently "tilted" toward Iraq and away from Iran, except of course when it was selling arms to the Iranians in a futile quest to persuade them to release the US and British citizens who were being held hostage in Lebanon and elsewhere. Once the Iraq-Iran War had come to an end, the first Bush administration aimed to convince Saddam Hussein not to invade another of Iraq's neighbors. To make this arrangement more appealing to the Iraqis, the first Bush administration floated the idea that maybe, if it remained on its best behavior, Iraq could have "normal relations" with the United States, upholding security and stability within and among the various states of the Persian Gulf region.[17]

When Iraq invaded Kuwait in 1990, the first Bush administration and subsequently the Clinton administration turned their attention back to the problem of containing Iraq. Why containment? Both of these administrations were concerned that an invasion of Iraq might cause it to shatter in unpredictable ways, which might endanger any US troops that happened to be in the vicinity when Iraq came apart. A US withdrawal from the Persian Gulf region was also ruled out on the grounds that Saddam was highly unlikely to give up his ambition to conquer his neighbors and make Iraq the dominant regional power. If invasion and withdrawal were both unlikely, then containment was all that was left.[18] There were also several secondary reasons why the Bush 41 and Clinton administrations found containment attractive.

First, Iraq had suffered terribly during the eight-year-long war it had waged against Iran. To justify those losses to the Iraqi people, Saddam's regime claimed that it was actually preempting an inevitable war that was to be inflicted on Iraq by Iran. Saddam's government made these expansive claims even though there was little or no evidence that Iran was plotting any such thing. Indeed, the same arguments that made war against Iran attractive to the Iraqis—the turmoil in the Iranian armed forces and Iran's inability to buy replacement weapons and spare parts from the United States—strongly suggested that Iran was nowhere near ready to fight Iraq and likely would not be ready for war against Iraq for at least several more years.[19]

Second, during the run-up to the start of the Iraq-Iran War in September 1980, the Ba'ath Party regime in Iraq tried hard to convince the Iraqi people that war with Iran would be preventive as well as preemptive— preventive in the sense that the weaker state, Iraq, attempted to resist the "hegemonic aspirations of its stronger neighbor, Iran, to reshape the regional status quo according to its own image."[20] As Efraim Karsh observes, "Faced . . . with Iran's determination to reshape the regional status quo according to its own design and with the bitter memory of armed conflicts with Iran in the early 1970s, the Ba'ath leaders seriously doubted that the Iraqi political system could sustain another prolonged, exhausting confrontation with Iran."[21]

A third reason why Saddam proved to be risk-accepting rather than risk-averse can be traced to actions that he undertook in order to keep the Iraqi people under state control. "Saddam understands," Miller and Mylroie wrote in 1990, just after the Iraqi invasion of Kuwait, "that his ability to project power outside [Iraq] helps maintain his authority inside the country. Threatening and intimidating other states contributes to an aura of invincibility at home."[22]

Fourth, the war against Iran proved to be far costlier than any sober fore-caster might have predicted. Iraq suffered casualties that ran into the hundreds of thousands, and economic costs that climbed into the tens of billions of US dollars.[23] Iraq and Iran were fighting to win, but the Reagan and Bush 41 administrations were hoping that the war would end in a stalemate. As seen from Washington, the greater danger was that Iraq—the weaker party—would quit first, thereby removing the first line of resistance to Iranian schemes to export their Islamic revolution to more states, which they hoped could then be brought under Iranian control. In an attempt to avoid this outcome, the United States offered diplomatic support to Iraq, and it extended credits to Iraq that could be used to purchase grain and other agricultural exports from the United States. The United States also shared intelligence information with Iraq, so that Iraq could shift its forces to wherever the Iranians were concentrating their forces for their next offensive against the Iraqis.

Iraq thus came out of the war with Iran greatly weakened, at least compared to 1980, when the war began. Even so, Iraq's forces were still intact, and they could have continued to fight if the cease-fire had not been signed. More important, Washington clearly favored Iraq over Iran during the war between them, which contributed to an Iraqi delusion that the United States just might look the other way if and when Iraq moved against Kuwait or some other gulf state. How did the United States find itself in such a position? More to the point, how did the architects of dual containment find themselves accepting Saddam Hussein's Iraq as a kind of junior partner in an ongoing effort to gang up on Iran?

A large part of the answer to these questions is that the Reagan, Bush 41, and Clinton administrations neither forgot nor forgave the Iranians for all the trouble that they had caused for the United States both during and after the hostage crisis of 1979 to 1981. Compared to Iran, Iraq—even an Iraq led by a "brute" like Saddam Hussein—didn't look so bad.[24] In order to contain Iran, the Reagan and Bush 41 administrations encouraged Iraq to continue to follow a moderate course, which would allow it to work more closely with the United States. Conversely, Iraq would likely be lost as a prospective regional ally if the United States were to impose additional sanctions on it in retaliation for using chemical weapons against Iranian forces during the war with Iran, and against the Kurds too. The Reagan and Bush 41 administrations both urged continued restraint by Iraq, so that it could help contain Iran. In the meantime, it was US policy to stand by Iraq, particularly during the second half of the Iraq-Iran War. As a result, there was little or no controversy within the US foreign policy establishment concerning the wisdom of cozying up to Saddam Hussein. Everyone knew Saddam's reputation, but what other choices were there? As seen by the first Bush administration, the choices open to the United

States were basically two: continue to press Iraq to moderate its policies, or stand on the sidelines and watch Iran run wild.[25]

The Iraq-Iran War

The Iraq-Iran War began in September 1980 when Iraq invaded Iran, expecting a quick and easy victory that would win for Iraq control over both banks of the Shatt al Arab waterway and portions of Iran's Khuzestan Province and the oil fields located underneath them. In the United States, both the Carter administration and its replacement, the newly installed Reagan administration, were caught by surprise when the widely anticipated quick and easy victory for Iraq failed to materialize. Iraq's inability to translate its initial military successes into a lasting and advantageous peace did, however, provide the Reagan administration with an opportunity to reexamine US policy toward the Persian Gulf region as a whole and the Iraq-Iran War in particular. This policy review, along with the Iranians' evident determination to fight on until every Iraqi soldier had been pushed back across the international boundary from where they had come, led to the unremarkable conclusion that, to contain and deter Iran, the United States should help Iraq. Indeed, by the end of 1981, a growing body of evidence suggested that Iraq's war against Iran "was rapidly turning from a victory to a near calamity. Increasingly, the Iranians penetrated into Iraq's territory."[26] By mid-1982, the Iranians had managed to drive out all the Iraqi forces who were still in Iran. By the end of 1982, the Reagan administration had formally concluded that "it was in the national interest to develop closer ties with Iraq." The United States extended agricultural credits to Iraq and shared military intelligence too.[27]

On the other hand, it soon became apparent that even these steps likely would not be enough to prevent an Iranian victory against Iraq. Facing an opponent with three times the population of Iraq and much more strategic depth, Iraq needed a partner who could help it sustain its war effort. In practical terms, Iraq needed help from the United States, which was the only state with the number and kinds of resources that could make a difference with regard to when and on whose terms the war would end. To get that support, Iraq silenced its criticisms of Egypt's peace treaty with Israel, thereby partly rehabilitating itself, at least in the eyes of the US government. Perhaps even more important in this regard is that the Iranian hostage crisis was still being played out when Iraq attacked Iran, and it would continue in effect until President Reagan's inauguration in January 1981. Timing was important here, because it meant that the hostage crisis was still fresh in the minds of the senior ranks of the newly installed Reagan administration, which saw Iran as a pariah state whose very existence called out for a robust containment policy. These events, and the conclusions that the Reagan administration drew from them, meant that "the Americans were very receptive to the notion . . . that Iraq was changing" for the better. The Reagan administration viewed Iranian words and deeds as so abhorrent that just about anything that came out of Baghdad would be better than what was coming out of Tehran. By the end of 1984, these changes of policy and attitude opened the door to the resumption of full diplomatic relations between Washington and Baghdad.[28]

For an administration that thought of itself as filled with tough-minded, unsentimental conservatives, the Reagan administration did not try very hard to exploit Iraq's weakened position and desperate need for US help (especially the satellite photography that gave the Iraqis advance notice of where the next Iranian offensive would be staged). What stands out in retrospect is how little the Reagan administration asked of Iraq. To qualify for US support, Iraq did not have to make peace with Israel; it had only to signal that the Iraqi position on the Arab-Israeli conflict was changing. For Iraq to qualify for US support, Saddam's regime and the Reagan administration did not have to like one another, and they certainly did not. "As the immediate aftermath of the Iran/Iraq war would reveal, Iraq remained just as hostile [to America and Israel] as it had been before." It wasn't Iraq that had to change to satisfy the Americans; it was instead the Americans who changed their view of Iraq. Overall, the Reagan administration preferred Iraq to Iran. Saddam Hussein was a brute to be sure, but he was our brute, often cited as the only barrier standing between Iran's Ayatollah Khomeini and the rest of the Middle East.[29] The Americans, Avner Yaniv subsequently wrote, "were very receptive to the notion . . . that Iraq was changing."[30]

And it wasn't just the Reagan administration that was almost pathetically optimistic about the prospects for US-Iraqi relations. In 1977, Jimmy Carter's national security adviser, Zbigniew Brzezinski, stated publicly that Iraq and the United States both wanted the same thing: "a secure Persian Gulf." Three years later, in May 1980, Brzezinski's view remained largely unchanged: "We see no fundamental incompatibility of interests between the United States and Iraq."[31] If, however, Brzezinski was correct about the United States and Iraq both wanting the same thing, then what was the rationale for "dual containment," supposedly aimed as much at Iraq as at Iran? It wasn't Iraq's and the United States' liking or admiring or identifying with each other that drew them together. It was instead Iraq's reckless conduct of the Iraq-Iran War that had caused its position to become so perilous that Iraq by and large could get away with not having to say or do much in order to secure greater support from the United States. Iraq did not have to obtain US consent to each and every facet of Iraq's war effort, nor did Iraq did have to make peace with Israel. About all the Iraqis had to do to obtain greater support from the United States was to signal that their position on the Arab-Israeli conflict was changing.

Toward this end, the Iraqis invited prominent American scholars and journalists to visit Iraq and to write about what they saw. In retrospect, Iraq by
and large achieved its goal of being seen in a new light. "Gone were the
charges of brutality and tyranny. If Iraq was not yet presented as a civilized
pluralist democracy, the thrust of these reports was that a 'new' Iraq was
emerging that had learned its lesson the hard way in the war with the Iranian hordes."[32] But this was all that the Iraqis offered—vague "indications"
that Iraq was changing. Proponents of this view of Iraq had little or no hard
evidence that they could cite to support their claim.[33] Instead, absence of evidence was seized on as evidence of absence. Iraq was not even close to being
a moderate, secular state that accepted Western values like civil liberties,
human rights, and free commerce. There were, however, lots of conservative
intellectuals in the United States who were eager to tell the world what they
had seen, which was an Iraq that was moving in the right direction.[34]

More important, the top ranks in both the Reagan and Bush 41 administrations formed an important audience that was eager to buy what the
Iraqis were selling. For example, George Shultz, who served as President
Reagan's second secretary of state, wrote in his memoir, "There had been a
period of 12 to 18 months in the mid-1980s when I, and American foreign
policy, gave the benefit of the doubt to the Iraqi regime of Saddam Hussein."[35] Shultz described himself as someone who was skeptical of whether
and how much Saddam had really changed. "Iraq's ambitions and activities," he subsequently wrote, "were not of a kind to breed confidence in
Saddam Hussein." On the other hand, Shultz continued, "a radical Iran
now posed an immediate threat to the strategic Gulf area, and Iraq was the
only military machine that could block the path of Khomeini's forces."[36]
Even as the United States was engaging in various military moves that benefited Iraq but not Iran, such as reflagging and escorting Kuwaiti oil tankers
into and out of the Persian Gulf, and fighting an undeclared war against the
Iranian navy in the gulf, it became more and more apparent that Saddam
was responding not with gratitude but instead with continued pursuit of a
military option against Israel. Saddam was also "seeking to construct a
regionally dominant military machine that could not be explained by his
fear of Iran alone."[37]

These developments, in turn, were enough to convince Secretary Shultz,
among others, that Iraq had not changed, which meant that the United
States would have to make changes of its own. By the end of the Reagan
years, Shultz wrote, "it was clear to me that no further reasons existed for
the United States to give Iraq the benefit of the doubt for balance-of-power
purposes against Iran." "We were at sword's point with Iraq: over chemical
weapons, the difficulty of obtaining compensation from Iraq for the victims
of the attack on the U.S.S. Stark, and signs of Iraq's support for terrorists."
Shultz concluded that "a new and tougher policy toward Saddam Hussein's Iraq was now appropriate."[38]

Shultz may have seen enough of Iraqi duplicity, but his successor as secretary of state, James A. Baker III, was not fully convinced that Iraq under Saddam was irretrievably lost, at least not yet. As Baker pointed out in his memoir of the first President Bush's term in office, there were lots of demands on policy makers in 1988 and 1989. "In this environment, at that time," he wrote, "none of us considered policy toward Iraq to be an urgent priority. And it was simply not prominent on my radar screen, or the President's." Besides, any sanctions that the United States might impose would almost certainly affect US grain sales to Iraq (backed by US credit guarantees), which were "immensely popular" in Congress and among farm state politicians.[39] As a result, policy toward Iraq remained unsettled until October 2, 1989, when the first President Bush signed the presidential directive NSD-26, which sought to codify US policy toward the Persian Gulf region. NSD-26 set normal relations as the goal for the United States and Iraq. Friendlier relations, it was hoped, might lead Iraq to modify its behavior. And if the Iraqis did not modify their behavior, political and economic sanctions would likely follow. The flexibility to move from incentives to disincentives and back again was a "central component" of US strategy toward Iraq.[40]

Seen this way, American foreign policy toward Iraq and Iran during President Reagan's two terms and the first President Bush's first year in office was largely the product of hopes that Iraq could still be salvaged and fears of what the Iranians might do if there was no Iraq blocking their path. Saddam Hussein's regime got much of what it wanted from the Reagan and Bush 41 administrations, such as US military support, satellite imagery, reflagging Kuwaiti oil tankers in 1987, and a short but intense naval war between the US Navy and Iran, during which the Iranian Navy was effectively destroyed as a fighting force. The first Bush administration continued and indeed expanded upon its predecessor's policy of drawing closer to Iraq. Specifically, the first President Bush opted for a policy of constructive engagement toward Iraq, hoping that this would contribute to the goal of moderating Iraq's policies. As NSD-26 and other documents explain, "Iraq was becoming a pillar of U.S. policy in the Persian Gulf, a bulwark against Iran, and a possible ally of U.S. interests" in other matters, such as the Arab-Israeli dialogue.[41]

There was, however, at least one obvious problem with a policy that aimed both to engage and contain Saddam's Iraq more or less simultaneously. Once the Iraqis had secured US military support for the war against Iran, they had no reason to make any additional concessions to the United States. As the "immediate aftermath of the Iran-Iraq war would reveal, Iraq remained just as hostile [to Israel and the United States] as it had been before."[42] And while there was lots of evidence suggesting continued Iraqi hostility to the West in general and the United States in particular, even the most perceptive assessments would be of little help if they weren't heeded. The first President Bush and his national security adviser, Brent Scowcroft, claimed in their jointly written memoir that it was apparent soon after the Iraq-Iran War had ended that Saddam had not changed his policy toward the United States and Israel. The more ruthless Saddam's regime appeared to the West, the harsher the criticism of Iraq in the West, especially in the United States. The more vocal the criticism of Iraq on issues such as human rights, corruption, and WMDs, the more determined Saddam became to acquire WMDs, and to do so quickly, before the United States and its allies might resort to coercion or even brute force, to compel Iraq to give up its WMD programs.[43] Saddam himself appears to have believed that this backlash against Iraq was being orchestrated by the United States, Britain, and Israel. In response, Saddam threatened to attack Israel with chemical weapons, "a threat that pushed entirely the wrong buttons in the United States."[44] For its part, the first Bush administration dropped plans for a second round of agricultural credits to Iraq, worth five hundred million dollars. "If our analysis [that Iraq had changed its stance] was correct," Bush and Scowcroft later wrote, "then our current policy was not appropriate." Still, it didn't seem necessary at that time to actually *do* anything right away regarding Saddam and Iraq. Saddam was so mercurial, Scowcroft reflected, that the United States could wait a bit before changing policy itself.[45] Or could we? Hindsight has a lot to offer on this matter.

A strong case can be made that the first Bush administration was doing the right things, albeit for the wrong reasons. US statesmen and policy makers should try—indeed, try hard—not to jump prematurely into a quarrel that is taking place on the other side of the world, seven thousand miles from the United States. A policy that takes as its starting point the judgment that hesitation is acceptable because the full nature of the threat is not yet well understood is often a sensible way to avoid unnecessary casualties. Containment, as envisaged by US strategists such as George Kennan, William Kaufmann, and John Lewis Gaddis, was not a blueprint for fighting another war. It was instead an attempt to exploit the leverage that comes with being able to fight if need be.

Precisely because the United States was and is a superpower with vast resources at its disposal, it could realistically keep up the pressure on a relatively small adversary for years and maybe longer, all the while waiting for signs that the target of containment had changed and could take its place in the community of law-abiding and peace-loving states like the United States and its allies. In the case of the Iraq-Iran War, however, as the war progressed it became harder to spell out who was manipulating whom in order to induce important policy changes by the target states. The Reagan and Bush 41 administrations resisted any and all pressures for retribution toward Iraq. Saddam continuously denigrated the US, and Washington's refusal to respond looked like weakness to Baghdad.[46]

In addition, Saddam's regime was ready to compete. "Iraq's leaders," as Barry Rubin recalls, "were armed, desperate, and dangerous," and the US did not make Saddam pay for his behavior. As Rubin rightly points out, "the word for this approach" is "appeasement."[47]

The first President Bush's hesitation in this regard was not the first time that the United States had stumbled on the issue of what to do about Saddam and Iraq. As evidenced by President Reagan's willingness to sell arms to Iran in order to ransom US citizens who were being held hostage in Lebanon and elsewhere, the Reagan administration never fully resolved what to do about Iraq and Iran. The first President Bush attempted to resolve this problem by deciding in favor of a policy of constructive engagement toward Iraq, hoping that this would moderate Saddam Hussein's policies toward the United States and Israel. On October 2, 1989, the first President Bush signed NSD-26, "which reaffirmed our strategic interests in the [Persian Gulf] region and, with caveats conveying our concerns, generally confirmed the previous policy of engaging Iraq." As seen by the first President Bush, "the problem was how to encourage Saddam Hussein to be at least a minimally responsible member of the international community and yet not accept or ignore his depredations."[48]

Here indeed was a problem worthy of presidential attention. Was constructive engagement of Iraq the best solution available? Even as more and more evidence accumulated that Saddam Hussein was not modifying his actions and his stance vis-à-vis the United States and the West, the first Bush administration continued to cling to constructive engagement as its chosen policy toward Iraq. Both the Reagan and Bush 41 administrations recognized that there was a problem with Saddam Hussein, but was containment the solution to this particular problem? A strong case can be made that containment did not fail, and it did not fail because it wasn't tried, or at least not very well.[49]

Iraq Invades Kuwait

The shah of Iran had been the first choice of three American administrations—Nixon, Ford, and Carter—to serve as principal US ally and stabilizing presence for the Persian Gulf region. The Reagan administration let it be known a bit too frequently that it preferred the shah to the clerical regime that took control of Iran in 1979. In view of the fall of the shah and the animosity felt by the United States toward the clerical regime in Iran (for tolerating the abuse of the Americans held hostage there for more than a year), the United States turned to a policy of dual containment of Iraq and Iran.[50] In practice, this meant that the Reagan administration would, in Bush and Scowcroft's words, "tilt toward Baghdad during the Iraq/Iran conflict, not out of preference for one of two reprehensible regimes, but because we wanted neither to win the war and were worried that Iraq would prove to be the weaker." Once the war had ended in a stalemate, which was the outcome that the United States had wanted all along, "the Reagan administration set out to institutionalize this somewhat improved relationship with Iraq. It was an attempt to encourage acceptably moderate behavior on the part of Saddam Hussein."[51]

Unlike Colonel Qaddafi in Libya and Ayatollah Khomeini in Iran, Saddam Hussein appeared to US policy makers as the proverbial someone we could do business with, and thus someone who would be relatively easy to contain. On April 12, 1990, for example, Saddam met with a delegation of six US senators, who returned to Washington describing him as "a leader with whom the United States could work."[52] This view appears to have been widely held in the upper ranks of the first Bush administration, although not everyone shared it. As recounted by James Baker, on August 3, 1990, Dennis Ross and Robert Kimmitt cited the "illusion we can moderate this guy [Saddam]." Ross and Kimmitt argued that, to the contrary, "these [Iraqis] are tough guys. We have to treat them toughly."[53] US officials assumed that Iraq had been so weakened by the exertions required to achieve a cease-fire and a return to the status quo ante, that even an incorrigible troublemaker like Saddam Hussein would have little choice but to moderate his behavior in order to stay in the good graces of the Americans, whose support the Iraqis would need if Iraq were to recover from the war. Even if Saddam had not been virulently hostile to the United States and the West (and he was), Iraq's losses during the war with Iran had been so great that Iraq would almost certainly be consigned to observing international norms so as not to jeopardize the flow of petrodollars and agricultural credits from the United States. If Saddam was to have any chance of rebuilding Iraq's armed forces, he would have to stay within limits on the sale of weapons and equipment set by the West—the very countries that Saddam claimed to despise.

Saddam was a highly motivated buyer, but were the Americans motivated sellers? One outcome of these conflicting views of Persian Gulf security was that American officials, during the interval between the end of the Iraq-Iran War and the Iraqi invasion of Kuwait, tried harder to insert themselves into Saddam's good graces so that they could contain, block, or thwart whatever schemes Saddam was continuing to pursue in order to transform Iraq into a regional hegemon that dominated the Persian Gulf and its surrounding territories. The clerical regime in Iran likewise aspired to regional hegemon status, and of the two Iran was seen as the greater long-term threat because of its aspiration to oust incumbent governments and replace them with religiously observant governments that would be amenable to following Tehran's lead. Iraq's invasion of Kuwait resolved the issue once and for all, or at least until Iraq had nowhere left to fight.

After Iraq invaded Kuwait in August 1990, policy makers in the United States and elsewhere were quick to see the errors apparent in how they had approached both Iraq and Iran. They thus faced the problem of containing Iraq with greater vigor and determination than they had exhibited prior to the outbreak of the Iraq-Iran War in 1980. Seen this way, however, US policy toward Iraq and Iran was doubly flawed. On one hand, as Barry Rubin points out, "the whole purpose of U.S. support for Iraq had been to stop Iran's expansionism." US policy makers (mistakenly) saw Iran as the greater immediate threat, even though a strong case could be made that it was Iraq that was more likely to catalyze a new war aimed at elevating Iraq to the rank of regional hegemon. On the other hand, when the Iraq-Iran War finally ended in August 1988, US policy remained substantially the same. In the aftermath of the war, "Most U.S. officials and experts expected Iraq to concentrate on development and reduce military spending. They did not really understand that Saddam put a [high] priority on maintaining his power and realizing his ambition[s]. . . . After all, they reasoned, what country would be more likely to follow a pacific course than one that had just barely survived a terrible eight-year war?"[54]

In light of Saddam's expansive view of the kind of country that Iraq should strive to become, some limits on weapons purchases would be better than no limits, but even an extensive set of limits would likely accomplish only a little in terms of restraining Iraq. "In bilateral relations, [Saddam] shafted America at every opportunity, and the U.S. exacted no price from him for his behavior," as Barry Rubin observed. Instead, the Reagan and Bush 41 administrations resisted the idea of pressure or retribution against Iraq. "Thus, in response to Saddam's continued verbal attacks on the United States, Washington sent signals of weakness to Baghdad. . . . Each act of appeasement increased Iraq's boldness without ever convincing [Iraq] the United States wanted friendship."[55]

In effect, US policy remained static (tilted toward Iraq) when it should have been changing in anticipation of renewed warfare by Iraq (in the aftermath of the Iraq-Iran War). One result of this kind of thinking was that prior to the Iraqi invasion of Kuwait, the United States had tried hardly at all to contain Iraqi ambitions, in the sense of thwarting or blocking Saddam's scheming to transform Iraq into a regional hegemon.[56] As explained by Secretary of State Baker, "Our strategic calculation changed irrevocably on April 2 [1990], when Saddam explicitly threatened Israel in a speech to the General Command of his armed forces." As described by Baker, US concerns about Saddam and his policies should have changed over time, but not very quickly. The greater the worries and concerns on the US side, the more important it would be to actually do things to counter or thwart what Saddam might be doing. Did that actually happen? In retrospect, the course of events ran along a different track.[57]

At the time that these issues were being dealt with, Khomeini's Iran was seen as the greater danger to peace and stability in the Persian Gulf region. Saddam's Iraq, however, was arming at a rapid rate, which the first Bush administration was slow to recognize. By the summer of 1990, the Bush administration was becoming increasingly concerned about Saddam's ingratitude and belligerence, which continued to escalate, almost without any constraints on what Saddam might say or do.[58] In retrospect, Saddam was signaling that the status quo on the Arabian Peninsula was unacceptable and that he intended to change it. The first Bush administration, however, did not change its response to what Saddam was saying and doing. Saddam was intent on escalating his conflict with the other Arab gulf states, whereas the first Bush administration was intent on sticking with constructive engagement.

Flawed Implementation

After Iraq invaded Kuwait, policy makers in the United States and elsewhere were quick to see the error of their ways. "Our approach to averting conflict—to warn against belligerent behavior, to make clear we would stand by our friends, yet continue to offer good relations for good behavior—had failed."[59] Secretary Baker agreed. "Before Iraq's invasion of Kuwait," he wrote in his memoir of the first Bush presidency, "we had begun to stiffen our approach toward the regime in Baghdad. The policy of constructive engagement was giving way to a more sober and critical view of Saddam. This tougher line was sufficiently incremental, however, that those few Americans who were paying attention could be excused for having missed the shift. And then, practically overnight, we went from trying to work with Saddam to likening him to Hitler."[60] The greater the worries and concerns on the US side, the more important it would be to actually do things to counter or thwart what Saddam might be doing.[61] US officials thus approached the problems of rescuing Kuwait and containing Iraq with more determination and ingenuity than they had exhibited prior to the outbreak of the war in 1990.

Limited steps intended to demonstrate a willingness to continue working with Saddam, however, were as far as the first President Bush was prepared to go with Iraq. Prior to the Iraqi invasion of Kuwait, the first Bush administration had been willing to limit containment for the sake of constructive engagement. After the Iraqi invasion of Kuwait, the first Bush administration viewed containment as an even greater challenge than engaging Saddam, but also one that the United States could not and would not shirk.

In the immediate aftermath of Desert Storm, the first Bush administration decided that it was still in need of the coalition that had fought the war against Iraq, for two reasons. First, Saddam's WMD programs were more substantial and better concealed than the administration had realized at the start of the war. In Baker's words, "We were determined to use our victory in Desert Storm to put the Iraqis under the most intense glare of the most intrusive weapons-inspection regime ever developed, to root out every last bit of that program. We were also determined to maintain substantial economic and political sanctions against Iraq to restrict its aggressive tendencies." Baker and his colleagues saw that "to put Saddam Hussein in that cage, so to speak, we needed implementation of existing UN resolutions . . . and we needed all our coalition partners to be with us to achieve this."[62]

Second, the first Bush administration saw Saddam's overwhelming defeat as a clear repudiation of Arab radicalism, which in turn meant a new opportunity to pursue a lasting Middle East peace. To take advantage of that opportunity, however, "we needed to keep the coalition intact and focused on peace."[63] Iraqi armed forces had incurred huge losses during Desert Storm, but the war ended so quickly that a large share of the Iraqi Army had not been involved in the fighting at all. The Bush administration refused to march on Baghdad, for fear Iraq might implode in unpredictable ways. The first Bush administration also feared that American forces, with approximately five hundred thousand military personnel in Iraq, Kuwait, and Saudi Arabia, might be drawn into the fighting if Iraq collapsed.

In this situation, the Bush administration set out to reestablish containment, and this time do it right. The Iraqi Army was allowed to leave Kuwait at least partly intact, in what proved to be a vain hope that an army that had managed to maintain itself as an organized force would be more likely to stage a successful coup against Saddam than a motley assortment of small units and individual soldiers.

Saddam's Defeat

Despite the noise and confusion that accompanied the end of the first Gulf War, there are at least five reasons for believing that the outcomes achieved were very favorable to the United States and its coalition partners.

First, the armistice agreement that ended the war was very stringent. Under the terms of the agreement, Iraq promised to give up all its WMDs and the programs that produced them. No-fly zones were set up in northern Iraq (to protect Iraq's Kurdish minority) and in southern Iraq (to protect Iraq's Shiite majority). Iraq's oil revenues were put under the control of the United Nations, to ensure that those revenues were used to buy food and medicines for use by the Iraqi people, but not weapons. These limitations on what Iraq could buy may not have been perfect, but they were much better than nothing.

Second, the UN coalition, with the United States and Britain in the vanguard, accomplished its primary goal in remarkably swift and sure fashion—namely, keeping Iraq contained. In the years since the end of the first Gulf War, Iraq has not been able to attack its neighbors or other US allies, because of the US military presence on the Arabian Peninsula, economic sanctions, and other measures taken by the Americans.[64] As the UN weapons inspectors went about their work, more and more became known about the size and scope of Iraq's WMD programs and the size of its army too. In response, the first President Bush changed his view of what now appears as simultaneous failures of both deterrence (failure to prevent Iraq from invading Kuwait) and compellence (failure to convince the Iraqis to withdraw from Kuwait without having to drive them out). As the size and scope of Iraq's military programs became known, the first President Bush resolved not to settle merely for an unconditional Iraqi withdrawal from Kuwait. Instead, Bush wanted a military campaign and an overwhelming victory over Iraq (comparable to the overwhelming victory the United States had won over Manuel Noriega and Panama). As explained by the chairman of the Joint Chiefs of Staff, General Colin Powell, if the Iraqis withdrew now, it would be with impunity for their crimes. A pullback would also mean that Saddam could leave Kuwait with his huge army intact, ready to fight another day.[65] In the first Bush administration's view, attacking Saddam for the sake of finishing the job begun by Desert Shield and Desert Storm was preferable to containing Saddam, which might go on indefinitely. Secretary Baker was very candid on this point. "I feared that if we did not obtain congressional approval [for an attack on Iraqi forces in Kuwait and Iraq], we would be unable to sustain an attack on Saddam from a practical political standpoint and might have to settle for a policy of containment."[66] Secretary Baker makes a strong case, but his answer begs the question whether settling for containment would have been as fraught with difficulties as he suggested.

Third, "containment," as practiced by the Bush 41, Clinton, and Bush 43 administrations, is an elastic term that includes a wide range of behaviors. During the 1990s, containing Iraq included "U.S. and British pilots patrolling the no-fly zones in northern and southern Iraq. Iraqi provocations and subsequent allied reprisals against Iraqi military targets [occurred] almost daily."[67] In January 1993, while mounting air strikes against Iraqi air defense sites that threatened coalition aircraft patrolling the no-fly zones, US planes and pilots also attacked an alleged nuclear facility on the outskirts of Baghdad. Other coalition members dissociated themselves from this particular air strike, but these US strikes created facts on the ground that could be changed only with great difficulty.[68]

Fourth, as Daniel Byman notes, several military instruments proved "particularly effective during the decade-long effort to contain Iraq." Byman argues that "the use of force and the broader U.S. regional military presence . . . contributed to containment's success. Sanctions too . . . proved effective in containing Iraq."[69] In the aftermath of the first Gulf War, Iraqi forces were unable to perform routine maintenance on their vehicles and equipment, let alone modernizations and upgrades. Iraq's military capacity after the first Gulf War was less than 20 percent of what it had been in 1990, prior to Desert Shield and Desert Storm.[70] The United States, in contrast, had continually modernized and upgraded its forces, which made a substantial lead even greater than before the first Gulf War.

Fifth, a more patient and astute foreign leader might have attempted to slow the pace of events and thereby give his country some room within which to maneuver and maybe outwit the Americans. Saddam Hussein, however, was anything but patient and astute. He reportedly told his advisers, "The [UN] Special Commission is a temporary measure. We will fool them and we will bribe them and the matter will be over in a few months." As Byman remarks, "From the start, Saddam blocked the inspectors' access, lied to them about the extent or even existence of various WMD programs, and otherwise made a mockery of the process."[71]

But while Saddam was making boastful claims that he could never live up to on his own, the UN Special Commission (UNSCOM) that he had repeatedly derided was busy overseeing the slow destruction of Iraq's armed forces. Saddam talked a good game, but while he was boasting and bragging, it was UNSCOM that oversaw "the destruction of dozens of long-range missiles and missile warheads; tens of thousands of chemical munitions and 690 tons of chemical weapons agent; a biological weapons production facility; and nuclear weapons production facilities."[72]

In retrospect, our Iraq case study suggests that a great deal can be done to contain a rogue state like Iraq, even after hostilities have ended. Daniel Byman, for example, notes that since the end of Operation Desert Storm on February 28, 1991, "the U.S. and its allies repeatedly used limited force against Iraq, maintained tight sanctions, conducted intrusive inspections of Iraq's weapons of mass destruction (WMD) and missile programs, supported anti-Saddam oppositionists and otherwise strove to isolate and weaken Baghdad."[73] A superpower like the United States not only can engage in all these activities (simultaneously, too), but it can also keep them up and running for a decade or longer.

A more astute Saddam Hussein would likely have taken steps intended to make it more difficult for the US-led coalition to resort to these warlike activities, for example, by offering to negotiate. This might have divided the coalition and thrown US policy into confusion. But Saddam did not. In retrospect, Saddam was not bargaining hard; indeed, he was hardly bargaining at all. Saddam apparently believed that the coalition's position grew weaker and his own position stronger with each day that war was avoided. In doing so, he made another grave strategic error, just as he had in 1980 when he thought Iran would sue for peace or even collapse after a few weeks of fighting.[74]

How War Came to the Persian Gulf

The Reagan and Bush 41 administrations went to great lengths to improve relations with Iraq—for example, offering agricultural credits and access to US satellite intelligence. Early in 1990, the Iraqis embarked on a pattern of conduct that Secretary Baker later recalled as Saddam's "spring of bad behavior." By April it was clear that US policy had not produced the hoped-for results. There is no question Saddam's behavior changed for the worse in early 1990. A more confrontational stance toward Baghdad was now necessary.[75]

Saddam Hussein, on the other hand, "was thinking in terms of a very different scenario: an Iraqi assault on a U.S. ally in which he wanted to deter the U.S. help for his victim."[76] In effect, the Reagan and Bush 41 administrations did not try very hard to contain Iraq during the two-year hiatus between the end of the Iraq-Iran War and Iraq's invasion of Kuwait. During that two-year interval, the United States was seeking better relations with Iraq, rather than blocking and thwarting Saddam's latest scheme.[77] Because the Reagan and Bush 41 administrations preferred to woo Iraq rather than fight it, US officials took a relaxed view of these Iraqi moves, which subsequently proved to be the initial steps leading up to the Iraqi invasion of Kuwait in 1990. As the Iraqis built up their forces along the undefended border that they shared with Kuwait and Saudi Arabia, US officials reacted either by making excuses for the Iraqis or by dismissing these Iraqi actions as a bluff. Saddam's policies "were open to varying interpretations at the time," and Saddam's outrageous public behavior contrasted with his private diplomacy, which was more conciliatory. Instead of raising questions about just what the invaders of Iran might be trying to accomplish through these troop movements, US officials instead stressed all the steps the Iraqis had not yet taken but which they would need to take if war should come to the Persian Gulf (again). US officials not only made excuses for the Iraqis; they also questioned whether Iraq would engage in an old fashioned land grab at a time when that kind of behavior seemed out of touch with the post–Cold War world.

Once Iraqi forces had crossed the border into Kuwait and Iraq's intentions were unmistakable, the initial reaction at the highest levels of the first Bush administration was to downplay the severity of what Iraq had just done. "In many respects," Secretary Baker wrote in his memoir, "Iraq was the perfect candidate for economic sanctions. It relied heavily on [grain] imports [much of which came from the United States] to feed its people and keep its industry running." Iraq had only one significant export, which could be halted by shutting down the pipelines that carried Iraqi oil to export terminals in Saudi Arabia, Jordan, and Turkey. Iraq was also isolated geographically, surrounded by countries that were not particularly friendly to it.[78]

On the other hand, as Secretary Baker also pointed out, it was unlikely that sanctions alone would force Saddam to withdraw Iraqi forces from Kuwait. "Saddam's totalitarian regime" could reallocate resources at will, to lessen the pain from any shortages that might develop. Beyond that, any leader desperate enough to invade a neighboring state in blatant disregard for international norms (such as the Charter of the United Nations, to which Iraq was and is a party) would be likely to hold on more or less indefinitely. Last, but certainly not least, Kuwait's oil wealth was an enormously valuable prize for Saddam to claim, and he would likely demand a great deal more before agreeing to withdraw.[79] Because Iraq was (temporarily) in control of developments on the ground, every day that passed without an Iraqi withdrawal was another day that Iraqi soldiers could loot Kuwait of anything and everything they could stuff into their trucks and other vehicles. This suggested to the first Bush administration that there might not be a Kuwait for the Iraqis to loot and the coalition to rescue if the Bush administration did not move expeditiously to take back Kuwait quickly.[80]

Seen this way, it was taken almost as a given within the first Bush administration that time was on Saddam's side, to the detriment of the Americans and the other members of the anti-Iraq coalition. Was it really? What this school of thought—call it "containment pessimism"—overlooks is that Saddam had already acquired a roster of enemies by the time he invaded Kuwait in 1990. The purpose of the sanctions was to reduce, not eliminate, Iraqi military power. Anything that weakened the Iraqi Army made it less of a foe for the Americans, but it also made Iraq more vulnerable to the Iranians, who had not forgotten who started the Iraq-Iran War.[81] These circumstances suggested that the passage of time actually favored the United States, on the grounds that the more time available to it, the larger and more powerful the armed forces that the United States could send to the Persian Gulf region. Conversely, Saddam's only hope of actually winning this war would likely have required seizing Saudi Arabia before the United States could move enough forces to the Arabian Peninsula to make credible threats of retaliation if the Iraqis did try to seize part of Saudi Arabia. The first President Bush was very worried about this possibility. "In retrospect, if Saddam had wanted to make a go for Saudi Arabia he probably made a mistake in that he did not do it in this brief window—before my announcement that we would send forces. If he had, he would have had a free run."[82] Conversely, once the United

States had moved two hundred thousand military personnel to Saudi Arabia, Saddam's defeat was inevitable.

Move and Countermove

Containment, for reasons explained earlier, can very usefully be thought of as a game of move and countermove. One reason why Saddam Hussein was regarded as such a formidable foe can be traced to his reputation as an especially ruthless player of move and countermove. But even Saddam Hussein found it difficult to do well consistently against the United States, which had the resources of a superpower backed by dozens of coalition partners whose contributions would add legitimacy to the first President Bush's conduct of the war against Iraq.

How did the first President Bush conduct the war against Iraq? The question is important because, after the rout of the Iraqis in Operation Desert Storm, the United States and its allies would spend roughly the next twelve years (1991 to 2003) attempting to persuade Saddam to comply with various United Nations Security Council resolutions intended to disarm Iraq. For every move that Saddam made to escape the burdens imposed on Iraq by the sanctions, there was always at least one and usually several countermoves that could be taken by the United States and its allies. By 1994–95, for example, hyperinflation "had brought the Iraqi economy to the brink of collapse."[83] Saddam tried to win some breathing space from these UN sanctions by warning publicly that if the UN sanctions were not removed, he would "open the granaries of the world" to the Iraqi people by his own methods. When that didn't work, in October 1994 Saddam moved four divisions of Iraq's Republican Guard closer to Kuwait, in effect threatening to invade Kuwait again if the UN did not lift the sanctions.[84]

The US side, however, was not without moves of its own. The UN Security Council refused to remove or even to reduce the sanctions on Iraq. In addition, the UN, with the Americans, the British, and the French in the vanguard, launched some impressive military actions of its own. The United States rushed thousands of troops and hundreds of military aircraft to Kuwait and Saudi Arabia. The British and the French sent very capable forces too.[85] Saddam's threat to invade Kuwait again was thus exposed as hollow when the United States threatened to destroy the Iraqi armed forces unless they were withdrawn.[86] More important, the UN side, with the United States in the lead, threatened to destroy the Iraqi forces that were threatening Kuwait if they were not withdrawn to their previous peacetime locations. "Saddam quickly complied."[87]

In addition to issues played out on a grand scale—threats of war, troop movements, dramatic moments during meetings of the Security Council— the Iraqis were constantly raising lesser issues intended to hamper the work of weapons inspectors sent to Iraq with orders to unmask Iraq's programs to produce WMD warheads and ballistic missiles to carry them. For years the Iraqis resisted UNSCOM and International Atomic Energy Authority (IAEA) demands for access to inspection sites in Baghdad and elsewhere. The Iraqis also tried to reduce and even eliminate the presence of Americans in the inspection groups. They tried to compel UNSCOM to cease flights by U-2 reconnaissance aircraft over Iraq. Iraqi officials also tried to convince the inspectors that the extravagant presidential palaces Saddam had built for himself and his family should receive a kind of blanket immunity that would prevent visits of all kinds by the UN inspectors. In response to these Iraqi demands, the United States sent additional forces to Kuwait and threatened retaliation if Iraq did not cooperate fully with the inspectors. UNSCOM and the IAEA likewise resisted Iraqi demands. They could do so because their work was backed by the Security Council, which itself was backed by the threat of air strikes by the Americans and the British. Saddam ultimately agreed to compromises on these issues that fell far short of his original demands.[88]

In December 1997 Iraq once again impeded UN and IAEA inspectors, preventing them from visiting sites they had wanted to see (move). In response, the United States sent the aircraft carrier USS *George Washington* to the Indian Ocean, where it joined the USS *Chester Nimitz*. The Clinton administration also sent B-52s to Diego Garcia in the Indian Ocean, and more tactical air units and ground forces to Europe (countermove). In January 1998, Iraq again obstructed the international inspectors (move). In response, the Clinton administration sent the carrier USS *Independence* to the Persian Gulf followed by marines in February 1998 (countermove).[89] The Iraqis also increased the number of Russian-made surface-to-air missiles launched against US and British aircraft, in the vain hope that they might actually shoot down one of the American and British aircraft that were enforcing the no-fly zones over northern and southern Iraq. In 2001, Saddam again increased the number of surface-to-air missile attacks aimed against American and British aircraft patrolling the no-fly-zones in northern and southern Iraq (move). In response, in February, US and British aircraft launched air strikes against Iraqi command-and-control facilities in the suburbs of Baghdad, many of which were outside the no-fly zones (countermove).

Raymond Tanter has suggested that these episodes should be viewed as evidence of Saddam's ability to create crises that he could then use as opportunities to secure diplomatic gains.[90] This raises an obvious question about the wisdom of Saddam's tactics: What diplomatic gains might he achieve by antagonizing the Americans and the British (again and again)? The Iraqi surface-to-air missile attacks that Tanter cites invariably missed their targets. They did so because US and British warplanes were technologically far superior to anything the Iraqis possessed. Conversely,

American and British warplanes, armed with "smart" bombs and missiles, almost never missed. By allowing the Americans and the British opportunities to establish and then to reinforce the precedent that retaliatory strikes need not be confined to either of the no-fly zones, Saddam's ineffectual gestures opened the door to a substantial expansion in the scope and pace of the air war over Iraq.

The evidence available regarding the move-and-countermove competition is not quite as one-sided as the account provided here might suggest. Saddam did enjoy an occasional success in the game of move and countermove. For years after Desert Storm, Saddam pressed for the removal of the UN inspectors working for UNSCOM. In 1998 his wish finally came true. In practical terms, this meant there was "no monitoring or inspection of Iraq's capacity to develop and deliver weapons of mass destruction (WMD). The United Nations Special Commission for the disarmament of Iraq . . . effectively ceased to function; its inspectors [were] withdrawn and long-term monitoring systems abandoned."[91]

In effect, Saddam got some of what he wanted, but at what cost? Saddam's actions sparked an argument regarding what to do about UNSCOM and the IAEA. Would it be better to keep their personnel on the ground in Iraq and Kuwait, which was the only vantage point from which the inspectors could actually see and feel what their targets were, but where they might fear that their personal safety had been compromised?[92] Or should the inspectors be pulled back to London, where they would be much safer but also so far from Iraq that their contribution to the sanctions regime would be greatly reduced? To get around this problem, the Americans and the British planned a brief air war intended to destroy or at least damage those parts of Iraq's WMD programs that the Iraqis were trying hard to conceal. Once again, an Iraqi move was met by an Anglo-American countermove intended to impose on Iraq costs that were larger than what Iraq would have experienced if Operation Desert Fox had not been launched and UNSCOM and the IAEA had continued to function.

Desert Fox was a four-day bombing campaign carried out by the United States and Britain during December 1998. The purpose of the air attacks was to destroy or at least cripple Iraq's WMD programs. Desert Fox was followed by another expansion of the rules of engagement for US and British warplanes patrolling the no-fly zones in northern and southern Iraq. In the aftermath of Desert Fox, US and British reprisals against Iraqi military targets took place "almost daily."[93] In this instance, Saddam was able to get rid of UNSCOM and the IAEA inspectors, both of which conducted daily inspections on the ground in Iraq. In return, the Americans and the British conducted daily air strikes against targets that were both military and nonmilitary in nature, and which were no longer limited to the no-fly zones. If this is considered to be one of Saddam's triumphs, it would be interesting to know what one of his failures might look like.

Relinquishing the Initiative

If relinquishing the initiative is such a clever ploy, why didn't either or both sides make better use of it, for example, during the first Persian Gulf War? US political and military leaders were eager to identify a strategy that would minimize casualties, especially on the American side. Regarding the question why either or both sides didn't make more use of relinquishing the initiative, the answer is that both sides did use it, albeit not as effectively as they might have done. In retrospect, we can identify several points at which relinquishing the initiative (or failing to do so) shaped the conduct of the first Gulf War.

First, the Iran hostage crisis, the Soviet invasion of Afghanistan, and the Iraq-Iran War all imbued US officials with a healthy respect for the obstacles that would have to be overcome if US armed forces were called on to halt and maybe even repel a large-scale border-crossing operation in the vicinity of the Persian Gulf, which is seven thousand miles from the United States. In June 1979, officials in the Carter administration urged President Carter to strengthen the US military presence in the Indian Ocean and the Persian Gulf.[94] Carter's secretary of defense, Harold Brown, warned during congressional testimony that time would likely be a key factor in a future confrontation involving the Persian Gulf region. The *Washington Post* reported that "if the United States could get even relatively small ground forces into position before the Soviets got into the area then it would be the Soviets who would face the decision of whether to have a head-on confrontation with U.S. troops."[95]

Saddam Hussein, in contrast, appears to have made another of his colossal misjudgments by assuming that the Americans and their allies were so unimaginative that there was one and only one way by which they might hope to liberate Kuwait, which was to go straight through the Iraqi Army and its layers of defenses—berms, bunkers, and fortifications of all types. Judging from the way the Iraqis layered their defenses and then positioned their forces, Saddam apparently hoped to relinquish the initiative (but not Kuwait) to the coalition. Put differently, Saddam wanted the coalition to be faced with a choice between firing the first shot that would catalyze a bloody war for Kuwait and crafting a "compromise" that would leave Iraq in possession of most or all of Kuwait. For this strategy to work, Saddam needed to persuade himself[96] that the coalition would either fall apart or slip into a political coma when faced with a choice between doing something risky and doing nothing about Kuwait.[97] If the United States and its coalition partners did attack, Saddam's memories of Iraq's war of attrition against Iran provided him with a seemingly plausible basis for believing that this time his forces would construct more and better fortifications, which would enable Iraqi forces to win a war of attrition against "soft," casualty-averse Western democracies. In addition, Saddam could always dip into Iraq's stockpile of Scud missiles to threaten retaliation against Israel, Saudi Arabia, or Turkey.

Second, the first Bush administration expected the Iraqis to make an attempt of their own to relinquish the initiative. This was an Iraqi scheme that deeply concerned President Bush and his closest advisers because they were concerned that it just might work. The Iraqis could do this by seizing all or part of Saudi Arabia's undefended Eastern Province, in addition to seizing Kuwait. The first Bush administration was especially concerned that if Saddam's first move into Saudi Arabia proved successful, he might then be tempted to seize all of Saudi Arabia. "I was worried," the first President Bush wrote in a personal comment included as an afterword in the Bush-Scowcroft memoir, "that the Iraqis would indeed move across the border into Saudi Arabia. With so many tanks heading south, it seemed incontrovertible that Saddam had such plans."[98] Since there were no Saudi forces stationed in that part of the country, and sizable American forces were not expected to arrive for several weeks more, the Bush administration feared that US and Saudi forces would not arrive in time to prevent the Iraqis from consolidating their newly won territorial prize. Bush and Scowcroft recount in their memoir how they talked "about the possibility of a swift Iraqi strike at the Saudi oil fields. Saddam could move into Dhahran [Saudi Arabia] and stop, saying, 'Now what are you going to do.' This would be an enormously serious problem."[99]

Third, there is no small irony in the way the Scowcroft paper and President Bush's afterword put forward the goals for which the first Bush administration was prepared to fight in Kuwait. By the time the Scowcroft memo was circulating in Washington, Saddam had already relinquished the initiative to the United States and its allies. The Iraqis did this by seizing Kuwait, by building extensive but also flimsy fortifications intended to slow any advances by the Americans and their coalition partners, and by positioning Iraqi forces so that they could get off several shots at the advancing Americans and their coalition partners.[100]

Fourth, for Saddam Hussein, "relinquishing the initiative" meant positioning his forces more or less evenly along the border with Saudi Arabia and then waiting for the coalition to respond. For the Americans, "seizing the initiative" meant using the coalition's formidable reconnaissance assets to identify weak spots in the Iraqi defenses, followed by shifting coalition forces to places where they could inflict the most damage on Iraqi forces. Saddam had a very static vision of armored warfare—prepare defenses, position forces, and hope that the Americans would be easily discouraged. This was an approach that was well suited for use by the superpowers, both of which were constantly looking for new sources of leverage but not for a fight with the other, but Saddam's vision was almost cruelly out of touch with the demands imposed by fighting a superpower. A brief comparison of how relinquishing the initiative was used by the

United States against Libya's Colonel Qaddafi and Iraq's Saddam Hussein suggests that this is a strategy that works well when employed by states that are relative equals in military power (like the United States and the Soviet Union during the Cold War),[101] or when used by a state that is clearly superior to its target (for example, the United States and Libya during the Cold War).

Relinquishing the initiative worked well against Colonel Qaddafi because once the United States had deployed its naval and air forces above or adjacent to the Gulf of Sidra, the US side could not have withdrawn without being mocked and even ridiculed for its unwillingness or inability to take on a small power like Libya. This didn't happen. Instead, the United States relinquished the initiative, thereby shifting to Colonel Qaddafi's regime the responsibility for deciding whether and when to fire the first shot. When US forces remained in the background, the Libyans didn't seem to know what to do in response. When the Libyans did fire first, as they did in March 1981 and April 1986, they lost two aircraft in each clash. When the word got around that the Syrians and the North Koreans—the mercenary pilots who actually flew Libya's MiG aircraft—were refusing to take off as long as US Navy F-14s were in the vicinity, the Libyans were ridiculed for not having a clue how to fight the Americans.

In retrospect, relinquishing the initiative worked well against Libya during the Cold War in part because it was practically suicidal for Libyan aircraft to intercept and then fire at US aircraft. During the first Gulf War in 1991, once the United States had two hundred thousand military personnel in Saudi Arabia, it too was in a position to confront the Iraqis with an ultimatum: get out of Kuwait, or else. Because the United States was so much more powerful than Iraq, a US ultimatum would have been very credible. Iraq tried to relinquish the initiative during the first Gulf War, in the hope that the coalition would fall apart rather than opt for war, but the poor quality of the Iraqi conscript forces made them little more than speed bumps when matched against the US Army's heavy armored divisions. During the second Gulf War in 2003, the George W. Bush administration (Bush 43) did not worry much about touching off a wider war. Indeed, the second Bush presidency wanted a wider war against Saddam Hussein, because the president and his closest advisers expected to win.

Fifth, there can be no doubt that something failed with regard to Saddam, Kuwait, and the United States. Iraq crossed an international boundary, and assistance from the Americans arrived too slowly to prevent the looting and sacking of Kuwait. Saddam invested precious time and efforts to set the stage for a relinquish-the-initiative strategy, followed by a war of attrition if need be, but as usual his implementation was deeply flawed. Failure of this sort carried with it expensive consequences. In the first Persian Gulf War in 1991, Saddam lost control of more than half of his own country. By 2003 (the second Persian Gulf War), he had lost almost all of the rest of Iraq.

Even more surprising, Saddam appears not to have prepared an escape route that he could use to bribe his accomplices and outwit his pursuers. Saddam's actions during the second Gulf War also suggest that he had made no arrangements with other states that might allow him to seek asylum in another state. That would have been no fun to be sure, but to someone in Saddam's position, exile likely would have been preferable to facing the coalition's justice.

Others Will Help

The conventional wisdom about coalitions is that small states are reluctant to join, preferring instead to free ride on the exertions of the larger members. Yet in both Persian Gulf Wars, the United States was able to assemble coalitions of thirty or more members, although in both cases the Americans and the British did most of the actual fighting. What do these cases tell us about conventional wisdom's claim that coalitions are difficult to form and even more difficult to sustain? Guided by hindsight, several points come readily to mind.

First, during the Cold War, small states like the Persian Gulf sheikhdoms faced a choice between globe-spanning rival coalitions led by the United States or the Soviet Union. When the Cold War ended, small states faced a choice between aligning now and striving to remain neutral in the future. With the Cold War winding down but still not over, small states seeking a larger state's protection faced one more choice—namely, balancing versus bandwagoning. To a superpower these issues may have seemed trivial, but they were matters of life and death for the small states involved. The military tasks that could be offered to the smaller members of the two Gulf War coalitions were often minuscule, but even so these alignments were important to the larger members, especially the United States. What small states had to offer was more political than military. With not much of a military role open to the smaller members, these states opted instead to contribute legitimacy to the coalition's actions, on the grounds that when democracies work together unselfishly, their work gains a legitimacy not available to nondemocratic states.

Second, during the Cold War, small states were often accused of being free riders. This was an appellation that American officials preferred not be applied to US allies, thereby jeopardizing relationships that the United States had been cultivating for years, if not longer. For both of the Persian Gulf Wars, the Americans hoped they could recruit even more members into the coalitions that fought against the Iraqis, especially democracies. The greater the number of democracies that could be persuaded to join the coalitions formed to oust Saddam's regime in the two Gulf Wars, the greater the perceived legitimacy of the cause in the eyes of skeptical parliaments and electorates.

Third, among the small states participating in the two Gulf War coalitions, probably the deepest, the darkest, the most closely held fear experienced by America's partners in the coalitions was not that the United States would turn on them, like Iraq had done to Kuwait, but that it would ignore them. American policy makers were well aware that a superpower cannot pass the buck to smaller states, or even to a medium power (or two) like Britain or France. American officials paid careful attention to issues that might have been developing into something more serious. American officials were also sensitive to issues that, if left to fester, might have developed into a challenge to the existing order; and they were readily convinced that these new issues are serious matters indeed.

Furthermore, if a superpower were to find the military and other options available to it to be unsatisfactory, it could almost always come up with new and presumably better options. Who else but a superpower—the United States—could draw on such a wide range of capabilities, such as sending B-52s to overfly the sea lanes in the Indian Ocean? Alternatively, only a superpower like the United States could stage combined arms exercises, involving navy carriers, army brigades, and air force tactical fighters. Only a superpower like the United States could flood a potential combat zone with intelligence-gathering aircraft and satellites to overfly and eavesdrop on what was going on in the Persian Gulf, the Arabian Sea, and the Mediterranean too. Alternatively, when the Reagan and Bush 41 administrations wanted to send an attention-getting message of their own, they could deploy three aircraft carriers in the Mediterranean, the Persian Gulf, or the Indian Ocean. Everyone who lived through the 1980s knows what happens when the US Navy deploys three carriers in a contested area. Colonel Qaddafi knew too. The first Bush administration was more interested in impeding and undoing what the Iraqis had already done than in relinquishing the initiative to them. This was not for lack of concern on the administration's part. Not every strategy will be a good match for whatever predicament a superpower might have to face. In the case of Operations Desert Shield and Desert Storm, Iraqi forces were already in possession of Kuwait, which was being looted on a daily basis. In these circumstances, any strategy that included outwaiting an opponent was a nonstarter. Hence the Bush administration judged it necessary to drive the Iraqis out of Kuwait as soon as possible, before the Bush administration and the coalition could give additional thought to daring Saddam to do anything in particular.

Fourth, the two Gulf Wars fought against Iraq in 1990–91 and 2003 illustrate very nicely the roles typically filled by the United States and its small-state allies. Small states seek to ingratiate themselves to the United States by offering even token military deployments, because they much prefer sharing a continent with a friendly superpower rather than an unfriendly one, or even a would-be regional hegemon. Complementary needs encourage coalition formation by the United States and its smaller rivals. The United States seeks political cover for its own policies aimed at containing expansionist states like Libya, Iraq, and Iran. US forces during the two Persian Gulf Wars by and large outclassed the militaries of the states seeking US aid and protection. What the United States wants and what smaller would-be allies are able to give are often two quite different contributions. But since protection from a nearby superpower will almost always be valued more highly by a small state than economic or military aid, a superpower like the United States will likely make offers that smaller state would be foolish to refuse.

Fighting the Last War

Saddam Hussein's Iraq had numerous military assets and advantages at its beckoning, including a very large army made up of more than one million soldiers, dozens of divisions, and thousands of tanks, artillery pieces, and armored personnel carriers. Second, Saddam Hussein had at his disposal Iraq's enormous oil wealth, which could have done a lot to strengthen Iraq's armed forces and its civilian economy, provided the money was spent judiciously and not squandered on items that were beyond the Iraqi armed forces' capabilities. Third, Iraq was seven thousand miles from the United States, which suggested that Saddam had some room for maneuver, provided that he was careful about whom he provoked and for what reasons. Fourth and finally, Iraq's location meant a considerable asymmetry between the burdens that another Middle East war would place on Iraqi and US forces. US forces would have to fly seven thousand miles to reach Iraq; the Iraqis had only to drive across a desolate frontier to reach Saudi Arabia. The Americans had many interests that made repeated demands on the first Bush administration's full attention. Small states like Kuwait might occasionally topple off the Bush administration's radar screen. How much longer could the Americans be trusted to keep Iraq contained, at a reasonable cost? Would the Americans grow weary of protecting the gulf region again? American commentators and pundits were often in awe of Saddam's million-man, tank-heavy army, and the Iraqi Army did indeed look formidable on paper or at the parade ground. Even so, we can see now that there were indeed multiple reasons why Iraqi assets and advantages proved not to be worth much at all.

First, Saddam was seriously overconfident. Saddam *wanted* to fight the first Gulf War, and to fight it much the same way he had fought the Iranians, only this time against the United States and Britain. Saddam had not accumulated all those tanks and artillery pieces and the soldiers needed to run them by accident or inattention. Saddam instead wanted all those weapons to fill two roles: first, to allow Iraq to intimidate, or even invade, neighboring states; and second, to stop another state's counterattacks before they could penetrate too deeply into Iraq itself. Iraq's army may have been a good one (by Middle East standards), but the coalition's forces were much better. Much of Saddam's army consisted of poorly trained conscripts whose idea of a fortified position was a three-foot-high wall of loose gravel, which accomplished little other than providing the Americans with aim points. Conversely, most of the coalition's soldiers were long-term professionals, who expected to be sent on expeditionary campaigns rather than huddle in bunkers and wonder when the Americans would arrive.

Second, not even Saddam himself could hold together indefinitely a million-man army made up largely of teenage conscripts. How could Saddam hope to fight the Americans and still survive? One possibility here would be to resurrect what Saddam believed to be an Iraqi military triumph, and then fight it all over again.

In this regard, for Saddam and his generals, the "last war" was the Iraq-Iran War, during which the Iraqis constructed elaborate walls, barriers, and trenches. Behind these they had hoped to fight a war of attrition against the Iranians, until the Iranians grew tired and returned home, having lost parts of Khuzestan (an Iranian province that sits atop a very large oil field) to Iraq.

The first two years of the Iraq-Iran War went largely as the Iraqis had expected, but by 1982 the Iranians had beaten back the Iraqis' offensives. The Iraqis were able to save themselves because the United States gave them access to US satellite imagery which told the Iraqis where the Iranians were massing their forces for their next offensive. The Iraqis apparently hoped that the first Persian Gulf War would follow the same script, except of course without the satellite imagery, which was reserved for America's allies.

For the Americans, however, the "last war" was neither Vietnam nor Korea, but rather the Cold War, as it was played out in Europe. The choice of Europe was fateful, since in this conflict US forces took it for granted that they would be outnumbered and outgunned by the Soviet Red Army, with its notorious 175 line divisions, backed by enough reserve forces to put four hundred divisions in the field within the first thirty days of the war.[102] Faced with this disparity in forces available, US armed forces had spent virtually the entire Cold War practicing how to use combined arms operations to defeat a numerically superior foe, namely, the Soviet Union. Toward that end, US armed forces practiced using the army's heavy-armor tanks, navy aircraft carriers, air force tactical fighters, and marine amphibious forces, all the time expecting that their ultimate opponent would be Soviet forces in central Europe.

Surely it must stand as one of the great mysteries of the transition from the end of the Cold War to the new world order that Saddam and his generals appear to have believed that Iraq—which two years earlier had barely been able to expel from Iraq mobs of lightly armed Iranian conscripts—could be expected to hold its own in a war of attrition against a US Army that had just spent several decades practicing how they might fight against a heavily armed Red Army in Europe. In effect, Saddam and his generals took for granted that Iraq could and would fight the kind of war of attrition against the Americans that Iraq had fought against the Iranians during the Iraq-Iran War. Exactly why the Iraqis would have wanted to fight another war of attrition, this time against the Americans, is a question that remains unanswered.

Seen this way, the two Persian Gulf Wars stand as a warning to states and their leaders to avoid self-congratulation. In both cases, the US armed forces crushed their Iraqi opponents. This outcome was achieved in part because Saddam was not much of a foe. Saddam was directly responsible for the deaths of more than a million Iraqis and Iranians, and his actions strongly suggest that he was eager to unleash a war against the Americans as well.

Saddam Hussein was thus a very inept foe. He sought to cultivate the impression that he was the strongest, the meanest, and the most dangerous of what passes for leadership in the contemporary Middle East. Because he was essentially a thug in a suit, he didn't pose much of a challenge to the United States. Like Colonel Qaddafi and Ayatollah Khomeini, what seemed to many to be a stiff challenge to the Americans and their containment policy turned out not to be much of a challenge at all.

Invading Iraq

Was it unavoidable that the United States should invade Iraq in 2003? Were there no other ways to halt or at least slow Iraq's progress toward WMDs of its own, dismantle the labs and other facilities that Iraq was using to hide its WMD programs from the UN and IAEA inspectors, and overthrow Saddam Hussein's tyrannical regime? Was containment not up to the job?

Opinions on these matters have been forming, and hardening, since before the day in March 2003 when US forces crossed the border from Kuwait into Iraq, intending to march on Baghdad and free it from Saddam's murderous grip. Because the literature on containing Saddam Hussein and thwarting his quest for WMDs is both large and contentious, in this chapter I concentrate on the positions taken and the arguments made by observers of Saddam's Iraq during the decade-long interval between the end of Operation Desert Storm in 1991 and the start of Operation Iraqi Freedom (the US invasion of Iraq) in 2003. I pay particular attention in this chapter to the clash of views between those who believed that Saddam Hussein's Iraq could not be contained at a reasonable cost as long as Saddam himself remained on the scene (containment pessimists), and those who believed that containment was both feasible and sustainable, because the great disparity in resources between the United States and Iraq meant that the United States could pressure Iraq for years to come, if need be, without resorting to drastic methods, such as withdrawal or a resort to open warfare (containment optimists).

To buttress their case, containment pessimists argued that containment could not be counted on to last indefinitely because of the asymmetry between what was at stake for Saddam and his regime, and for the United States and its allies, in the years after Iraq's defeat in the first Persian Gulf War (1990–91). For Saddam Hussein and the rest of his repressive apparatus, the stakes were nothing less than survival. Saddam and his henchmen, pessimists argued, would *always* feel more strongly about whatever was at stake for Iraq, because Saddam and his followers lived there and had nowhere left to run or hide. Saddam too was powerfully motivated to escape the bonds of containment. Hence, it was only a matter of time, pessimists argued, before Saddam managed to break free of whatever constraints had been imposed on Iraq. As of March 2003, pessimists argued, containment had already been tried and found wanting; therefore more forceful policies should be utilized to deal with Saddam and his regime.

Optimists, on the other hand, conceded that containment wasn't perfect, but in their view perfection wasn't needed to bring down Saddam and his regime. In the optimists' view, a containment policy, especially one backed by the vast resources of the United States and its many allies, would offer multiple ways of pressuring Saddam but without crossing the threshold to outright war.

Background

Containment pessimists have often differed among themselves concerning exactly when the containment regime imposed on Iraq after the first Persian Gulf War either collapsed or eroded into insignificance. Containment pessimists are by and large agreed that, as of 2003, containment either had already failed, or was about to fail, which meant that something else would have to be found to take its place. Lawrence Freedman, for example, cites the mid-1990s as the period when "the Western strategy of containment began to erode."[1] Joseph McMillan takes a similar approach, warning that, by the second half of the 1990s, containment as played out in the form of sanctions, inspections, and no-fly zones could not bring about regime change in Iraq. Neither could containment "secure Iraqi compliance with its cease-fire commitments, or provide any degree of certainty that Iraq was not developing WMDs."[2]

Other writers, such as Daniel Byman, Kenneth Pollack, and Gideon Rose, were even more pessimistic than Freedman and McMillan. The "current containment regime," Byman and his coauthors wrote at the end of the 1990s, "is falling apart." In their view, the challenge facing the United States at the end of the 1990s was "not whether to abandon containment for a better alternative—there [was] none—but rather how to shore it up."[3] Kenneth Pollack, writing individually about a year before the US invasion of Iraq in March 2003, described containment as a "sensible approach to a situation in which there were few attractive options. It served its purpose well and far longer than most thought possible." But even good policies can sometimes lead to a bad end, and this was one of those times. Containing Iraq, Pollack wrote, should be replaced by invading Iraq, because "containment [had already] started to unravel." The only way to ensure that

Saddam, a "serial aggressor," never again attacked one of his neighbors was regime change, and the only sure way to bring about regime change in Iraq was by invading Iraq.[4]

Once Saddam was ousted, as he was in March 2003, opinions on containment changed hardly at all. "Containment *was* failing," Kenneth Pollack wrote in 2004. "The shameful performance of the United Nations Security Council members . . . in 2003 was final proof that containment could not have lasted much longer; Saddam would eventually have reconstituted his WMD programs."[5] Jackson Diehl, writing in 2011, conceded the point that the outcomes produced by the US invasion of Iraq fell short—indeed, far short—of what Americans and many Iraqis had expected it to accomplish. On the other hand, as Diehl put it, Iraq's "vicious dictator and his family are gone, as is the rule by a sectarian minority that required perpetual repression. The quasi-civil war that raged five years ago is dormant, and Iraq's multiple sects manage their differences through democratic votes and sometimes excruciating but workable negotiations. . . . All of these happened," in Diehl's view, "because the United States invaded [Iraq]."[6]

At the other end of the spectrum of opinions between invasion and containment, containment optimists credit President Clinton and the second President Bush with important accomplishments in this regard, most prominently "keeping Saddam's Iraq contained." Saddam, these scholars note, had not successfully menaced one of Iraq's neighbors since 1991—"a signal achievement," in view of his prior invasions of Iran and Kuwait.[7] Containment optimists often refer to the US invasion of Iraq as a series of disasters, and an unnecessary one at that. Adeed Dawisha, for example, described the US occupation of Iraq as essentially "one inept policy decision after another." The United States' continued reliance on containment, these scholars concede, may not have solved once and for all the problem of what to do about Saddam and his family, but at least it didn't make the situation worse, as did two especially damaging decisions made early in the US occupation of Iraq: dissolving the Iraqi armed forces and banning all Ba'ath Party members from public life, no matter how lowly and inconsequential their positions within Saddam's regime might have been.[8]

Was containment a viable alternative to preventive action like an invasion of Iraq? The Bush Doctrine[9] took it as a given that containment could not, would not hold, and therefore the United States would have to fight, sooner or later, to defend its vital interests against rogue states and terrorist fanatics. Saddam Hussein may have been a rogue and a scoundrel too, but he was also a rogue who had a lot to lose if he provoked the United States one time too many.

At this point an audience of containment pessimists might well cry out, "Like what?" in response to the claim that Saddam had a lot to lose if containment was superseded by war. What exactly did Saddam have to lose if he did not cut a deal with at least some of his many enemies? The question itself is not difficult to answer. Among the items likely to come readily to mind would be the iron grip that Saddam maintained on Iraq and its people, and the wealth that he and his extended family had accumulated during their time in power. There was also Saddam's aspiration to be the new Nasser who would unify the Arab world, to say nothing of all those presidential palaces and other monuments to Saddam's greatness.

Finally, there was Saddam's personal stake in his quarrel with the Americans over Kuwait. "[Saddam's] regime's legitimacy rested on intimidating its own citizens and neighbors. The Iraqi public's awe toward the ruling elite . . . could be shattered if Saddam appeared cowardly."[10] Likewise, if Saddam were to withdraw from Kuwait without first fighting hard against the Americans, this might appear to audiences in Iraq and elsewhere in the Arab world to be humiliating and unmanly; it would be an insult to his tribal honor and quite possibly cost him the respect of the Iraqi people. Note in this regard that, in Saddam's world, it was not necessary for him to defeat the Americans to retain the Iraqi people's awe and perhaps even their esteem. Quite the contrary, a few defeats at the hands of the Americans, with their vastly superior technologies and awesome weapons, would allow Saddam's sycophants to glorify their leader's heroic resistance, which would serve Saddam's purposes quite well.[11]

There remains the question of whether containment was a plausible alternative to preventive action in the form of invading Iraq. Containing Saddam Hussein's Iraq would not be easy, but it set more modest goals that should have been sustainable for a longer time and at less cost to the United States than the second President Bush's decision to invade and occupy Iraq.

Optimists and pessimists are unlikely to convert each other regarding the uses and limitations of containment as the foundation of US strategy for the greater Middle East. Hence, in the rest of this chapter, I argue that containment backed by the threat of further military action was indeed a plausible alternative to prevention by means of invasion. On what grounds do I make this claim? Conspicuous by its absence in the run-up to the invasion of Iraq in 2003 was the observation that Saddam turned sixty-six in 2003. Saddam may have been an especially vicious dictator, but he was not immortal, and with every cruelty and humiliation that he and his sons and their lackeys inflicted on their own people, the greater the likelihood that his enemies would soon catch up to him.[12] Maybe Saddam really did believe that he could outlive his foes, but even if he could do so, he was adopting a policy that one day would surely cause him to lose. And even if he somehow managed to stay one step ahead of his enemies both inside and outside Iraq, what exactly would he have accomplished besides staying alive one more day? After all the pain that Saddam had inflicted on the Iraqi people, his enemies would neither forget nor forgive; and with every day that Saddam ran from them, he got older, weaker, and more alone in a hostile world. Saddam's fate was sealed when the first Iraqi tank crossed the border into

Kuwait in 1990. After that, it was only a matter of time before his enemies or old age caught up to him.

In similar fashion, the UN Security Council resolutions embargoing the sale of weapons to Iraq meant that Saddam's armed forces would likely grow more decrepit and inferior to what the Americans and the British were using with every year that Iraq was barred from the international arms market. The morale of Saddam's soldiers would likely suffer too, which was hardly surprising after all those years of serving as target practice for US and British pilots enforcing the no-fly zones over northern and southern Iraq.

In effect, then, there was a dynamic dimension to the quarrel between the Americans and Saddam's regime, which has yet to receive the attention it deserves in the broader controversy over containment versus invasion. Saddam did not have an unlimited number of years with which to rebuild Iraq's armed forces and reconstitute its WMD programs. If there had been no invasion of Iraq in 2003, maybe Saddam would have found a way to cling to power long enough to fracture the coalition put together by the second Bush administration in 2002–3. On the other hand, the United States had already demonstrated that it could outlast the Soviet Union in a cold war that stretched over more than four decades, and the Soviet Union was by far a more formidable foe that Iraq. In retrospect, there was one side to this conflict between the United States and Iraq that was in a strong position to outlast the other, but it was not Saddam's side.

The Containment Regime

One senior analyst dates the initial US opening to Iraq to February 26, 1982, when the Reagan administration removed Iraq from its list of states that sponsor terrorism. Formal diplomatic relations between the United States and Iraq resumed in November 1984. The Reagan administration's goals regarding Iraq during the 1980s were for the most part opportunistic: to conclude an "alliance of convenience with Iraq against . . . Iran."[13] "Like [their] allies in London and Paris, the [Reagan and Bush 41 administrations] had gradually come to believe that Saddam's aspirations could be turned away from his past militancy and that Iraq could become a source of reason and moderation as well as valuable contracts." Seen from Washington, "Iraq's most promising feature was that it was Iran's enemy. . . . Hence if Iraq could keep Iran in check then that in itself was cause for commendation."[14]

The Reagan and Bush 41 administrations knew what they wanted from Iraq; it was how to get there that bedeviled the US side. US policy toward Iraq during the 1980s was erratic, to say the least. Sometimes the United States treated Saddam Hussein like a junior partner in an ongoing effort to balance and contain Iran.[15] Presidents Reagan and Bush 41 offered Saddam generous agricultural credits that Iraq could use to pay for food imports from the United States, thereby staving off discontent in Iraq over Saddam's ruinous policies.[16] But the Reagan and Bush 41 administrations also clashed with Iraq regarding issues like proliferation, human rights, and the Egypt-Israel peace treaty. During the Iraq-Iran War, the Reagan administration tilted toward Iraq by sharing imagery collected by US satellites that allowed the Iraqis to see where the Iranians were massing their forces for their next offensive.[17] Toward the end of the Iraq-Iran War, the US Navy helped both Iraq and Kuwait by keeping open the sea lanes through the Strait of Hormuz, despite Iranian efforts to interfere with and even halt oil tanker traffic into and out of the Persian Gulf. But at the same time that the United States was openly aligning with the Iraqis on the issue of freedom of the seas, the Reagan administration was secretly selling weapons to Iran that the Iranians used to wage war against Iraqi forces.[18]

The first Bush administration was deeply concerned about Iraq's tank-heavy army and especially about how Iraqi armored forces might be employed by Iraq in a future Middle East war. That same Bush administration was also deeply concerned that if the United States were to cut off or even restrict the flow of credits that Saddam's regime was using to buy food grains in the United States, the Iraqis might look for a new alliance partner.[19] The first President Bush went so far as to look the other way when the Iraqis diverted some of the agricultural credits they had received from the United States to pay for weapons that they could use against Iran.[20]

The run-up to war over Kuwait during the summer of 1990 offers a good illustration of how the first Bush administration clung to the hope that Saddam Hussein could be persuaded to give up his designs on Kuwait in favor of a closer alignment with the United States. On July 25, 1990, the CIA's national intelligence officer judged the evidence that Iraq was about to invade Kuwait to be "convincing." The officer's evaluation was accurate, to be sure, but it was hardly a stunning revelation considering that evidence of Saddam's hostility toward Kuwait had been accumulating for months or even years; what's more, it came too late to have much impact on US policy. As late as the last week in July 1990, the first Bush administration was still hoping to secure "Saddam's help in opposing terrorism and in promoting a moderate view of the Arab-Israeli dispute."[21] The last week in July was also the time when the US ambassador to Iraq, career foreign service officer April Glaspie, met with Saddam Hussein to inform him of her "direct instruction from the President to seek better relations with Iraq."[22]

As the first Persian Gulf War came to an end in 1991, the first Bush administration set about fashioning a containment regime that would take into account multiple US objectives in the Persian Gulf region: (1) deter Saddam Hussein from launching any more invasions of his neighbors, (2) make possible a robust defense of Iraq's neighbors so that Saddam could no longer intimidate them by threatening to start a costly and bloody war, (3) punish Iraq for its failure to comply with UN Security Council resolutions demanding that Iraq dismantle its WMD programs, and (4) deny Iraq the resources that it would need to reconstitute and then operate its WMD programs. A containment regime would be a very large undertaking, which would likely require substantial armed forces nearby or readily at hand in order to satisfy the requirements of deterrence and defense, punishment and denial, but without being so onerous that Saddam's neighbors might refuse to participate.

Could a containment regime keep Saddam's Iraq stymied more or less indefinitely? Would such a regime work as planned? Here was the heart of the matter. Even superpowers have been known to grow weary in the face of political-military challenges likely to require a decade or more to resolve.[23] What grounds were there for believing that this time the United States would get things right?

Earlier in this chapter, I presented the arguments made by containment pessimists, such as Lawrence Freedman and Kenneth Pollack, both of whom suggested that containment was about to fail as early as the mid-1990s.[24] On the other hand, Daniel Byman, while earlier a pessimist, working with much the same source material as Freedman and Pollack, would reach a strikingly different conclusion—that the United States had "accomplished the most important task: keeping Saddam's Iraq contained (or 'in the box,' in Washington parlance). Because of the U.S. military presence, sanctions, and other measures," Saddam was unable "to attack his neighbors or other U.S. allies." George Lopez and David Cortright, writing at the same time as Lawrence Freedman (the summer of 2004), likewise reached very different conclusions about how well containment was working. The "system of containment that sanctions cemented," Lopez and Cortright concluded, "did much to erode Iraqi military capabilities."[25] What exactly is going on here? These observers are all highly respected scholars. They can't all be right, can they?

In the rest of this chapter, I explore how and why scholars with stellar reputations, such as Freedman, Pollack, Byman, and Lopez and Cortright, can reach such differing conclusions regarding whether and how long containment might be sustained if applied to a difficult opponent like Saddam Hussein. Containment was doomed, Freedman and Pollack both argue, because it was oversold, particularly in the United States, thereby rendering it vulnerable to collapse once it became clear that containment entailed burdensome commitments that might last for years, maybe even a decade or more. Containment eroded as soon as it became clear just how burdensome it would prove to be.

On the other side of this argument, Daniel Byman, and George Lopez and David Cortright, focus on the synergies that could be achieved when the United States and its allies employed multiple military and diplomatic instruments to thwart whatever schemes a state like Saddam Hussein's Iraq might get involved with. Daniel Byman, for example, focuses on the military and diplomatic instruments that could be used to support and if need be enforce a Persian Gulf containment regime based on deterrence, defense, punishment, and denial. Specifically, Byman suggests that a robust containment regime, capable of sustaining itself for as long as Saddam Hussein and his ruling clique managed to cling to power in Iraq, would likely include, among other things, a substantial military presence that could be maintained in and around the Persian Gulf region for as long as Iraq continued to pose a military threat to its neighbors; no-fly zones over northern and southern Iraq, enforced by periodic air strikes on Iraqi armed forces; regular and frequent inspections of Iraqi laboratories and weapons factories intended to deny Saddam any opportunities to reconstitute his WMD programs; and finally, sanctions on Iraq, intended to punish Iraq for its refusal to comply with UN Security Council resolutions calling on Iraq to abandon its WMD programs and to deny the Iraqis the resources they would need to continue pursuing WMDs.[26] Lopez and Cortright likewise focus on how separate policy instruments, especially inspections and sanctions, can be expected to work in combination to increase the effectiveness of the containment regime.[27]

If these were the policy instruments available to the United States and its allies, how suitable might they be if the goal was to create and then sustain a containment regime built around deterrence, defense, punishment, and denial? How well did the United States do when it came to matching means (military presence, periodic air strikes, inspections of Iraq's WMD programs and facilities, and sanctions intended to weaken or even cause the collapse of Saddam Hussein's regime) to goals (deterrence, defense, punishment, and denial)? Was containment sustainable, or not?

1. MILITARY PRESENCE

During the first Persian Gulf War, the US armed forces needed roughly six months to transport to Saudi Arabia and other locations in the Middle East the forces needed to make Operation Desert Storm (the sequel to Desert Shield) ready to launch.[28] Saddam, to the endless amazement of his adversaries in the United States and elsewhere, made no attempt to interfere with the movements of these forces from North America to the Middle East.[29] There was a half-hearted effort by the Iraqis to disrupt the coalition's preparations for what would become Desert Storm, in the form of a short-lived border crossing into Saudi Arabia at Khafji and a handful of other points along the border between Iraq and Saudi Arabia.[30] If the Iraqis had managed to carry out some kind of strike at US forces while they were still assembling in Saudi Arabia early in the US build-up there, then an Iraqi defeat at the hands of the Americans might not have been as humiliating as it proved to be. Memories of how the Iraqis were overwhelmed by the Americans might not have seemed so overpowering *if* the Iraqis had struck sooner, and with greater impact.

Hindsight is helpful, but not always as helpful as we might like it to be, especially when dealing with hypothetical questions like these. Suffice it to say that, in view of the humiliating defeat suffered by Iraqi forces during their withdrawal from Kuwait, it seemed self-evident to the Americans that Saddam would not make the same mistake twice—in other words, allow the Americans the luxury of months of preparation that could be used to build up their forces around the gulf before engaging them on ground. Hence one of the first steps taken by the first Bush administration as part of its efforts to create a containment regime for the Persian Gulf region was the stationing of very large and capable US forces from all three services (army, navy, air force), ready to intervene on short notice. In addition to rotating army units through Kuwait and Saudi Arabia (for training and acclimatization), the United States stationed very powerful air and naval forces near the gulf itself. The first Bush administration also sent naval vessels into the gulf while flying military aircraft over it. In addition, the United States pre-positioned large cargo vessels at Diego Garcia (in the Indian Ocean) that carried enough weapons and equipment to allow US ground forces (who would be flown in if needed) to move quickly to a war footing.[31]

The purpose of all this activity was essentially twofold: to improve the US ability to fight another Persian Gulf War if need be; and to make plain for all to see—especially dictators with delusions of infallibility—that Desert Storm was no fluke. What had been done once could be done again, only this time US retaliation against Iraq for starting yet another Persian Gulf War would begin sooner and likely would inflict even greater damage on Iraq than had been the case in 1991. Keeping such a large force in the vicinity of the Persian Gulf was expensive, but there is no reason to believe that a superpower like the United States could not have maintained such a presence in and around the Persian Gulf until Saddam's time had run out. There was also an important side benefit that came from keeping large and capable forces close to Iraq: armed forces deployed to keep a close watch on Iraq could also be used to contain Iran, if need be.

2. MILITARY ACTION AGAINST IRAQ

The second element in the Persian Gulf containment regime took the form of an air war waged by the American and British air forces, ostensibly aimed at enforcing the no-fly zones that had been put in place over northern and southern Iraq in the aftermath of the first Gulf War. For roughly a decade after the end of the first Persian Gulf War, the Americans and the British retaliated in tit-for-tat fashion for Iraqi attempts to shoot down their aircraft enforcing the no-fly zones. "Sustaining the no-fly zones over Iraq," in

Byman's view, proved "draining" on the Americans and the British, but even so the Americans and the British managed to sustain the air war until the second Bush administration's invasion of Iraq in March 2003 rendered the point moot.[32] Sustaining the air war was more than just a matter of luck or good fortune. In retrospect, there are multiple reasons why the air operation was a very valuable asset, and the Americans and the British would likewise have strong incentives to find ways to keep it going for a very long time.

First, there was a great deal more to enforcing the no-fly zones than merely retaliating whenever the Iraqis tried to shoot down an American or British warplane enforcing the no-fly zones. Initially, the air war took the form of limited reprisal strikes against Iraqi air defense sites in retaliation for the Iraqis' having launched one or more of their surface-to-air missiles at an American or British plane. Over time, the Americans and the British expanded their target lists. Even a prominent containment pessimist like Kenneth Pollack conceded in this regard that "Operation Southern Watch has seriously degraded the capabilities and readiness of Iraq's air defense system."[33] By the end of the 1990s, the Americans and the British were selecting targets primarily because their loss would degrade the capability of the Iraqi armed forces across the board, as opposed to limiting the air strikes just to Iraq's air defenses. Broadening the target base, in turn, offered the Americans and the British an opportunity to chip away at the size and the effectiveness of those Iraqi forces that had managed to survive Desert Storm. Morale within the Iraqi forces was less than stellar because, while the Americans and the British could attack Iraqi targets with impunity, the Iraqis were unable to do anything to halt what the Americans and the British were doing to them.

Second, by using the air campaign to carry the war to the Iraqis, the Americans and the British were able to modulate their responses to whatever provocations the Iraqis were engaged in. In December 1998, for example, the Americans and the British retaliated for Iraq's expulsion of UNSCOM's weapons inspectors by launching Operation Desert Fox, a four-day bombing campaign that was much more intense than the attacks that they had been carrying out to date. In the aftermath of Desert Fox, the Americans and the British resumed their sustained albeit limited bombing campaign against Iraqi targets, including targets that were chosen to degrade the military capability of the Iraqis across the board. Desert Fox was followed by "an expansion of the rules of engagement for American and British pilots patrolling the no-fly zones in northern and southern Iraq. Iraqi provocations and subsequent allied reprisals against Iraqi military targets [occurred] almost daily."[34] The provocation and reprisal cycle worked in one direction only. The Americans and the British could and did strike Iraq almost daily, but the Iraqis could not retaliate against America and Britain. In this way the United States and Britain were able to chip away at and thus erode Saddam's forces while avoiding being struck themselves.

Third, an air war that struck at Iraqi targets across the length and breadth of Iraq was one way to signal to Saddam's supporters and enemies alike that this was a war that Iraq could not possibly win, and that the quicker Iraq rid itself of Saddam and his family, the sooner the Iraqis could begin work on rebuilding Iraq. Saddam's mind may have been irrevocably closed but not so the minds of his enemies and his friends. Barry Rubin points out that Saddam believed that "every day as the sun rose his position was stronger. America could not fight and lacked the stamina to continue the confrontation for very long."[35] One way to impose a reality check on a deluded dictator like Saddam would be to continue with and even expand a provocation-and-reprisal cycle that ran in one direction only. The Americans and the British could strike Iraq at will, but Iraq had no way of striking the United States and Britain. In effect, Saddam had transformed Iraq's armed forces, once the envy of the Middle East, into a list of targets that the Americans and the British could strike, strike, and strike again, until the weaknesses in his position became obvious, if not to Saddam, then to prospective coup leaders.

Fourth, the air operation provided the Americans and the British with some tangible military benefits too. The intent behind the no-fly zones was two-fold: first, to make it more difficult for Saddam to reassert his authority over rebellious Kurds in the north and Shiites in the south, in effect denying him access to about two-thirds of the population and other resources of his own country. That, in turn, made it more difficult for Saddam to reconstitute the armed forces that he had used to invade Iran in 1980 and then Kuwait in 1990. The no-fly zones were also intended to preclude any American and British casualties by destroying enough of the Iraqi air defense network to render it unusable against American and British aircraft flying overhead. The air war was so one-sided that the Americans and the British could expand the scope of their coverage and the list of targets available to be struck. As the target list expanded, the need for some kind of plausible connection to the no-fly zones was relaxed to the point of disappearing. What started as a humanitarian gesture intended to protect Iraqi Kurds and Shiites gradually transformed into an air war. It may not have been a big air war or an intense air war, but it was an air war nonetheless. The Iraqis were essentially powerless to fight back against the sophisticated weaponry employed by the Americans and the British, who suffered no losses in these engagements with the Iraqis, even as they struck with impunity targets such as Iraqi surface-to-air missiles, radar installations, and command-and-control centers.

3. UN-MANDATED INSPECTIONS OF IRAQ'S WMD FACILITIES

The third element of the containment regime created for Iraq in the aftermath of the first Persian Gulf War took the form of UN Security Council resolutions that required that the Iraqi government cooperate with UN inspectors (UNSCOM) and inspectors from the IAEA, who had been sent to Iraq to locate and then take possession of the labs, factories, and storage sites Iraq had built for its WMD nuclear programs. The goal of the inspectors' work was to disarm Iraq, voluntarily if possible, but backed by UN sanctions if needed to ensure that Iraqi compliance would be forthcoming.

No one doubted that Saddam and his regime would make strenuous efforts to conceal their activities aimed at acquiring WMDs, and especially their programs to make progress toward an Iraqi nuclear weapon. The question at issue in the post–Gulf War controversy over Iraq's quest for WMDs of its own was, How well were they doing? Etel Solingen reports that Suroor Mahmoud Mirza, a brother of Saddam's senior bodyguard, was sent to Vienna to serve as "scientific attaché" on the Iraqi embassy's staff, with orders to penetrate the IAEA. Mirza subsequently alerted the Iraqi government "to the successes of satellite remote sensing in uncovering clandestine, and especially underground, activities."[36] By using informants in this fashion, Iraq's government became more proficient at concealment and deception, but the UN inspectors got better too. The "new safeguards system ('93 + 2') set up in 1993 strengthened the IAEA's mandate; UNSCOM effectively dismantled much of Iraq's nuclear infrastructure; and UNMOVIC's 2003 assessment of Iraq's capabilities proved right. These were significant achievements." (UNMOVIC was the UN Monitoring, Verification and Inspection Commission.) The Iraq experience, Solingen concludes, was "both one of institutional failures but also of learning and accomplishments."[37]

4. UN-MANDATED SANCTIONS

The sanctions issue proved to be difficult political terrain for the United States and its allies. This was in no small part because of their continued insistence that they intended no harm to befall the Iraqi people, who were presented as victims of Saddam's regime just like the Kuwaiti people. If the sanctions were indeed causing serious distress among the Iraqi people, then they would be harder to sustain over the long haul. If there was no distress, the sanctions would likely be judged ineffectual.[38] In effect, "the battle of wits between Saddam and the rest of the world was about short-term survival. If Iraq could keep going under siege long enough then, Saddam might hope, he could eventually obtain a settlement on tolerable terms."[39]

Saddam was both clever and dangerous, but his opponents were not exactly slouches when it came to matching wits with a determined opponent. For the democracies that made up the US-led coalitions (one coalition for each of the two Persian Gulf Wars) that were formed to wage war against Saddam, the stakes were lower than those that Saddam faced, but significant nonetheless. Mishandle the sanctions issue—for example, let Saddam escape from his box—and the result just might be defeat in the next election. The political imperative not to mishandle the sanctions issue gives us an opportunity to admire the skill and ingenuity that coalition partners brought to their dealings with Saddam. There is no doubt, Freedman and Karsh subsequently wrote, that the sanctions in Iraq "were a remarkable technical success and exacerbated Iraq's economic problems."[40]

Was Containment Failing?

If containment really was failing, and multiple scholars have asserted that this was indeed the case as of the mid-to-late 1990s,[41] then there are certain events involving the United States and Iraq that probably should not have occurred, but which did indeed occur nonetheless. Consider in this regard the following eight cases, all of which occurred during the period between the end of the first Gulf War in 1991 and the US invasion of Iraq in March 2003.[42]

1. IMPOSING THE NO-FLY ZONES

Shortly after the cease-fire that ended the first Persian Gulf War in 1991 was put into place, "the United States and its allies, acting through the United Nations, intervened on the ground to protect the Kurds in Iraq's north." The United States and its allies also established no-fly zones over northern and southern Iraq to protect Iraqi Kurds and Shiites from attacks by what remained of Iraq's air force. The no-fly zones were enforced by combat air patrols flown by US and British pilots and occasionally by air and cruise missile strikes against Iraqi radars, surface-to-air missiles, and command facilities. Over time, the no-fly zones were expanded in ad hoc fashion by adding Iraqi air defense targets located outside the geographical limits that had been set when the no-fly zones were first imposed in Iraq, and by launching air strikes against lucrative targets other than those associated with Iraq's air defenses, even if they were located within the geographical limits of the no-fly zones.[43]

This is not to suggest that enforcing the no-fly zones was easy. No-fly zones "are dangerous, expensive and extremely complex." They "require huge planning efforts, strategic cooperation, allied basing privileges, overflight rights, significant intelligence preparation and substantial commitments of strike, air-refueling and command-and-control aircraft, search-and-rescue platforms and intelligence, surveillance and reconnaissance assets."[44] If containment really was failing during the mid-to-late 1990s, the first signs that this was so should have taken the form of a growing weariness and a diminished commitment to sustain the no-fly zones over Iraq. Precisely because no-fly zones are difficult and expensive to sustain over a period of years, any weakening of Anglo-American resolve to continue containing Iraq should have been apparent in a growing inability on the part of the United States and Britain to sustain the no-fly zones month-to-month and year-to-year. This, however, appears not to have happened. Instead, the British and the Americans maintained the no-fly zones for more than a decade (1991 to 2003), during which both the no-fly zones themselves and the target lists employed were gradually expanded, both geographically and in terms of the value of the targets covered.

2. IRAQ CHALLENGES THE CONTAINMENT REGIME

Beginning in December 1992, Iraq moved to challenge the containment regime put in place by the United States and its allies. The Iraqi challenge took several forms: (1) flying aircraft over the southern no-fly zone, (2) moving additional surface-to-air missiles into the southern zone and threatening to shoot down US aircraft enforcing the no-fly zone, (3) blocking UN weapons inspectors from visiting sites that were believed to be part of Iraq's WMD programs, and (4) sending two hundred Iraqi troops to make repeated crossings of the border into Kuwait, where they seized items that they claimed belonged to Iraq. In response, US, British, and French aircraft conducted air strikes on Iraqi command-and-control facilities and air defense sites in the southern no-fly zone. The United States also struck the Zaa'faraniyah nuclear facility outside Baghdad with forty-five cruise missiles. This attack was followed a few days later by additional strikes against Iraqi military targets in the no-fly zones. Faced with the likelihood of more, and more intense, air strikes by US and allied aircraft, which had the capability to strike Iraqi targets seemingly at will, the Iraqis backed down. The Iraqis did not challenge the no-fly zones, nor did they actively challenge UN weapons inspectors for several years to come.[45]

3. IRAQ PLOTS TO ASSASSINATE THE FIRST PRESIDENT BUSH

Iraq's lack of success regarding the no-fly zones did not stop them from searching for other ways of challenging the United States. In 1993, for example, the Iraqis prepared an exceedingly foolish and ill-conceived plan to assassinate the first President Bush while he was visiting Kuwait.

The Clinton administration unearthed evidence of the plot's existence; its response was to launch cruise missiles at military and intelligence targets in Iraq.[46]

4. DETERRING ANOTHER INVASION OF KUWAIT

In August 1994, Saddam moved two of Iraq's Republican Guard divisions, bringing them closer to and pointing them toward Kuwait, much like he had done in 1990 when he repositioned his best forces as part of Iraq's preparations to invade and occupy Kuwait. In response, both the United States and Britain warned Iraq "that they would use force to stop any Iraqi buildup south of the 32nd parallel."[47] These threats were credible because the United States "had been building up its capabilities and facilities in the Gulf ever since the 1991 [first Gulf] War." The Clinton administration "used the occasion of these Iraqi armored movements to reinforce [the US] presence there to deter any new invasion of Kuwait." As a result, "the Iraqi units that were threatening Kuwait were withdrawn soon after the U.S. reinforcements arrived, and the Clinton administration claimed that its threats had succeeded"—in other words, containment worked.[48]

What should we make of this claim? Daniel Byman credits the Clinton administration with an outright success. In response to the US buildup, he points out, "Iraq drew back its forces, recognized Kuwait's independent status, and accepted the revised Iraq-Kuwait border." In addition, "the United Nations Security Council also passed resolution 949, which limited the Iraqi presence near the Kuwaiti border—the so-called no-drive zone."[49]

Barry Blechman and Tamara Wittes, on the other hand, take a more circumspect view, dismissing the Clinton administration's claims of success to be "uncertain," on the grounds that "many observers [have] maintained that the Iraqi leader could not possibly have contemplated an invasion given the experience in 1991, the much weaker state of the Iraqi armed forces, and the much greater preparedness of the United States and its allies three years later."[50] Even if Saddam never contemplated another invasion of Kuwait, he still ran enormous political and military risks (specifically, a US preemptive strike) by appearing to challenge the United States. In return, Saddam received essentially nothing, except looking foolish in the eyes of the world and, more important, his own people.

5. OPERATION DESERT STRIKE (1996)

In September 1996, the United States once again struck air defense sites in southern Iraq, this time in response to an Iraqi intervention in a conflict between the two principal Kurdish factions in the north. The United States maintained that the Iraqi military action was unacceptable, and it responded both by reinforcing its forces in the gulf region and by launching cruise missile attacks on newly rebuilt Iraqi air defense sites in the south. The Clinton administration also extended the no-fly zone in the south, which previously had ended at the thirty-second parallel, to the thirty-third parallel. The reasons for extending the no-fly zone in the south were partly to make it harder for Iraq to move its forces from one part of Iraq to another, and partly to improve the US-led coalition's ability to monitor events in Iraq.[51]

The Clinton administration's efforts to control events were relatively modest in this case. Neither the Saudis nor the Turks cared much about the Kurds, which meant that neither of them was willing to help the United States coerce Saddam's regime into leaving the Kurds alone. Attacks on surface-to-air missile sites, radar installations, and command-and-control centers in southern Iraq were militarily useful in the context of a years-long containment policy, but they were also unlikely to have much effect on what the Iraqi Army and secret police did while they were temporarily in control on the ground in northern Iraq. When Saddam Hussein seemed to defy US injunctions regarding the need for Iraq to respect the no-fly zone in the south, the United States threatened more devastating air strikes against Iraq and moved aircraft into the region that would be capable of carrying them out. This time, Saddam Hussein appears to have taken notice of the Clinton administration's threats. Prior to the US cruise missile strikes, the Iraqis had concentrated their forces near Chamchamal, a Kurdish-held city. After the cruise missile strikes, Saddam dispersed the Republican Guard divisions that had been used to intervene in Kurdish-held territory in northern Iraq and pulled his forces back to the cease-fire line.[52]

6. IRAQ CHALLENGES THE CONTAINMENT REGIME (AUTUMN 1997)

As 1997 drew nearer to a close, Iraq chose to challenge the Persian Gulf containment regime once again, this time by refusing UN inspectors access to facilities they deemed suspicious, and by otherwise hindering the inspection process. In response, the Clinton administration moved the aircraft carrier USS *George Washington* to the Persian Gulf region, where it joined the USS *Chester Nimitz*. The Clinton administration also sent B-52s to Diego Garcia, deployed tactical fighters and bombers to Kuwait and Bahrain, and sent more troops to Kuwait, bringing the US total there to thirty thousand.[53]

While these military moves were being carried out, Iraq continued to impede inspections. In response, the Clinton administration sent the USS *Independence* to the Indian Ocean to join the two carriers already there. This was potentially an important signal, because during the 1980s, the presence of three carriers in the Mediterranean had been a sign that the United States was preparing to strike Libya. The Pentagon announced that the United

States was prepared to launch air strikes against Iraq if it continued to defy the United States and the UN on the inspections issue. This time Iraq allowed the UN inspectors to return, by means of an agreement negotiated by the UN secretary-general Kofi Annan, which allowed the weapons inspectors to return but also placed limits on where they could go and what they could see. "Despite its favorable terms, Baghdad's agreement was only temporary, and Saddam soon refused all cooperation."[54] Saddam Hussein scored a short-term, tactical success when his regime persuaded the UN Security Council to withdraw the UNSCOM inspectors from Iraq. In response, the Americans and the British intensified and widened their air strikes on Iraq.[55]

7. OPERATION DESERT FOX (DECEMBER 1998)

On November 13, 1998, Iraq expelled the six remaining American arms inspectors; to protest this action, the UN withdrew all the other inspectors in Iraq. On November 21, Iraq readmitted the arms inspectors, including four Americans, although it still tried to bargain over what the inspectors could and could not see. In response, UN weapons inspectors were removed from Iraq and sent home. The Iraqis thought they had outwitted the Americans and the British, but once again the US-led coalition had options the Iraqis appear not to have taken into account. While the UN and Iraq engaged in verbal sparring over which inspectors could look where, the Americans and the British planned and then executed a four-day campaign of aerial bombing—approximately six hundred sorties by aircraft and four hundred cruise missile launches—intended to degrade Iraq's WMD programs, thereby compensating at least in part for the absence of the UN inspectors. More important, whatever respite Saddam's regime earned by attempting to rid itself of the inspectors was only temporary. UN inspectors, this time under a new name—UNMOVIC—returned to Iraq in 2002 as part of the effort to forestall a US invasion of Iraq.

8. OPERATION DESERT FOX, AFTERMATH

In 1999, Iraqi forces made repeated challenges of the no-fly zones while continuing to deny UN weapons inspectors access to suspicious sites. Daniel Byman reports that during 1999, the Iraqis launched "over 400 separate attacks on coalition aircraft, and over 140 violations of the no-fly zones; the figures for 2000 are similar." Coalition forces responded with air strikes, "primarily against Iraqi air defense sites, but also against communications nodes and other targets." Taken together, Byman concludes, "the various military strikes since the end of the Gulf War [in 1991] have helped the United States make marginal progress in keeping Iraq contained."[56] McMillan takes a more expansive view of the US response. "In response to stepped up Iraqi challenges to the no-fly zones following *Desert Fox*, the U.S. Central Command was given flexibility to strike targets related to air defense in southern Iraq. The use of this authority seriously degraded Iraqi air defense capabilities in the south and left coalition forces in an enhanced position to conduct additional operations on short notice if directed."[57]

Move and Countermove

There are at least three themes that run throughout these eight cases. First, during the decade that followed the end of the first Gulf War in March 1991, Saddam Hussein launched multiple challenges to the Persian Gulf containment regime, but after a decade of these challenges what did he have to show for his efforts? Iraq's economy barely functioned; its infrastructure was in ruins; and its armed forces had learned the hard way the same lesson the Libyans and the Iranians had already learned about fighting the Americans head-on. On the other hand, who else besides Saddam had the nerve to stand up to the Americans after the trauma inflicted on Iraq during the first Gulf War? Seen this way, Saddam's need to retain control of Iraq practically required him to challenge America's positions over and around the Persian Gulf. To keep his grip on Iraq, Saddam had to be seen standing up to the Americans. If there were no challenges to the containment regime, what use was Saddam?

Second, for every move taken by the Iraqis in an attempt to break free of the restraints imposed upon them by the United States, there was always at least one countermove available to the Americans. In December 1997, to cite one example, Iraq obstructed the work of the UN weapons inspectors by preventing them from visiting sites that they (the inspectors) wanted to see. Iraqi obstructionism was intended in part to deny the inspectors access to "palaces and official residences" reserved for use by Saddam and his immediate family.[58] In response, also in December 1997, the United States sent two carriers (the *George Washington* and the *Nimitz*) to the Arabian Sea. The United States also sent B-52s to Diego Garcia, and more troops and tactical aircraft to bases in Kuwait and Bahrain. In January 1998 the United States send a third carrier (the *Independence*) to the vicinity of Iraq, and a marine expeditionary force. This time, Iraq agreed to allow the UN inspectors to return to their work. This sequence of move and countermove is important because it suggests that the United States and Britain could have sustained containment of Iraq for some time to come.

Third, it should come as no surprise that the move-and-countermove dynamic played itself out this way. Superpowers have such enormous resources at their disposal that they are able to compete in many different ways. The United States could afford to relinquish the initiative to Saddam and Iraq; but Saddam could not relinquish the initiative to the United

States, because it would make him seem cowardly in the face of America's pummeling of his regime and armed forces. Saddam could only hope that his forces could hold on long enough for the Americans to grow discouraged about the prospects for winning in view of the extensive fortifications the Iraqis had already built. Saddam believed the Americans had no stomach for the kind of bloody war of attrition that Iraq had fought against the Iranians. Even if the Iraqis had fought longer and harder than they actually did, the best Saddam could hope for was a long-term stalemate that could prove fatal to his claims that he alone knew how to stand up to the Americans.

In effect, for nearly thirteen years (1991–2003), relations between the United States and Iraq were characterized by ambiguous outcomes—that is, "military triumph for the United States but political survival for Saddam Hussein."[59] Whenever US and Iraqi forces fought against each other head on, the outcome was invariably an Iraqi defeat, and even annihilation of the Iraqi forces involved. "Yet in the larger strategic sense," Blechman and Wittes claim, containment "failed" because Saddam continued to cling to power in Baghdad, from which he also skirted the demands made by the UN Security Council, terrorized Iraq's minority populations, behaved belligerently toward Kuwait, and challenged the United States politically. "In short," Blechman and Wittes conclude, "the United States . . . had to settle for a lesser objective: containment. In the words of one U.S. official, U.S. diplomacy and military activity . . . served at best 'to put Hussein back in the box.'"[60]

In the case of Saddam Hussein's Iraq, for years and years Saddam defied the United States, and for what? "Non-cooperation with the UN allowed Saddam to demonstrate that he had not been cowed." On the other hand, Saddam was constantly expending scarce resources on ineffectual schemes, such as attempting to shoot down American or British aircraft enforcing one of the two no-fly zones.[61]

Relinquishing the Initiative

Viewed in retrospect, a decade or more of enforcing the no-fly zones over northern and southern Iraq by means of air strikes and other forms of pressure certainly gives the appearance that the United States and its allies took the fight to Iraq rather than vice versa. Events in and around Iraq, however, suggest that US policy was more subtle than that and included an element of relinquishing the initiative to the Iraqis. How could this be so, in view of the diverging paths the Americans and the Iraqis were taking in anticipation of more fighting in the future?

Bear in mind that the Americans and the British had established the no-fly zones and the rest of the containment regime in 1991, as the first

Persian Gulf War was coming to an end. They then dared the Iraqis to do something about them, like the Americans had done to Colonel Qaddafi during the 1980s. Precisely because Saddam had boasted so much of his ability to handle the Americans and the British, every overflight of Iraq and every attack on an Iraqi target inevitably raised questions along the lines of, Why did we stop? Relinquishing the initiative played an important role here, by entangling Saddam in a nasty dilemma. On one hand, if Saddam were seen to be frittering away Iraq's remaining military assets, such as its stockpile of surface-to-air missiles, in a vain attempt to shoot down even one American or British aircraft, he would likely diminish his standing in the eyes of the Iraqi people, thereby raising more questions among the Iraqi people regarding what exactly was he (Saddam) good for, besides leading Iraq's armed forces into punishing defeats at the hands of the Americans and the British. On the other hand, if Saddam tried to seize the initiative by attacking coalition forces, he risked additional crushing defeats inflicted by the Americans. If he acted impetuously, he risked being portrayed as someone who sent Iraq's young men off to war while his own sons terrorized the Iraqi people. If he held back, he might well be seen as giving in to Anglo-American demands upon him, thereby diminishing his reputation and his standing in the eyes of his people.

Was there any way out for Saddam? One possibility would have been a Qaddafi solution—namely, surrender Iraq's WMD programs and this time do it for real. It likely would take years for the UN weapons inspectors to comb through the remnants of Iraq's WMD programs. In the meantime, Saddam could obtain a respite from the air war by calling attention to Iraq's offer to surrender its WMD programs, followed by quibbling over what parts of Iraq would be open to the inspectors and what parts would not. The Iraqis could keep these negotiations tied up in knots for months if not years. But Iraq was no Libya and Saddam was no Qaddafi. By 2003, Qaddafi was willing, indeed eager, to turn over Libya's WMD programs to the Americans and the British, thereby gaining a measure of protection for his regime. Saddam appears not to have prepared a fall-back option in case the negotiating agenda proved to be more contentious than Saddam had anticipated. For Qaddafi, surrendering Libya's WMD programs was the ticket he needed to protect his regime from enemies both within and outside Libya. For Saddam, surrendering Iraq's WMD programs would at last answer the question of what Saddam was good for. Qaddafi could switch sides and live to tell about it (at least until the Arab Spring of 2013). For Saddam, surrender meant the destruction of his regime and everything he had aimed to accomplish. Indeed, the longer Saddam clung to power, the greater the damage likely to be inflicted on Iraq's armed forces by the Americans and the British, and the fewer the ticks of the clock remaining to Saddam.

More important, what if one of Saddam's schemes had actually worked? What exactly would he have accomplished if Iraq's tattered air defense network had somehow managed to shoot down an American or British fighter jet? The Americans and the British would likely find it easier to intensify their efforts vis-à-vis Iraq than would be the case for Iraq against the United States and Britain. Iraq in 2003 was poorer, weaker, less safe, and less respected than it had been in 1990 (just prior to the first Gulf War), which is exactly the outcome that a determined pursuit of a containment policy should have produced.[62]

Neither was it a coincidence or a fortuitous set of events that accounted for the ability of the United States to pursue a containment policy against a middle power like Iraq for nearly two decades. The Persian Gulf security regime, as explained earlier in this chapter, contained multiple elements, which is why the failure of any one would not necessarily mean failure of the regime as a whole. The more difficult judgment would be how to respond to the failure of several, but not all, of the elements of the gulf security regime. If two or more of these elements of the Persian Gulf security regime could be shown to be failing to carry out their principal objective—namely, thwarting, denying, or impeding progress by Iraq toward reconstituting its WMD programs—then containment could be said to be failing too. In that case, a much more intense air war or an invasion might well be required to accomplish what containment had failed to do. Similarly, if it could be shown that Saddam and his underlings were making progress toward reconstituting Iraq's conventional armed forces, which Saddam could then use to browbeat or intimidate Iraq's neighbors, that too could be considered evidence of failure of the security regime, because it would put Saddam in a stronger position to mount another invasion of one of Iraq's neighbors, or to threaten such an invasion for the sake of intimidating one of Iraq's neighbors in order to pressure that neighbor to be more accommodating on issues such as debt forgiveness or economic aid. In view of Saddam's track record, it would likely be a short step from intimidation to extortion to another invasion of one of Iraq's neighbors.

What all this meant in practice was that, even after his defeat in the first Persian Gulf War, Saddam was still a formidable opponent, and a bloodthirsty one at that. If he could somehow undermine or escape the web of sanctions and restraints that the United States and its allies had put in place around him, the result would likely be renewed warfare, in part because Saddam had already invaded two of his neighbors, causing great hardship and suffering, and in part because in 2003 Saddam was a sixty-six-year-old tyrant, distrusted and even hated by his own people, running out of options and, more important, running out of time. If Saddam was somehow allowed to resume and even to escalate the conflicts between Iraq and much of the rest of the world that had begun on his watch, the outcome would almost certainly have been renewed warfare. The question was, Could he do it? Could Saddam somehow escape the obstacles put in place by the United States and its allies in the hope that he could somehow be coaxed or enticed to get "back in his box," like the United States had done to Libya's Colonel Qaddafi?

How Long Could Containment Last?

In this section, I argue that Saddam was so hampered and restrained by the sanctions and other constraints imposed on Iraq that his opportunities to resume his role as chief troublemaker in the Middle East ranged between not very many and almost none. I argue further that, while it may have been desirable to capture Saddam, conquer Iraq, and then dismantle his WMD and ballistic missile programs brick by brick and warhead by warhead, it was not essential to do all that to effectively contain Saddam. Iraq was much weaker in 2003 than it had been in 1990, in part because of all the damage and destruction suffered by the Iraqi armed forces during the Iraq-Iran War and the two Persian Gulf Wars, and in part because of all the years after the first Gulf War that Iraqi armed forces had served as involuntary practice targets for American and British warplanes. Conversely, the United States was better prepared for war against Iraq in 2003 than it had been in 1990. In 1990, "the U.S. had no adequate [military] response to the Iraqi invasion [of Kuwait]." As Freedman and Karsh point out, "the armed forces necessary to force Iraq to leave Kuwait were simply not in place. The United States had nothing in the region capable of such a task."[63] By 2003, in contrast, the United States had bases in the region hosting ground, air, and naval forces, plus equipment and supplies pre-positioned within range of Iraq. In 1990 the United States had no nearby forces capable of striking Iraq, and it would take months to deploy the forces necessary to eject Iraq from Kuwait. In 2003, air strikes would have started within about twenty-four hours of the outbreak of hostilities.

By 2003, Saddam's regime in Iraq was in decline and on the run. Keeping in mind Saddam's advanced age, the United States did not need to invade and occupy Iraq. All that the United States and its allies had to do was to keep Iraqi scientists and engineers on the run from the UN weapons inspectors and to keep Iraqi armed forces vulnerable and demoralized until Saddam, his sons, and his lackeys could ruin Iraq no more.

Evaluating Failure

From 1982 to 1989, US-Iraqi relations improved some, but this was essentially a by-product of the Iraq-Iran War. In 1982 the Reagan administration took the first steps in this regard by formally removing Iraq from its list of states that support international terrorism, followed by the resumption of diplomatic relations in November 1984. In October 1989, the first President Bush signed NSD-26, which made an improvement in US-Iraqi relations an explicit foreign policy goal for the United States.[64]

On the other hand, there is a considerable gap between committing a goal to paper and achieving that same goal. Iraq had stumbled across the finish line for its war with Iran broke and exhausted; it needed US agricultural credits to keep the Iraqi population fed. Iraq also wanted to buy atomic bomb components in the United States and elsewhere. Every dollar of agricultural credits that Iraq received from the United States was one dollar more of Iraq's limited resources that Saddam's regime could devote to building an Iraqi nuclear weapon. The Reagan administration and the first Bush administration sought to entice Iraq into joining the civilized world, with entry conditional on renouncing any further pursuit of a nuclear weapon. In retrospect, there were warning signs that US policy had become deeply flawed, with too much appeasement and not enough containment.[65] This was not a suggestion to return to pre-1982 levels of hostility toward Iraq; it was instead a call to firm up and balance the overly accommodating policy found in NSD-26. The Reagan and Bush 41 administrations were so intent on enticing the Iraqis to give up their quest for an Iraqi bomb that they had failed to notice that Iraq was going through the motions in a way that told the Americans what the latter wanted to hear.

By the end of the 1990s, however, increasingly the argument was being made that containment, which once had worked very well against Iraq, was now failing. In an article published in *Foreign Affairs* in 2002, Kenneth Pollack argued that containing Iraq was a sensible policy at the time it was imposed (after the first Persian Gulf War, 1990–91), but more recently containment had started to unravel.[66] Five years later, Pollack was more certain—"containment was failing." In his view, "The shameful performance of the United Nations Security Council members . . . in 2003 was final proof that containment could not have lasted much longer; Saddam would eventually have reconstituted his WMD programs."[67]

Are these judgments correct? How would we know? Pollack's answer suggests that containment worked reasonably well until 1998 or so, which was the year that the UNSCOM and IAEA inspectors were withdrawn from Iraq at the request of the Iraqi government, which meant there would be no inspectors available to enforce the UN Security Council resolutions banning Iraqi WMDs and ballistic missiles to carry them in the event of another Persian Gulf War. Lawrence Freedman's assessment of containment took much the same position: "Containment eroded during the 1990s because members of the Security Council became increasingly unwilling to sustain a porous and counterproductive sanctions regime and endorse enforcement action that appeared to be more punitive than decisive."[68] The view that containment was failing was "the accepted view among many of the key members of the [second] Bush administration."[69] The second President Bush devoted much of his first eighteen months in office to stemming "the precipitate decline of the sanctions regime."[70]

What does it mean to say that a policy like containing Saddam Hussein's Iraq is unraveling? During the 1990s, the conventional wisdom about Saddam was that he had "a number of pathologies that [made] deterring him unusually difficult."[71] When dealing with Saddam, the possibility of another Persian Gulf War could never be excluded, even after Iraq's humiliating defeat in the first Gulf War. The conventional wisdom also suggests that, if we were to reexamine efforts by the United States to contain Iraq since 1991, we would likely find our dealings with Saddam to be divided into two more or less distinct periods: one in which containment worked reasonably well, followed by one in which containment had started to unravel. If and when containment had begun to fail, would we know it when we saw it? Why might it not be obvious that containment was failing?

This is actually a very contentious issue because, at the same time that scholars such as Kenneth Pollack and Lawrence Freedman were suggesting that containment was eroding or even collapsing, the United States and Britain were acting quite vigorously to keep Saddam "in his box," just like Colonel Qaddafi in Libya. Daniel Byman notes in this regard that, during the decade following the first Persian Gulf War, the United States could and did rely on multiple instruments to keep Saddam and Iraq contained, including sanctions, weapons inspections, a large military presence in the Persian Gulf region, frequent use of limited military power against Iraq, and support for the Iraqi opposition.[72]

In similar fashion, the Bush Doctrine, as applied to post-9/11 Iraq (and Afghanistan too), was a recipe for action, not for sitting around and waiting for something to happen. As summarized by Robin Wright, the Bush Doctrine specified that the United States should, first, be prepared to act preemptively to prevent strikes on US targets. Second, Washington should also be willing and able to act unilaterally if called on to do so. Third, since Iraq was the next cornerstone in the global war on terrorism, Washington should give special attention to ensuring that any vulnerabilities would be recognized and repaired promptly. Finally, Baghdad's transformation into a new democracy was expected to spark region-wide change, but only if the United States ensured that action was taken.[73]

In effect, Daniel Byman and Robin Wright have each provided alternative ways of enumerating the many and varied activities that the second Bush administration was using, under the guise of containment, to chip away at Iraq's ability to do harm to the United States or Iraq's neighbors. The most important point here is not that Byman's list differs from Wright's, but that all these actions on both lists could have continued more or less indefinitely even if the United States had not invaded Iraq.

Seen this way, the art of choosing which of these varied actions could still have been included even if the United States had not invaded Iraq suggests that deciding which could have been included as "containing Iraq" involves more than just scoring debating points. These actions and the outcomes they caused constitute a powerful case for sticking with containment while deferring a judgment on invading Iraq until sometime in the future. In this regard, there are at least five reasons why containment, as it was practiced in the aftermath of Iraq's crushing defeat in the first Persian Gulf War, could have remained a viable strategy for coping with Saddam Hussein's regime for a very long time.

First, US policy toward Iraq during the decade after the first Persian Gulf War was more successful than generally realized. Iraq was contained, and while the French and the Russians quickly grew weary of the burdens that containment entailed, there is every reason to believe that the Americans and the British could have provided the necessary fortitude while time ran out for Saddam. As of 2001, the United States was maintaining a "robust U.S. regional presence, a rapid surge capability, and a willingness to use limited force." Conversely, also as of 2001, Saddam's Iraq was far weaker than it had been in 1990.[74] Since the Iraqis didn't know whether and when the Americans and the British might strike next, it was the Iraqis who were being run ragged by the Americans and the British. In effect, the United States had seized the initiative and was using it to outwit Saddam and his helpers. The Iraqis were for the most part reacting to what the United States and other coalition members were doing. The Iraqis were so intent on outrunning their many pursuers (UNSCOM, the IAEA, and the CIA, to name a few) that they appeared to have almost no time left to design and then pursue programs that could produce WMDs. The United States, in contrast, could use its vastly superior intelligence-gathering resources to determine where and when to demand access to a suspected Iraqi WMD facility. Since the Iraqis had very little advance notice of where the UN inspectors would want to look next, frequently they had to improvise, making snap judgments about how to delay or sidetrack the inspectors.[75]

Second, the Iraqis spent a great deal of their time on the run from the Americans, the British, the UN inspectors, and the IAEA inspectors (who were accepting tips from Western intelligence agencies about where to look). Life on the run for the Iraqis meant that they faced an increased risk that they would be caught in a lie. Being caught in a lie would damage Saddam's carefully cultivated reputation for being the only leadership figure in Iraq and throughout the Arab world capable of standing up to the Americans. As Saddam's regime weakened, it would be exposed to ridicule all over the world, and this would damage the regime's legitimacy among the Iraqi people. Saddam, moreover, had a personal stake in all this, at least in the sense of not being seen to be giving up too much, too soon. In 1961, 1973, and 1990, Iraq laid claim to territories that were already claimed by others. Especially in 1990–91, Saddam could not understand why the Americans would fight so hard to rescue a country referred to derisively by Arabs as the world's largest shopping mall. Iraq was "a restless power: the legitimacy and credibility of the Ba'athist regime, and of Saddam Hussein in particular, depended upon his attaining new foreign policy successes and enhancing Iraq's international position."[76]

This is why Saddam preferred to let the world think that he did have some WMDs, to keep the Iraqi people and his enemies in Iran and elsewhere in awe of his ability to bamboozle the Americans and their helpers. On the other hand, gambits rarely last forever, and this one was no exception. Saddam's innermost circle may have known that there were no WMDs in the Iraqi arsenal, but not so President George W. Bush. The second Bush presidency accepted the conventional wisdom that Saddam was hoarding some WMDs. More important, the second Bush administration was determined to solve the problem of Iraqi WMDs, and this time for good.

Third, because the Iraqis were constantly on the run from UN inspectors on the ground and US spy planes (U-2s) and imaging satellites in the sky above them, they rarely had time to build anything new, like better storage facilities for their WMD programs.

Fourth, there was more to containing Iraq than just pursuing Iraq's WMD programs. When the Iraqis increased the number of surface-to-air missiles that Iraq's armed forces were launching against US and British aircraft, the Americans and the British took this not just as a threat but also as an opportunity to add to the target lists that they were maintaining as part of their enforcement of the no-fly zones over northern and southern Iraq. It was the Iraqis who made the first move, by adding to their stockpile of Soviet-made surface-to-air missiles. This was followed by a US countermove (expanding the number and value of the targets struck). By going first, the Iraqis gave the Americans and the British lots of targets to shoot at, and the Anglo-American partnership took advantage of the opportunities before them. More important, while the events recounted here were being played out, Saddam was growing older, and he would keep on growing older, unless he provoked the United States one time too many, in which case he wouldn't need to worry any longer about growing older.

Fifth, containment and preventive action (an invasion of Iraq) were both rival strategies and complements. A decision to stick with containment now did not preclude an invasion later. Indeed, the threat of an invasion could be a powerful incentive to the Iraqis not to challenge containment too vigorously now. The second Bush administration took it as a given that the United States would have to fight to defend its vital interests against rogue regimes and terrorists. Saddam Hussein was certainly a rogue, but he was also a rogue with a lot to lose. The more Saddam had to hide, the greater the likelihood he would take care not to provoke the Americans to the point that they would opt for war. Conversely, the more cautiously Saddam behaved, the less likely the Americans would push disputes with Saddam to the point of fighting.

Others Will Help

I suggest toward the end of chapter 3 that if the Persian Gulf containment regime was indeed crumbling into ineffectualness, then the likelihood of one or a few of the smaller Persian Gulf states bandwagoning with Iraq or Iran should increase. Why bandwagon? Small states, like the Persian Gulf sheikhdoms, must take into account whether and when the United States might withdraw its forces from the Persian Gulf and Indian Ocean regions, leaving the gulf Arab states to fend for themselves. In 1998, Saddam had compelled the departures of the inspectors from the UN and the IAEA. As of 2002, Saddam had spent roughly a decade attempting to reconstitute Iraq's WMD programs and to rebuild Iraq's conventional forces too. Last but not least, Saddam had already invaded two of Iraq's neighbors, and there was no good reason to believe that he might not try again.

In this situation, the appeal of bandwagoning with Iraq or Iran (rather than balancing against them) was that it offered the gulf states the prospect of escaping involvement in a future gulf war by doing the minimum necessary to keep the Iranians or the Iraqis at arm's length. States bandwagon in the hope that they can avoid involvement in a future war. In this case, they would have done it by sending Iraq or Iran conciliatory messages while avoiding commitments to any meaningful military support. Bandwagoning also would have kept open the option of defecting to the United States, just in case Iraq or Iran should demand too much of its nominal "ally." Iraq's assorted weapons programs were progressing, but only very slowly. This raises the question, What, if anything, were the United States and the rest of the West prepared to do about these developments? Iraq and Iran were not the only threats to peace and stability, and bandwagoning was not the only strategy open to the small Arab states. There are several reasons to believe that the Americans could and would continue to compete vigorously (and effectively) to win the cooperation of the Arab gulf states, and that the latter would be receptive to American offers of greater military cooperation.

First, barring a near-complete collapse of political will, the United States would almost certainly win this competition, because it had so much meaningful military support that it could offer to the smaller gulf states. There had been attempts at bandwagoning prior to the first and second Gulf Wars, but considering what the United States could offer, the Arab gulf states would have been foolish to align with any state other than the United States. In the end, there would be no bandwagoning with Iraq or Iran prior to either of the two Persian Gulf Wars.

Second, geography matters. As seen by one of the small Arab gulf states, or even from Saudi Arabia, the United States was far away, while Iraq and Iran were close at hand. If the United States ever were to withdraw from the Persian Gulf and Indian Ocean regions, the gulf sheikhdoms would be left to face Iraq and Iran by themselves. But since the United States was a much more benign superpower, at least when compared with Hitler's Germany or Stalin's Soviet Union, the Arab states concluded that the path to safety for them was to share some burdens rather than shift them to the United States. Hence the smaller gulf states provided the United States with access to sophisticated and spacious air and naval bases which, not coincidentally, made it easier for the United States to protect them too. Hence the suggestion mentioned earlier—that the best strategy for the Arab gulf states was to chain themselves to the United States as tightly as they could.[77]

Third, domestic politics might cause another round of containment to blow up in the faces of the designers. During the congressional debate on whether Congress should authorize force to evict the Iraqis from Kuwait, the Senate majority leader George Mitchell (D–Maine) warned against "a war in which Americans do the fighting and dying while those who benefit from our effort provide token help and urge us on."[78] The US experience in the two Persian Gulf Wars, and more than a decade of hindsight gathered between those two wars, all suggest that, contrary to the predictions of collective action theory,[79] others will indeed help, but they will find it easier to help when the United States is defending, deterring, and in general leaving it to the opposing side to fire the first shot. Doing so provides both legitimacy and political cover to whatever the United States is asking of its allies. Others will especially want to help when the vast resources of the United States (which greatly improve the chances of success) can be coupled to a politically legitimate undertaking (like something blessed by the UN Security Council). But when the United States invades another state without UN warrant or the support of numerous other democracies, the United States will likely find it more difficult to persuade other states to take on meaningful roles. Compare, for example, the roles of France and Germany in the two Persian Gulf Wars. Both contributed to the US-led, UN-sanctioned effort in the first Gulf War; neither contributed to another US-led invasion of Iraq. Indeed, both tried hard to prevent the United States from going through with the invasion of Iraq in the second Gulf War.[80]

To better understand the relative strengths and weaknesses of containment versus the Bush Doctrine, I conclude this chapter with a brief counterfactual case in point. Suppose that the United States had not invaded Iraq in March 2003. What would have been the likely consequences if the United States had chosen to pursue a diplomatic rather than a military solution?

First and foremost, if the United States and Britain had not invaded Iraq in 2003, there still would have been lots of military and diplomatic actions taking place. Almost all these ongoing activities would have been planned and executed by the United States. At long last, the United States would have the initiative, and Saddam's regime would be reacting to what the United States was doing. The historical record, however, suggests that the United States was already doing quite a lot. UNSCOM and the IAEA would continue looking for Saddam's forbidden weapons, and anything that was found would be confiscated by the coalition, like Iraq's stockpile of Scud missiles. The UN would supervise use of Iraqi oil revenues to pay for medical and humanitarian uses. Saddam's regime would continue to engage in smuggling. The American and British air forces would continue striking lucrative targets wherever they could be found in Iraq. The Kurds in the north and the Shiites in the south would continue to foment revolution against Saddam's continued rule.

Second, the list in the previous paragraph could go on and on if need be. The sheer number and variety of the actions that were then being taken by the United States and Britain is a reminder of how much a superpower can bring to bear on an ongoing struggle. Because the Iraqis were reacting to what the United States and other coalition members were doing, they had little or no time to plan how best to lead the United States and its allies astray when the latter were demanding access to Iraqi facilities that the Iraqi side would prefer the Americans not see. The Americans could use the enormous resources of the US intelligence community to estimate where and when to demand access to an Iraqi facility. The Iraqis had to improvise, making snap judgments that they hoped would mislead the Americans but without activating the rest of the coalition. More important, every minute that the Iraqis had to devote to improvisation was one less minute that they could devote to carefully planning how to mislead the Americans.

Third, Saddam's regime lived on a bed of lies, and because the Iraqis were improvising, they faced a heightened danger that they would be caught in a lie. This was a sensitive matter for Iraq's officer corps, its diplomats and bureaucrats, all of whom worked for a leader whose continued hold on power depended in part on his ability to convince the Iraqi people that he knew what he was doing and that he could run the coalition in circles looking for Iraqi WMDs, which always seemed to be just a little beyond the grasp of the UN inspectors, Western intelligence agencies, and the like. And if that didn't work, Saddam could always threaten to turn the weapons and interrogatory skills of his police state on anyone who wasn't showing enough enthusiasm for the survival of Saddam and his regime.

Fourth, because the Iraqis were constantly on the run from UN inspectors, they were greatly hampered by their inability to build anything new, especially because Iraq was being photographed every day by US reconnaissance satellites looking for exactly that—evidence of new construction associated with Iraq's WMD programs.

Fifth, the Americans and the British were waging an ongoing air war with the Iraqi air defense forces. In the immediate aftermath of the first Gulf War, these air attacks took the form of reprisals against Iraqi forces that made the mistake of attempting to shoot down US and British aircraft. Later on, in the air war over the no-fly zones, the Americans and the British greatly expanded the target lists that their aircraft could strike if the opportunity to do so presented itself.

In the Iraqi case, then, containment was neither static nor slow-paced nor limited in what US forces could do. Instead, there was a great deal of activity ongoing. Because the costs of containment were relatively small compared to those of invading Iraq, it seems likely that the Americans and the British could have kept it up more or less indefinitely. Containment may have proven difficult to extend beyond 2003, but it is crucial to remember that political imperatives are not solely the domain of the United States. All the while that the Americans and their allies argued the relative merits of containment versus invasion, Saddam grew older, his armed forces became more decrepit, and the morale of his soldiers dropped even lower.

Sixth, what if the second President Bush had chosen to follow the advice and policy prescriptions offered repeatedly in this book—namely, that the United States refrain from invading Iraq, choosing to focus on containing rather than destroying Saddam's regime? What, if any, would have been the likely consequences if the United States had chosen to defer a decision on invading Iraq until sometime in the future, perhaps even the distant future? Four responses to these questions come readily to mind. First, the air war over and around the no-fly zones would have continued, as would the sanctions on Iraq's economy. Second, Saddam would rule only those parts of Iraq with majority Sunni populations, which were concentrated within those parts of Iraq where Sunnis traditionally lived. Third, Saddam likely would continue his attempts to shoot down a US or a British fighter plane, which would have given the Americans and the British an opportunity to expand or intensify reprisal strikes against the Iraqis. Fourth, Saddam would grow older; his enemies would grow in number, and even Saddam's most vocal supporters would find it harder to conceal from the rest of the Iraqi population that Saddam was no longer a young man, or even middle-aged.

This is more than just whimsical thinking. During his first eighteen months in office, the second President Bush reportedly devoted much of his available time not to preparing for war with Iraq, but rather to trying to fix "the precipitate decline of the sanctions regime."[81] Even the second President Bush occasionally took a more relaxed view of the threat to US interests posed by Saddam's regime, especially prior to 9/11. The view of Condoleezza Rice, who served as national security adviser and later secretary of state, was perhaps the most relaxed among the second Bush administration's senior policy makers. The counterfactual suggests that even if Saddam had opted for more fighting—for example, trying harder to break the naval embargo imposed on Iraq by the United States and its allies immediately after the cease-fire that ended the first Gulf War in 1991 by sending ships to attempt to do so, the United States and its allies responded by persuading the UN Security Council to pass Resolution 665, which authorized any UN member state to stop an Iraqi ship trying to defy the embargo. In effect, "Iraq was forced again to recognize that the international community was unimpressed by its bluster, and that it had little choice but to respect the naval embargo."[82] Even if the sanctions imposed at this time should prove to be leaky, sanctions were only one part of a broader security regime that was being prepared for Iraq. If the sanctions should prove to be a disappointment, there were always other ways the United States could continue to pressure Iraq.

Containing Iran

Like Colonel Qaddafi's Libya and Saddam Hussein's Iraq, Iran under clerical rule was widely thought to be a difficult target for a strategy based on containment. "If Iran gets nuclear weapons," a senior Israeli official told a Western newsmagazine in 2010, "the Middle East will look like hell. I cannot imagine that we can live with a nuclear Iran."[1] Strong words indeed, but what were the alternatives? In January 2006, a past and future Israeli prime minister drew an analogy with the 1930s to call attention to Iran's potential: "It's 1938 and Iran is Germany."[2] Also in 2006, Israel's deputy defense minister predicted, "War with Iran is inevitable."[3] Four years later, Israeli sources let it be known that 2010 was the "year of decision"—the year when Iran's aspirations and Israel's fears would likely collide head-on.[4] War did not break out in either 2006 or 2010, but this was likely small consolation to those charged with preventing such a war. With every year that passed, Iran *seemed* to draw closer to becoming a nuclear power and therefore harder to deter and to contain, or so the conventional wisdom proclaimed. As one analyst argued in 2009, "Official Washington has resigned itself to pursuing a containment policy that some argue will limit Iran's ability to proliferate, terrorize and otherwise exploit being a nuclear power. But it is wrong to think a nuclear Iran can be contained."[5]

In this chapter, I focus on the political-military rivalry between the United States and Iran between 1991 (the first Persian Gulf War) and 2016 (when Iran accepted strict limits on its use of the nuclear fuel cycle to produce fissionable materials).[6] In 2015 and in 2016, "Iran . . . shipped 98 percent of its nuclear fuel out of the country, dismantled thousands of centrifuges used for enriching uranium, and destroyed the core of a major nuclear reactor. Instead of being two to three months from acquiring a [nuclear] weapon," President Obama announced, it was "now a year away."[7] In return, the United States and its allies agreed to phase out economic sanctions aimed at Iran, some of which had been in place since the 1980s.

If containment pessimists are correct about Iran being undeterrable and uncontainable, then many of the events recounted in this chapter probably should not have occurred. But they did occur, which suggests that a closer look at the historical record will likely reveal some additional interesting twists and turns.

Why Iran Matters

There are at least five reasons why the United States and its allies, especially Israel, consider Iran to be an existential threat and therefore in need of being contained.

First, the Islamic regime that succeeded the shah in 1979 was and still is undeniably hostile to the West in general and the United States and Israel in particular. Islamic Iran has "worked consistently to undermine U.S. interests in the Middle East," while Washington has worked hard to contain Iran.[8] The Iranians proved to be determined competitors. "Iran is on the move," Charles Krauthammer wrote in 1993, "and makes no effort to hide its ambitions."[9] Also in 1993, two well-connected US journalists wrote in their syndicated column that "in Sudan, the mullahs of Iran are building a formidable structure of terrorist schools, military training camps and intelligence."[10] With the shah no longer in the picture, there seemed to be no limit to Iran's aspirations. Martin Indyk, for example, accused Iran of pursuing offensive weapons, which it could then use "to dominate the [Persian Gulf] by military means."[11] The US secretary of state Warren Christopher told an audience of European leaders in 1993 that "Iran is 'the most worrisome' of the nations buying arms today."[12]

Second, religious fervor endowed the clerical regime in Tehran with considerable staying power. During the 2000s, for example, George W. Bush's administration found itself confronting a hostile regime in Tehran that was doing many of the things that its predecessors had done during the 1980s and the 1990s, such as fomenting revolution in nearby states, pursuing weapons of mass destruction, and strengthening Iran's nonnuclear forces. In response, the second Bush administration used many of the same arguments about Iran's aspirations and capabilities that the Clinton administration had used more than a decade before. In its 2006 *National Strategy for Combating Terrorism*, the second Bush administration echoed claims made during the 1990s by Martin Indyk and Warren Christopher, who judged Iran to be "the most active state sponsor of international terrorism." Through its Islamic Revolutionary Guard Corps and its Ministry of Intelligence and Security, the regime in Tehran planned terrorist operations and supported groups such as Hizballah, Hamas, and Palestinian Islamic Jihad (PIJ). Iran was unwilling even to account for, much less bring to justice, senior al Qaeda members that it had detained in

2003. "Most troubling is the potential WMD-Terrorism nexus that emanates from Tehran."[13]

Third, Islamic Iran consistently pursued multiple lines of policy, any one of which could be deemed a threat to important US interests. As mentioned above, during the 1980s, 1990s, and 2000s, Iran sought to export its Shiite-led Islamic revolution to nearby states, acquire WMDs, and expand and improve Iran's nonnuclear armed forces, all more or less simultaneously.[14] Any one of these would likely be considered a threat to vital US interests in the vicinity of the Persian Gulf. The combination of all three within Iranian foreign policy presented what seemed to be an especially grave danger to the United States and to Israel too, all the more so because everyone knew that the Iranians were unpredictable and might strike at the United States or Israel while providing little or no warning that an attack was imminent.

Fourth, Iran's ruling clerics rarely missed an opportunity to flaunt their disinterest in and contempt for Western norms, rules, and principles for managing international affairs. Islamic Iran, for example, signed the Chemical Weapons Convention, and then acted as if the treaty didn't exist. As of 1996, Iran was continuing "to upgrade and expand" its ability to produce and use poison gases and "spending large sums of money on long-term capital improvements," which, in the eyes of the CIA, indicated Iran's intention "to maintain a chemical weapons capability well into the future."[15] Test-firing medium-range ballistic missiles after the UN Security Council passed a resolution prohibiting such launches was a second opportunity for Iran to flaunt its contempt for the West.[16] Hostage taking was yet another way of showing "Iran's heedlessness of international law and its penchant for the humiliation of its enemies."[17]

Fifth, Islamic Iran posed an especially vexing challenge because of a certain never-say-die quality that permeated its policies toward the rest of the world and especially the United States and Israel. The mullahs and other religious zealots who have ruled Iran since the overthrow of the shah in 1979 seemed never to grow tired or even discouraged. Vali Nasr and Ray Takeyh, for example, describe Islamic Iran as presenting "serious problems for the United States. Its quest for a nuclear capability, its mischievous interventions in Iraq, and its strident opposition to the Israeli-Palestinian peace process constitute a formidable list of grievances."[18] Colin Dueck and Ray Takeyh likewise call attention to the clerics' "strident anti-Israel rhetoric." As seen by Iran's militant mullahs, Israel was and is an illegitimate state, and Israel's military power is the product of a pernicious conspiracy. "In its opposition to Israel, the Islamic Republic has violated all prevailing international norms." Islamic Iran "frequently denies that the Holocaust occurred, calls for the elimination of a member state of the United Nations, and actively supports terrorist organizations plotting against Jerusalem."[19] When the governing elite of a state like Iran holds such extreme views, it can be very hard not to believe that today's irresponsible words might well be tomorrow's catalyst for war. As seen by Iran's ruling elite, any day is a good day to cause trouble for America (Israel too). In this case, Iran's contempt for the United States was reciprocated by the Reagan, Bush 41, Clinton, and Bush 43 administrations, which neither forgot nor forgave the abuse inflicted on the American diplomats formerly stationed at the US embassy in Tehran.

Whatever else students of the US-Iranian relationship may or may not agree on, one belief shared by almost all of them is that Iran continues to pose an exceptionally difficult problem for the United States—too big to invade, too wealthy to bribe, too powerful to ignore, deeply hostile toward the United States—and this situation seems likely to continue for years to come.[20] In the meantime, what should the United States be doing to resolve the West's "Iran problem"?

A good place to start in this regard would be to remind ourselves that the "Iran problem," while deeply troublesome, is by no means insoluble. During the Cold War, the United States learned to live with a Soviet Union that was very large, very powerful, and very hostile to Western notions of human rights and civil liberties. In response, the United States waged, successfully, a four-decade-long Cold War against the Soviet Union (and China too, during the 1950s and the 1960s). If the United States could successfully contain the Soviet Union and China during the Cold War, why should it be deemed incapable of containing a middle power like Iran, which, while dangerous, was and is much less of a threat to the United States and its allies than was Stalin's Soviet Union and Mao's China?

This is not to make light of the challenge a nuclear-armed Iran would pose. If Iran should proclaim itself a nuclear power, other nations might question the U.S. government's power and resolve to shape events.[21] On the other hand, even if Iran were to catch the world by surprise by unexpectedly testing a nuclear weapon, that would not change the fact that containment has already bought time—indeed, a lot of time—to find a better foundation on which a US-Iranian relationship could rest. The United States and Iran don't have to like each other, but they do need to understand each other's grievances and respect each other's power. What, if anything, can containment optimism and pessimism tell us about learning to live with Islamic Iran?

Can Iran Be Contained?

Containment pessimism begins with the assumption that an ambitious regional power like Iran will never accept permanent second-class status relative to other nearby states that have already acquired nuclear weapons of their own (Israel, India, and Pakistan). Containment pessimists likewise believe that an Iran that possesses nuclear weapons will be very difficult to deter. Containing Iran through military deployments and antagonistic alliances is not a tenable strategy. An Iran that cannot be deterred, pessimists conclude, is an Iran that cannot be contained.[22] These are controversial claims, but containment pessimists have advanced multiple reasons why they believe that Islamic Iran has proved itself to be more than just another ambitious regional power and therefore more difficult to contain than the Soviet Union or China during the Cold War.[23]

First, containment pessimists argue that Iran—ruled by clerics—is not a normal state and therefore will likely prove harder to contain than the Soviet Union during the Cold War. Charles Krauthammer, for example, describes Iran as a state led by "religious fanatics seized with an eschatological belief in the imminent apocalypse and in their own divine duty to hasten the End of Days. The mullahs are infinitely more likely to use these weapons than anyone in the history of the nuclear age."[24] John Bolton's views are very similar to Krauthammer's: "When you have a regime that would be happier in the afterlife than in this life, this is not a regime that is subject to classic theories of deterrence."[25]

Second, containment pessimists highlight the ways in which Muslim clerics have used religious fervor to mobilize their followers, vanquish their secular foes, and capture the Iranian state, which they then used to subvert Iran's neighbors and export Iran's Shiite-led Islamic revolution throughout the Middle East and the Persian Gulf regions. In effect, the religious militants who ousted the shah in 1979 have used their capture of the Iranian state to redefine what they believe to be Iran's vital interests vis-à-vis the West in general and the United States in particular. "Iranian conservatives see their defiance of the Great Satan as a means of mobilizing nationalist opinion behind a revolution that has gradually lost popular legitimacy."[26] An influential cleric explains: "Our national interests lie with antagonizing the Great Satan. We condemn any cowardly stance toward America and any word on compromise with the Great Satan."[27]

Third, the Iranians proved to be clever foes. During the hostage crisis (1979–81), "Iran watched and learned." The Iranians especially "learned how obsessively engaged our news media becomes when U.S. prisoners are taken."[28] The Iranians also learned from Iraq's mistakes. In 1981, Israel destroyed Iraq's Osirak nuclear reactor, using only eight F-16 aircraft. Roughly twenty years later, the Israeli pilot who led the strike on Osirak noted that "the Iranians are clever. They learnt well from Osirak. . . . There is no single target [in Iran] that you can bomb with eight aircraft."[29] Iran's clerics did not just stand idly by while the United States fought two wars— one against the Taliban in Afghanistan in 2001 and 2002 and a second against Saddam Hussein's regime in Iraq in 2003. Iran's ruling clerics had "plenty of opportunity to learn lessons on beating the IAEA inspection regime from watching Iraq and North Korea, which both cheated successfully against IAEA inspectors."[30]

Fourth, revolutionary Iran has proven to be a difficult target for a containment policy because some of the West's own policies have encouraged the Iranians to raise their sights regarding what they might get away with in their dealings with various Western audiences. It was widely known during the 1970s that the shah of Iran had nuclear ambitions of his own. Washington wanted the shah's Iran to serve as one of two pillars that would look after US interests in the Persian Gulf region (Saudi Arabia would be the other pillar). Because imperial Iran had something that Washington wanted, the latter declined to make an issue of why an Iran rich in oil and natural gas should require twenty or more power-generating reactors, which is what the shah's program called for. The Europeans didn't ask questions either. Indeed, the same European states that during the 1990s and 2000s called on Iran to suspend its nuclear enrichment activities were in the 1970s and 1980s eager to sell to the shah (and later to the clerical regime that ousted him) the technology needed to construct a network of nuclear plants that could without much difficulty have been used for military purposes. Since the fall of the shah, "belated Western concerns regarding Iran's proliferation tendencies [have only reinforced] Tehran's arguments regarding the hypocrisy of the great powers and the iniquitous nature of the Nuclear Non-Proliferation Treaty (NPT)."[31]

What Kind of State Is Iran?

First, in order to sustain their claim that Islamic Iran poses a new and more threatening challenge to the nonproliferation regime in particular and to peace and stability in general, containment pessimists have often portrayed Iran as fanatical, irrational, and even suicidal. Containment pessimists almost have to make these claims if they are to sustain their case against Iran. Take away the references to religious fanaticism and suicidal tendencies and the like, and about all that's left of revolutionary Iran is another aspiring middle power trying to claw its way up the international ladder of status and prestige.

A second, potentially more serious problem for containment pessimism is that Islamic Iran has proved to be more agile and more ingenious than the qualities attributed to it by containment pessimists might suggest. Religious fanatics they may be, but the Iranians learned early on how to frame their arguments in ways that made it difficult for their Western negotiating partners to say no to whatever the Iranians were selling. The Iranians have also proven to be shrewd negotiators. When talking with the West, it has been one of their goals to split the Americans and the Europeans by putting forward proposals that the Europeans would find attractive but which the Americans would not. A good example in this regard would be the offer made by the Iranians to the Europeans in March 1995 (specifically, the

EU-3: Britain, France, and Germany). In this case, the Iranians offered to limit their nuclear-related activities to those that could be done without violating the NPT. To add substance to their proposal, the Iranian side offered "to produce only low-enriched uranium; to limit the amount of uranium enriched; to convert all low-enriched uranium to fuel rods for use in reactors (fuel rods cannot be further enriched); to limit the number of centrifuges in Natanz; and to make the full operation of the fuel cycle incremental, beginning with the least sensitive part of uranium conversion; to refrain from reprocessing spent reactor fuel, and to give the International Atomic Energy Agency a permanent on-site presence at all sites for uranium conversion and enrichment."[32] All these activities were already open to Iran as a signer of the NPT, but these were also activities that would allow the Iranians to get closer to mastery of the entire fuel enrichment cycle, and in that way put Iran into a position to break out of the constraints imposed upon it.[33] The Europeans, however, found it hard to say no to Iranian proposals that were couched in terms of staying within the limits of the NPT, which likely accounts for why the Europeans never responded in public to this particular Iranian proposal.[34]

Eight years later, the same four states (Britain, France, Germany, and Iran) were talking once again about essentially the same set of issues. In September 2003, the IAEA circulated a ten-page paper that provided damning evidence that the Iranians had undertaken a secret, crash program to enlarge and improve their ability to produce fissionable material and, ultimately, nuclear weapons. The paper also accused Iran of trying to mislead UN investigators.[35] Iran's negotiating position was not very strong at this time. Even the Europeans did not believe the lame excuses that the Iranians were offering. All the parties to these talks (the EU-3 and Iran) were facing an imminent deadline, October 31, 2003, orchestrated by the United States and accepted by the IAEA's thirty-five-member board of governors. The terms proposed by the United States and accepted by the IAEA's board were that Iran should be given a choice between fully disclosing its nuclear program and a referral to the United Nations Security Council, where the United States had been lobbying vigorously for more and stricter sanctions to be imposed on Iran. The Iranians were expected to give a full accounting of what they had been doing in their nuclear program. If the Iranians did not provide a full and accurate description of what they were doing, including any violations of international law that might have occurred in their nuclear program, then they should be referred to the UN Security Council, where the Americans were still waiting for them, with plans for additional sanctions that could be imposed on Iran for its lack of truthfulness regarding its nuclear program.

What was the Iranian response to all this? Instead of huffing and puffing like mad mullahs eager for a confrontation with the West, the Iranians' response was to revive a tactic they had used with some success in the past.

On October 21, 2003, the Iranians signed—along with the British, the French, and the Germans—another vaguely worded document calling for more openness within Iran's nuclear program and more cooperation with those Europeans eager to impose greater international supervision on the Iranian nuclear program. The agreement also gave more details regarding what Iran could and could not do while remaining within the limits set by the NPT.[36]

In retrospect, it's not surprising that the Iranians preferred to deal with the Europeans rather than the Americans. The Europeans, hindsight suggests, were more easily satisfied than the Americans. The agreement signed by the Europeans and the Iranians was essentially a ploy to sign something, thereby creating the appearance of progress in these negotiations, and in that way head off the more insistent demands of the United States. The document signed by the EU-3 and Iran on October 21, 2003, may indeed have been a ploy, but in this case the ploy worked, in the sense of heading off a referral to the Security Council, where the Americans were still trying to arrange for more sanctions on Iran for not being open enough about its nuclear program.

In effect, the Europeans, the Iranians, and even the Americans were content to buy time with which to plot strategy for future moves. But as Fareed Zakaria wrote in August 2004, "The only problem is, Iran has recently announced that it isn't going to abide by the deal." According to Zakaria, "As the IAEA's investigations got more serious, Tehran got more secretive. One month ago the agency condemned Iran for its failure to cooperate. Tehran responded by announcing that it would resume work in prohibited areas."[37] It's not surprising to see a group of democracies acting to buy time (to forge a consensus on future goals and how to achieve them), but it is at least mildly surprising to see Iranian policy makers—spurned in the West as irrational, suicidal, and so on—acting in ways similar to their Western counterparts.

A third way in which exaggerated claims have limited the pessimists' ability to account for what the Iranians have already done, and to offer some modest predictions regarding what they likely will do in the future, can be traced to an apparent inconsistency within containment pessimism's view of Iran. Pessimists see Iran as unpredictable, undeterrable, and thus uncontainable, whereas the historical record since 1979 often portrays Iran as a careful, calculating actor that isn't afraid to provoke its enemies, but not too much. Containment pessimists take it as self-evident that containment has failed—indeed, more than once—since the fall of the shah in 1979. Ray Takeyh's view is typical of what pessimists think about Iran. Ever since the shah departed Iran for exile, the United States "has pursued a series of incoherent policies toward Tehran," he writes. "But none of these approaches has worked, especially not containment." In fact, "containment [has] never worked—and it has even less of a chance of working in the future."[38]

If Takeyh is right, and containment has never worked against Iran in the past and likely won't work in the future, then why didn't the Iranians try harder to take advantage of their own claims of incoherent policies and incompetent governance on the US side to press ahead with their own plans to make Iran into a nuclear power? This issue is particularly intriguing because it tells us a lot about how containment pessimists advance their claims and build on one another's findings.

On December 3, 2007, a new US National Intelligence Estimate, representing the view of the entire US intelligence community, concluded that Iran had ended its nuclear weapons program four years earlier. In the words of the intelligence estimate, "Tehran's decision to halt its nuclear weapons program suggests it is less determined to develop nuclear weapons than we have been judging since 2005. We do not know whether [Iran] currently intends to develop nuclear weapons."[39] In turn, the Iranians made it clear that Iran would never accept an agreement "that would single out Iran, forcing it to forgo activities other countries were allowed to pursue and subjecting Iran to restrictions not applied to other NPT signatories. These positions have been repeatedly stated in the Iranian press."[40]

If Takeyh and others in the pessimists' camp are right, then the events just discussed probably should not have been played out in just this way. Iran's goal was to join the ranks of the declared nuclear powers. The US goal was to thwart, delay, or impede Iran's progress toward mastery of the nuclear fuel cycle. The Iranians sought to define any limitations on their nuclear program as narrowly as possible. The United States pressed for the broadest possible interpretation of impermissible activities. The release of the intelligence estimate in 2007 suggests that Iran's progress has been anything but swift and smooth. Negotiations regarding the limits that Iran would have to accept or else risk renewed sanctions had first been taken up with the Iranians in the 1980s. Those talks continued off and on for more than thirty years. Containment pessimists are at a loss to explain how a democracy like the United States could have shown such tenacity. If containment pessimists are right, the United States should have grown weary of the conflict with Iran sometime in the 1980s, the 1990s, or the 2000s, but it did not. Instead, it was the Iranians who conceded first, signing an agreement with the United States and its allies that singled out Iran by placing additional limits on the work the Iranians could do regarding the nuclear fuel cycle. The agreement also mandated additional on-site inspections that other signatories of the NPT did not have to undergo. This was the kind of outcome (singling out Iran) that the Iranians themselves repeatedly claimed they would never accept. Why did the Iranians make the kind of agreement that they had repeatedly said they would never sign? In retrospect, one reason why these talks continued for so long was that both sides were content to go slow on the question of reimposing the sanctions first imposed by the nonproliferation regime in the 1980s. Even if they could not get an agreement now, both sides could at least hope that future elections would bring to power an Iranian government capable of more than just reiterating the same arguments about the same issues.

A fourth problem for containment pessimism is that, by portraying Iran as firmly in the grip of fearless and even reckless clerical rulers, it often overlooks that there are two sides to this story. In effect, pessimists beg the question of how to apportion responsibility between Iran and the United States for the unsatisfactory state of US-Iranian relations. Containment pessimism's response to this challenge is that it's all Iran's fault. The way to solve the Iran problem, pessimists suggest, is to change the composition of the government in Tehran. When Iran has a different government, improved US-Iranian relations will be easier to accomplish. Or will they? The second Bush administration invaded Iraq, even though it was not yet a nuclear power. That same Bush administration refrained from invading North Korea, which did have a nuclear weapon. Is it any wonder that the Iranians are likely to see an Iranian nuclear weapon as the only viable deterrent of US military action?[41]

In effect, the second Bush administration wrote off Iran without making much of an effort to see whether it might be engaged constructively—for example, in the aftermath of the 9/11 attacks on the United States, when the Iranians dropped multiple hints that Iran's relationship with the United States was open to reexamination.[42] Prior to the second Gulf War, the second Bush administration sent US representatives to talk with the Iranians, but only about narrowly focused issues, like search-and-rescue missions, or humanitarian aid for refugees fleeing the fighting in Iraq.[43] These were relatively modest steps but, even so, the US side broke off those talks in May 2003 because it thought Iran was harboring al-Qaeda members who had been involved in a recent bombing of residential compounds in Saudi Arabia.[44] The second Bush administration apparently saw no inconsistency between labeling Iran part of an "axis of evil" and asking for Iran's help in a future war against Saddam Hussein's regime in Iraq. These were exceedingly modest requests by the American side, which meant there would be no grand bargain between the United States and Iran, only occasional talks about lesser issues. On the whole, the second Bush administration's conception of diplomacy was so restrictive that it seemed to rule out just about any negotiated solution except Iran's capitulation. Instead of engaging Iran, the second Bush administration clung to its belief that Iran could not "be a constructive actor in a stable Middle East and that its unsavory behavior" could not be altered "through creative diplomacy."[45]

Fifth, what have the parties—the Americans, the Europeans, and Iran—learned from their dealings with each other? The Iranians likely have learned that the United States does not invade nuclear-armed opponents, and that stalling tactics can be made to work effectively against the Americans and even more so against the Europeans. If the road to Tehran really does run through London, Paris, and Berlin, Iran could take advantage of the Europeans' eagerness to sign something to argue the same issues over and over again, since the Europeans' desire for an agreement likely will collide head-on with their reluctance to do anything or threaten anything even remotely forceful.

On the US side, until 2016 containment pessimists were critical of containment, which they portrayed as an unqualified failure, mainly because the Iranian nuclear program was still in place and under way, and still in pursuit of an actual bomb. Pessimists were also concerned that with every passing day the Iranians came closer to asserting control of the entire nuclear fuel cycle. More important, many of the Islamic fanatics who took control of Iran in 1979 were still there, despite decades of sanctions and occasional military action.[46] Containment optimists, on the other hand, argue that containment has had only limited accomplishments in large part because it hasn't been used very well. States—even states governed by Islamic extremists—rarely burn every bridge behind them. Instead, states almost always leave themselves some kind of exit strategy. Contrary to the views of Krauthammer and other neoconservatives, "Iran is not . . . seeking to create disorder in order to fulfill some scriptural promise, nor is it an expansionist power with unquenchable ambitions. Not unlike Russia and China, Iran is a growing power seeking to become a pivotal state in its region."[47]

Containment Optimism

Containment pessimists have marshaled an impressive body of evidence suggesting that Iran cannot be considered a normal state, capable of sophisticated calculations of risk and reward as it plots future moves against its enemies in the Middle East and the Persian Gulf. Containment optimists have amassed a comparable body of evidence of their own, suggesting that Iran's behavior may have been misrepresented and may even have been misunderstood. Hindsight suggests that there are at least four reasons why containment optimists and pessimists differ so much concerning Iran as a rational international actor.

First, containment optimists take as their starting point their belief that what Iran does is a better indicator of future behavior than what Iran says. Iran "is sometimes portrayed as an 'un-deterrable' state driven by the absolute imperatives of religion, rather than by the pragmatic concerns of statecraft."[48] Tehran has indeed been aggressive and anti-American, but its behavior "has been neither irrational nor reckless. It has calibrated its actions carefully, showed restraint when the risks were high, and pulled back when threatened with painful consequences. Such calculations suggest that the

United States could probably deter Iran even after it crossed the nuclear threshold."[49] The US National Intelligence Estimate released in December 2007 took a similar view of Iran: "Tehran's decisions are guided by a cost-benefit approach rather than a rush to a weapon irrespective of the political, economic, and military costs."[50] Using arguments like these, containment optimists conclude that "the perception of Iran as an irrational, undeterrable state with a high pain threshold is wrong. Iranian decision-makers are generally not inclined to rash action."[51]

Second, careful, cautious observers—in this case, the Iranians—would likely find multiple reasons not to provoke the United States the way Colonel Qaddafi did during the 1980s and Saddam Hussein did prior to and during the two Persian Gulf Wars, in 1990–91 and 2003, respectively. More important, the Iranians could hardly fail to notice that, during the second Persian Gulf War, the Americans and the British pulverized what was left of the Iraqi armed forces, accomplishing in about one month what Iranian forces had been unable to do in eight years of war with Iraq between 1980 and 1988. "Tehran cannot fail to appreciate that Iranian conventional forces would have little chance of resisting a U.S. military assault."[52] Put differently, the Iranians appear to have concluded that fighting the Americans head-on would be suicidal, not sensible. On the other hand, knowing how little could be accomplished by provoking a showdown with the Americans would likely make other options seem more attractive simply because the military option looked so bad. In this regard, "a strategy offering strong rewards and severe penalties has a reasonable chance of discouraging Tehran from its nuclear plans."[53]

Third, the historical record suggests that decisions to pursue or even to acquire nuclear weapons are reversible. "The nuclear dam that U.S. President John Kennedy and his successors from both U.S. political parties worked with international partners to build has largely held. Indeed, more countries have abandoned nuclear weapons programs over the past fifteen years than have tried to acquire them."[54] South Africa built six nuclear warheads and then voluntarily dismantled those weapons after white minority rule there had ended. Argentina and Brazil both gave up efforts to build nuclear weapons and medium-range ballistic missiles to carry them. Taiwan and South Korea likewise gave up their efforts to acquire fissionable materials that could be used to build a nuclear warhead. More recently, Libya gave up its WMD programs, and North Korea has offered to give up its nuclear weapons program, although the latter has behaved so belligerently and erratically that nobody believes what North Korea says anymore.

Fourth and finally, the historical record suggests that even if Iran does acquire nuclear weapons, it likely will remain containable and deterable. The Cold War is testimony to what a patient, long-term program of containment and deterrence can accomplish, even against a formidable foe like the

Soviet Union. "Iran is not, despite common depictions, a messianic power determined to overturn the regional order in the name of Islamic militancy; it is an unexceptionally opportunistic state seeking to assert predominance in its immediate neighborhood."[55] Saddam Hussein's Iraq is also relevant here. There were no WMDs in Iraq when the United States invaded in 2003, and Iraq's WMD programs were in stasis. Containment and deterrence were working and, indeed, working quite well.

Evaluating Success

Did containment work against Islamic Iran? How would we know? These are questions for which the relevant literatures on coercion and containment do not yield consensus, at least not yet. Containment pessimists especially treat questions such as these as if their answers are almost self-evident.[56] In this section, I argue that there are at least five reasons for reexamining what has become the conventional wisdom regarding containment and Iran.

First, consider the range of views expressed during the prolonged negotiations over Iran's nuclear program in particular and its place in the global fuel cycle in general. Nasr and Takeyh, for example, saw Iran as an especially difficult foe, one that posed "serious problems for the United States." The aim of US policy, they wrote in 2007, was "to eliminate Iran's influence in the Arab world by rolling back Tehran's gains to date and denying it the support of allies." This would not be easy, because "Washington's containment strategy" was "unsound," could not be "implemented effectively," and would "probably make matters worse." In Nasr and Takeyh's view, "the ingredients needed for a successful containment effort simply [did] not exist."[57] Maybe that was the case in 2007, but within a few years the controversy over containing Iran would flare up again. Writing in 2010, Lindsay and Takeyh conceded that "containing a nuclear Iran would not be easy," but "even if Washington [failed] to prevent Iran from going nuclear," it could still "*contain and mitigate* the consequences of Iran's nuclear defiance."[58]

"Contain and mitigate" proved to be as far as containment pessimists were willing to move, short of conceding outright that containment might be working. By 2012, a more orthodox view was again on the rise in the United States. Charles Krauthammer asserted that "deterring Iran is fundamentally different from deterring the Soviet Union. You could rely on the latter but not on the former."[59] Matthew Kroenig, also writing in 2012, cited reckless behavior by the Iranians—for example, plotting to assassinate the Saudi ambassador to the United States—as the source of "the real and growing risk that the two sides could go to war sometime soon—particularly over Iran's advancing nuclear program."[60]

Containment pessimists have argued very persistently that containment failed repeatedly during the 1990s, the 2000s, and the 2010s. But if pessimists are right about containment's multiple failings, why has there not been more progress on the Iranian side toward an Iranian nuclear weapon? Has Iran's bomb project proceeded slowly because of the obstacles that the United States and its allies have placed in Iran's way to block and thwart Iran's final push to produce a bomb? This approach would suggest that Iran is a normal state using the tools and techniques available to any state. Alternatively, if Iran was (and is) ruled by religious fanatics, and containment has repeatedly failed, then why did the Iranians finally accept an agreement with the United States and the other leading states in 2015 (Britain, France, Germany, Russia) that required them to ship much of Iran's stockpile of low-enriched uranium out of the country, dismantle thousands of uranium-enriching centrifuges and then place them in storage, and dismantle Iran's sole plutonium-producing reactor?[61]

Second, if Iran really was on the rise and containment was indeed failing repeatedly, then why didn't one or more of the Persian Gulf sheikhdoms choose to bandwagon with Iran rather than continue balancing against it?[62] "For some," Bruno Tertrais wrote in 2010, "bandwagoning with the new major power of the region might be preferable to alignment with the West."[63] Why bandwagon with Iran? If Iran were to become "increasingly aggressive once it acquired a nuclear capability, [then] the United States' allies in the Middle East might feel so greatly threatened and so would increasingly accommodate Tehran, [and] that the United States' ability to promote and defend its interests in the region would be diminished."[64]

As "Iran's power increases, the local sheikdoms are likely to opt for accommodating Tehran rather than confronting it."[65] Even a nonnuclear Iran would tower over the Persian Gulf ministates and be a formidable foe for the United States. A nuclear-armed Iran, Lindsay and Takeyh wrote in 2010, would be seen as a "major diplomatic defeat for the United States. Friends and foes would openly question the U.S. government's power and resolve to shape events in the Middle East. Friends would respond by distancing themselves from Washington; foes would challenge U.S. policies more aggressively."[66] "Some states in the region," Matthew Kroenig wrote in 2012, "are doubting U.S. resolve to stop the [Iranian nuclear weapons] program and are shifting their allegiances to Teheran."[67]

Even if bandwagoning with Iran really did appear preferable to containment, which of the Persian Gulf states would be willing to put their relationships with the United States on hold and realign with Iran? Recent trends in the Persian Gulf and Middle East regions have been the opposite of what the bandwagoning hypothesis predicts. "The smaller Gulf monarchies—Bahrain, Qatar, Kuwait, the United Arab Emirates—take a different view. Some have a burgeoning relationship with NATO. . . . All these states seem to be interested in increased consultations with the

Alliance. By most accounts, Bahrain and Qatar are currently the most eager to deepen their relations with NATO."[68]

Third, hindsight reminds us that none of the scenarios discussed in the two previous sections actually happened. The gulf sheikhdoms did not bandwagon with Iran, and the United States did not strike Iran. The bandwagoning controversy suggests that the mostly unelected leaders of the Persian Gulf sheikhdoms are more afraid of allowing Iran's Shiite-led Islamic revolution to put down roots in their societies than they are of confronting Iran, which they might be called on to do as an ally of the United States. The Persian Gulf sheikhdoms did not bandwagon with Iran; instead, they balanced against Iran, which is what we would expect if containment was still working.[69] This is not just an isolated example. The historical record suggests that the United States has given no sign— with the exception of the marines' withdrawal from Lebanon in 1983—of backing away from the military instruments of containment. The Iranians, for their part, have moderated their behavior so as not to give the United States a pretext to strike Iran. The absence of bandwagoning (by the smaller states) suggests that containment continues to be viable rather than failing.

Fourth, if containment of Iran really was failing, we would expect to see the United States and its allies back away from the kind of military options that they had brandished earlier in the long and turbulent relationship between the United States and Iran.[70] Aircraft carrier battle groups and marine amphibious warfare groups would visit the Indian Ocean and Persian Gulf regions less often, and maybe not at all. If containment really was failing, it would be very much in Iran's interest to provide the Americans with a graceful exit. Once the Americans were gone, there would be more opportunities for the Iranians to play some cards of their own, such as threatening to close the Strait of Hormuz, or increasing pressure on the smaller Persian Gulf states, which had been de facto US allies for decades but now would be encouraged to reconsider their political alignment.

Fifth, there is an additional way to evaluate claims that containment is working (or not). This approach searches for indicators that should be present in an ongoing nuclear program, like the one formerly operated in Iraq, or the one currently under way in Iran. One such indicator would be reports by intergovernmental agencies, such as the IAEA or the intelligence community in the United States, regarding how soon an aspiring nuclear power like Iran might be able to build a bomb of its own. If containment is working, then the target dates incorporated in those estimates should be pushed farther into the future, as intelligence analysts work to incorporate into their estimates the most recent information about whether and when Iran is likely to have a bomb of its own. Hindsight suggests that this is by and large what happened.

In 2003, Iran was believed to be two or three years away from having a bomb, even under the Israeli government's worst-case scenario.[71] In 2005, however, the US intelligence community extended to 2015 its previous estimate of how long it would take Iran to build key components for a bomb, "roughly doubling the previous estimate of five years."[72] In December 2007, a US National Intelligence Estimate judged with "high confidence" that Tehran had halted its nuclear weapons program in the fall of 2003, meaning no progress toward an Iranian nuclear weapon for several years at least.[73] These estimates suggest that nuclear weapons are still very hard to build. "Cost considerations aside, it would take years for nuclear aspirants to develop indigenous nuclear capabilities."[74] Despite years of effort by Iranian scientists and engineers, the expected date for the arrival of an Iranian weapon continues to be pushed farther into the future.

Move and Countermove

In this section I argue that superpowers have so many resources at their disposal that they will almost always have more options to choose from than do lesser powers. Following the by-now-familiar script, for every Iranian move, there was a countermove (or more) available to the United States. "Successive U.S. administrations," Colin Dueck and Ray Takeyh wrote in 2007, "have sought to thwart Iran's nuclear ambitions. Over the years, Washington has scored some impressive gains and managed to delay and frustrate Tehran's quest for nuclear technology."[75] If the United States has indeed managed "to delay and frustrate Tehran's quest for nuclear technology," would this not constitute a success for containment? In retrospect, a strong case can be made that America's containment policy showed that the answer to this last question was yes, for multiple reasons.

In this regard, consider how the Iranians (and the Iraqis and the Libyans before them) engaged the Americans and the British in a high-stakes game of move and countermove. Was it just a coincidence that every time the Iranians (or the Iraqis and the Libyans) tried to change the location of their nuclear programs from one set of buildings to another, the US intelligence community responded by generating new leads that could be pursued by UN inspectors on the ground and US reconnaissance aircraft and satellites up above? Was it purely coincidental that the United States just happened to have multiple servings of carrots and sticks that it could brandish for the Iranians' benefit (as already had been done for the benefit of the Libyans and Iraqis)? I argue that there was nothing coincidental about the competition between the United States and Iran concerning who would have how much control over the nuclear fuel cycle. The United States had already mastered the fuel cycle, which allowed it to build more than thirty thousand nuclear warheads over the course of the Cold War (both strategic and tactical).[76] Iran had very little control of the fuel cycle and no weapons either, at least not yet. Iran wanted them both—control over the fuel cycle and a warhead too. The United States wanted to deny Iran control over both. Since it was a superpower, it should have been able to place multiple roadblocks and barricades in Iran's path in order to deny the Iranians access to a bomb that might never come. Or so the Americans wished. Both the United States and Iran acted as if they preferred to continue the rivalry between them, rather than stumble into an unwanted war. Looking backward, we can see that there were multiple reasons (again) why the rivalry between the United States and Iran went on for so long.

First, the United States brought to the table both a superpower's resources and the ambitions shared by high-ranking officials, both elected and appointed, whose continuation in office would likely depend on their ability to convince the voters that they knew what they were doing, where they were going, and how they wanted to get there. Concerning Iran and its well-known nuclear ambitions, there were indeed problems that called out for political solutions and solutions that offered political credits to their inventers. The Reagan administration "succeeded in obtaining Europe's agreement to rigorous export controls with respect to dual-use technologies and in getting Germany to abandon its cooperation with Iran's nascent nuclear program. In a similar vein, by 1996, persistent American pressure managed to get China to cease its nuclear cooperation with Iran."[77]

Second, a containment strategy based on move and countermove can be said to be succeeding when the range of options available to the state doing the containing expands over time. As the range of options increases, so too does the likelihood that the state doing the containing will find options that it can stay with for years if not longer. Conversely, when the options available decline in number and effectiveness, that would indicate a looming failure for containment, because a state with only a few options to choose among is likely to be cautious about pressing ahead, especially if there are few or no fall-back positions available.

Third, there is more at stake here than just splitting diplomatic hairs. "Iran is not a marginal state like Libya or Syria, but neither is it a great power. It has few friends and fewer allies. By alienating the United States and Europe, Iran increased its dependence on Russia for diplomatic support, nuclear and other technology and conventional arms. It has thus compromised its vaunted 'independence,' inhibiting the pursuit of its interests in the Caspian and Caucasus. Iran has neither hard nor soft power."[78]

The US side has had its disappointments too. "Ever since the revolution that toppled the Shah in 1979," Ray Takeyh wrote in 2007, "the United States has pursued a series of incoherent policies toward Iran. At various points, it has tried to topple the regime. . . . At others, it has sought to hold talks on a limited set of issues. Throughout, it has worked to box in Iran and to limit its influence in the region. But none of these approaches has worked, especially not containment." Furthermore, "Tehran's power," Takeyh observed, was "being steadily enhanced by its nuclear program," whose progress was "unhindered despite regular protests from the international community." This is hardly surprising because, on the whole, "containment never worked—and it has even less chance of working in the future."[79] This approach, however, carries with it at least two additional problems.

First, if Ray Takeyh's assessment that "containment [has] never worked" is correct, and if the United States has no realistic military option against Iran, then why is there no Iranian bomb? Alternatively, if the American side really was as feeble and incompetent as Takeyh and others have repeatedly claimed, then why did the Iranians accept the terms of the 2015 arms agreement that essentially traded Iran's nuclear program for the removal of the sanctions? After years of insisting that Iran would never allow itself to be treated differently than any other state, "Iran agreed to a nuclear deal that closes every single one of its paths to a nuclear weapon, and Iran is now being subjected to the most comprehensive inspection regimen ever negotiated to monitor a nuclear program."[80]

Second, if "Tehran's power [was] being steadily enhanced by its nuclear program," why did Iran agree to give up its most valuable asset—namely, its nuclear program? If the Iranian nuclear program really has been making "progress unhindered" toward possession of a nuclear weapon, shouldn't the "progress unhindered" assessment likewise be nearing the finish line?[81]

Our Iran case study is a reminder that when it comes to competition among states, superpowers are different. Superpowers have so many resources at their disposal that they can afford to call on multiple kinds of capabilities and multiple allies to aid in the pursuit of whatever political outcome they are chasing. "Now it is time to see Iran for what it is: a political threat and regional nuisance with many weak points, which can be played on. Neither a colossus nor a failed state, its primary focus is regime survival."[82] Superpowers have the luxury of being able to draw on many instruments of coercion or containment; small states are prisoners of their limited resources. In the context of alliances, if they don't do much at all, they run the risk of alienating their superpower protector. If small states do too much, they risk exhausting themselves even though the size of their contribution may not seem like very much because they are (and always will be) small states. Superpowers have enormous resources, but they are also likely to believe that their smaller allies are taking advantage of their generosity. Superpowers must constantly choose between doing too much and doing too little.

Others Will Help

During the early 2000s, the Iranians were still trying to keep hidden much of their nuclear infrastructure. In September 2003, the IAEA produced an important paper that provided considerable evidence that Iran had undertaken a secret, crash program to acquire its own nuclear weapon. The paper accused Iran of trying to mislead UN investigators with contradictory and implausible explanations.[83] The Iranians responded by moving much of their program underground. The Iranians never gave up (at least not until 2015), but neither did the Americans.

Iran has tried repeatedly to drive a wedge between the United States and its European allies, but Iranian efforts in this regard have not fared well. To illustrate the point, consider the Reagan administration's efforts to thwart or block Iran's attempts to acquire the nuclear infrastructure needed to supply highly enriched uranium, which is a prerequisite to building a nuclear weapon. These efforts date back to the early-to-mid-1980s, when the Reagan administration secured the European allies' consent to rigorous export controls aimed at limiting Iran's attempts to acquire the hardware that could eventually be assembled into a bomb.[84] The first Bush administration succeeded in obtaining Europe's agreement to rigorous export controls on dual-use technologies; it also persuaded Germany to abandon its cooperation with Iran's nascent nuclear program. In 1992 the first Bush administration persuaded Argentina and China not to sell to Iran a twenty-megawatt research reactor that would have allowed it to convert natural uranium into the highly enriched uranium used in nuclear weapons.[85] In similar fashion, by 1996, persistent US pressures persuaded China to cease its nuclear cooperation with Iran.[86] With the Chinese option denied to them, the Iranians turned to the Russians for help, but so too did the Americans. The Russians tried to bring in the Ukrainians, apparently in the belief that the more parties involved, the harder it would be for the United States to stop the project, but the Americans had other ideas. In March 1998, the Ukrainians, under heavy pressure from the United States, agreed to withdraw from their agreement with Russia to supply the turbines needed to complete the two Russian-designed and Russian-built power generating reactors at Bushehr in Iran.[87] Also in March 1998, the United States persuaded Russia to cancel a contract with the Russian missile firm NPO Trud to jointly develop a new engine to power Iranian ballistic missiles.[88]

In addition to winning cooperation with the United States regarding the imposition of sanctions on Iran, the Americans persuaded France, Germany, and Britain to support referring Iran's case from the IAEA to the United Nations Security Council. This move highlighted the determination of the major Western powers to contain Iran's nuclear ambitions. This episode has come to be seen as a "major defeat" for Tehran and a "major victory" for Washington.[89]

This is not to suggest that thwarting Iran's attempts to continue its nuclear program was easy or cheap. A denuclearized Iran would be a collective good for all states in the Persian Gulf and Indian Ocean regions, but the United States would likely feel more strongly about this issue than other states, for two reasons. First, there were lingering memories of the abuse of US diplomatic personnel, who were unjustly taken prisoner when the Iranians seized the US embassy in Tehran in November 1979. Second, US capabilities were much greater than those of the other states involved in the Iran issue. Put differently, what could the United States do and not do? This suggests that other states would attempt to shirk responsibility here, preferring to pass the buck to the Americans. The United States did indeed do much of the work needed to keep containment working, but it also received help from Britain, France, Germany, India, China, and Russia at crucial points in its attempts to thwart Iran's progress toward making a bomb, as the following three episodes suggest.

The first of these centers on China's decision, already alluded to above, to withdraw its offer to sell nuclear reactors to Iran, an outcome warmly welcomed by the Clinton administration, which had lobbied the Chinese intensively to withdraw their offer.[90] Nonetheless, "weeks after winning a Chinese pledge to halt assistance to Iran's nuclear program, the Clinton administration discovered and protested secret negotiations between China and Iran for hundreds of tons of material used in enriching uranium and weapons." This discovery led conservative members of Congress to say that "the episode suggested a Chinese effort to feign compliance with arms control agreements while proceeding covertly with years of nuclear assistance to Iran." China, several members of Congress said, was engaged in a "denial and deception campaign."[91] The key point here, however, is that China did not sell the reactor to Iran, which was the outcome the United States was pursuing all along.

A second episode centered on the "concession" offered by Boris Yeltsin's government in Russia to withdraw Russia's offer to sell the Iranians gas centrifuges that can enrich uranium to weapons grade. There was speculation throughout the Clinton administration that this was a gratuitous concession because Yeltsin's government had no intention of ever going through with it; instead, the Russians included it in their offer so that they would have something that could be used to make a present for President Clinton.[92]

A third outcome that was inconsistent with claims that containment was failing was a by-product of Iran's attempt to strengthen its nonnuclear forces. The Iranians had projected a substantial increase in their conventional forces, but they could not sustain their buildup because a US-led embargo on trade with Iran made it impossible for them to acquire the hard currency needed to pay for the weapons they hoped to purchase.[93] And even if the Iranians had been able to acquire and then sustain a larger navy, what exactly would they have accomplished? Iran bought two diesel-electric submarines from cash-strapped Russia (move). In response, US sources let it be known that a US nuclear-powered submarine (the USS *Topeka*) had entered the Persian Gulf, roughly a week or two before the Russian subs were scheduled to enter the Persian Gulf (countermove). The message was clear and unmistakable—even two Iranian subs were no match for a single US submarine, because the Iranians would not know where to look for it. And even if they did know where to look, they could never keep up with the combination of speed and endurance that rendered the US Navy untouchable.

If we had a time machine that allowed us to return ten years or even twenty years into the past, we would likely notice that many of the arguments that are still being used today were also used in the past. In all three of these episodes discussed above, we would also find representatives of the United States working diligently to halt or at least slow Iran's progress to a bomb. If containment had already failed, or was about to fail, would it not seem unusual that after more than twenty years of trying, Iran still does not have a warhead at its disposal, much less a miniaturized warhead that could fit on the ballistic missiles that Iran has purchased from North Korea? This is not to suggest that thwarting Iran's nuclear ambitions has been easy or cheap, or that it could be continued indefinitely. Even if Iran detonated a nuclear weapon tomorrow, there would still be questions about why it took so long for Iran to cross the finish line. The second President Bush reportedly did not try very hard to pursue reconciliation with Iran, so we cannot say for certain what Iran might have done with its bomb program had it been handled differently by one or more of the US administrations charged with managing and overseeing US foreign relations with Iran. On the other hand, twenty years can be an eternity in international relations. If containment bought for the United States twenty years of time with which to work on Iran, but US officials did not put that time to good use, then it is US policy that has failed, and not containment.

A fourth outcome inconsistent with containment pessimists' claims that containment was failing would be the 2015 agreement between Iran on one side and the United States, Britain, France, Germany, and Russia on the other. The 2015 agreement was intended to greatly limit Iran's ability to produce highly enriched uranium, which is one of two fissionable materials that make possible a nuclear explosion (plutonium is the other). The agreement took years to negotiate, during which the United States and its allies and negotiating partners maintained extensive sanctions intended to compel the Iranians to dismantle much of their nuclear enrichment program. The agreement with Iran was signed in July 2015, thereby putting

Iran into a position it had said repeatedly it would not accept—namely, singled out for special treatment, meaning more restrictions and more inspections for Iran's nuclear facilities. This was an outcome that the Iranians repeatedly said they would never accept, but then they did.

Of all the issues raised during the nearly four-decades-long effort by the United States to contain Iran, perhaps the most important of these was whether containment works and, if so, what constitutes firm evidence of its success. Previous sections of this chapter have shown that containing Iran first achieved prominence in US policy at the end of the 1970s, coinciding with the Iranian revolution and the seizure of the US embassy in Tehran in November 1979. With no promising military options available, successive administrations since Jimmy Carter's have turned to containment as the option of choice for dealing with Iran.

Containment pessimists, however, have repeatedly derided containment as a failure, proclaimed it not to be working, and berated several US administrations for their apparent inability to do something more about Iran.[94] But if pessimists are correct and containment has indeed failed on multiple occasions, doesn't that tell us something about Iran's nuclear program? If containment has indeed failed repeatedly, should we not expect those episodes of failure to produce more and better opportunities for the Iranians to push ahead with their own attempts to master the nuclear fuel cycle, in the form of sudden spurts of progress in the Iranian nuclear weapons program? Alternatively, if containment has indeed repeatedly failed, wouldn't that have afforded the Iranians opportunities to push forward with their nonnuclear programs while also attempting to rebuild their conventional forces, which had been badly mauled during the war against Iraq during the 1980s? And if containment has indeed failed—repeatedly—why have Washington's efforts to thwart, deny, and defeat Iran's schemes shown such staying power?

More important, even after thirty-plus years of move and countermove with the United States, Iran appears not to have acquired a reliable miniaturized nuclear warhead (something that Israel, South Africa, China, India, and Pakistan all were able to build, albeit largely on their own). Does this constitute a containment success for the United States—buying time that the United States and its allies could use to develop new lines of resistance? After all this time and effort invested by the United States in containing Iran, how many more years will be required before US policy can be judged a success? If thirty-plus years of blocking, thwarting, and denying Iran a bomb of its own do not constitute grounds for concluding that containing Iran has worked, then one can't help but wonder what exactly would be required to proclaim containment a success. If US officials responsible for containing Iran (or Iraq or Libya) are able to restrict or defeat their opposite numbers in a move-and-countermove game that spans nearly forty years and culminates in an agreement such as the one signed by the United States and Iran in 2015, does that not constitute a victory for containment?[95]

These are more than just word games. Containment pessimists argue repeatedly that containment has failed. They have repackaged and repeated these judgments, moreover, even as their own claims in this regard seem to lose credibility and conviction with each year that they continue. If containment pessimists do what they accuse containment optimists of doing—that is, make the same arguments over and over again (that containment is failing)—then they are likely to face an unwelcome choice of their own. In effect, they can argue that Iran was and still is a difficult foe that presents serious problems even for the United States.[96] Or they can argue that the Iranians and other anti-US actors are, for whatever reason, pulling their punches, as they search for new and better ways to weaponize their programs. America's foes (Israel's too) can wage a vigorous campaign against the United States and Israel and accept the losses that will be inevitable once the latter two retaliate, as they surely will. Alternatively, America's foes can lie low and wait for better opportunities to arise. If they choose to do so, would this not be indistinguishable from containment?

In sum, proliferation pessimists view Iran as a very difficult case for a strategy based on containment. "Difficult," however, is not the same as "impossible." First, containment works when a superpower fends off, thwarts, or blocks aggressive actions by lesser powers (Libya, Iraq, or Iran). Second, containment can also be said to be working when *nothing happens* that might alert governments worldwide that something is about to happen or has already happened. Third, there is an obvious problem with the NPT, which Iran signed years ago during the reign of the shah. The flaw in the NPT, as Jessica Tuchman Mathews explains, is that "it is legal to do lots of things that move a nation right up to the brink of a nuclear weapons capability."[97]

Iran's strategy has been to keep itself openly in compliance with the NPT (at least in ways that could be measured), which means that, under article 4, it was and is entitled to nuclear cooperation from other NPT members. The United States, on the other hand, has good reasons to believe that Iran is violating the spirit, if not the letter, of the NPT, but it is hard to line up others to oppose (and maybe impose sanctions on) a state that repeatedly proclaims itself in compliance with the NPT. This doesn't mean that the Iranians are off the hook. Because they have positioned themselves roughly twelve months from producing an actual weapon, any new evidence that points to an Iranian bomb will likely lead to sanctions more intense than ever before, pressures for preventive action by the United States and its allies, threatening force deployments that would make possible punitive air and naval strikes, and fierce resistance by the United States and Israel. Would such resistance lead to open warfare? Pessimists would likely say yes, while optimists would likely opt for a combination of sanctions and threatening military gestures. War is almost never an attractive policy option, whereas containment still has possibilities. And anyone who believes that containment is preferable to war should start work at whatever options might be suitable for another game of move and countermove, right away.

Containment Reappraised

In chapter 1, I make the case that the Bush Doctrine, recast as a theory of victory, includes six propositions:

1. Containment can't hold indefinitely.
2. Deterrence is not enough.
3. Time is not on our side.
4. Acting is better than waiting.
5. Offense is better than defense.
6. Preventive action works better than the alternatives.

I then use these propositions, both individually and as a group, to generate more specific guidance to political leaders, such as seizing the initiative is better than letting it be claimed by a foe, preempting may be better than waiting, striking first is better than being struck first. In the right circumstances, seizing the initiative, preempting, and striking first all may offer important military and political advantages, such as catching an opponent off guard and unprepared to fight or avoiding the political perils that may come with merely reacting to what an opponent is doing or reducing the political danger that comes with having a reputation for being timid, unimaginative, and not up to the job. On the other hand, acting preventively, striking first, and seizing the initiative all carry important risks too. Preventive action may widen a conflict that might otherwise have remained limited. A declaratory policy that proclaims (repeatedly) that time is not on our side, that acting is better than waiting, and that going on the offensive is better than staying on the defensive may have unintended consequences of its own, such as convincing an opponent that its choice is between war now and war later (by which time the international situation may have become even more perilous).

Conversely, waiting rather than attacking, strengthening defenses, and relinquishing the initiative all contribute to deterrence and war avoidance by shifting to an opponent the awesome responsibility of firing the first shot in anger. During the Cuban Missile Crisis, "by the time [President Kennedy had] determined to resist . . . , the Russian missiles could sit waiting and so could Cuban defense forces; the next overt act was up to the President."[1] President Kennedy's response was a move the Soviets had not anticipated—namely, the imposition of a naval "quarantine" around Cuba. The quarantine was an action that the United States could have sustained indefinitely, but which the Soviets probably could not. If the quarantine were left unchallenged by the Soviets, the United States would decide what cargoes could or could not get through to Cuba. Soviet forces in Cuba would remain there at the sufferance of vastly superior US forces, both nuclear and nonnuclear. And if the Soviets wanted to change this situation, they would either have to accept US demands to withdraw their missiles and any other offensive weapons they might have managed to sneak into Cuba, or they could fight. But since US military superiority rendered the second option practically suicidal, the United States could concentrate on maintaining or even tightening the quarantine while waiting for the Soviets to succumb to US demands.

The Cuban Missile Crisis offers exceptionally vivid and revealing insights into the interplay between challenger and defender, but it is still only one case. If we are to have greater confidence in our own judgments of the relative merits of striking first versus striking second, we need to know more about what the historical record tells us about cases in which US policy makers sought to contain troublesome states like Libya, Iraq, and Iran. How well did American policy makers strike a balance between acting versus waiting, deterring rather than striking first, and seizing the initiative versus relinquishing the initiative during other international crises?

It is not my intention to use these cases to rewrite history. Instead, I concentrate on how those in charge of US foreign and defense policy both during and after the Cold War responded to warnings of impending danger. In the rest of this chapter, I reconsider containment and the Bush Doctrine, particularly as they were applied to the case studies presented in chapters 2 through 6. How well did American policy makers handle the challenges posed by these varying theories of victory? What do these cases tell us about when, where, and why containment works or fails? As we have seen so far, these cases tell us a lot.

Containment Can't Hold Indefinitely

What stands out in retrospect about the Cold War and how it was waged by the United States is the number and prominence of those, insiders and outsiders alike, who proclaimed containment to be either already failing or about to become a failure. During the Truman administration, for example, Secretary of the Air Force Stuart Symington argued that, as of 1947, the United States was already at war with the Soviet Union—a life-or-death struggle that the United States was losing. The United States was losing, Symington claimed, because it was relying on a purely defensive strategy (containment), it sought to "localize" aggression wherever it appeared, and it had drawn back from dealing with the problem—the Soviet Union—at its source.[2] Foreign policy commentator Walter Lippmann was likewise sharply critical of George Kennan's version of containment, which Lippmann called a "strategic monstrosity," because it "would allow Moscow to determine the time, the place, and the nature of the competition," thereby seizing the initiative and risking the commitment of US resources on unsuitable terrain.[3]

On the other hand, during the Cold War the United States and its allies around the world successfully waged a multi-decade struggle to contain the Soviet Union (1947–89) and a twenty-year struggle to contain Communist-ruled China (roughly 1949–71). Similarly, during the post–Cold War era, the United States waged a twenty-year-plus struggle to contain Libya, a twenty-year-plus struggle to contain Iraq, and a thirty-five-year effort to contain Iran. Libya became a high-priority target for the United States in December 1979, when a Libyan mob trashed and burned the US embassy in Tripoli. Containing Libya lasted until 2003, when Libya offered to surrender to the United States all its programs intended to produce WMDs, including both stockpiles and production facilities. The United States also waged a twenty-year-plus struggle to contain Iraq—from 1980, when Iraq invaded Iran, thereby threatening the regional balance, until 2003, when the United States invaded Iraq and deposed Saddam Hussein. Regarding Iran, the United States has imposed sanctions upon it in one form or another since 1979, when an Iranian mob seized the US embassy in Tehran and held the embassy staff captive. More recently, the United States has maintained sanctions on Iran over the issue of an Iranian nuclear weapons program. These UN sanctions were kept in place until July 2015, when the United States, Britain, France, Germany, and Russia signed an agreement with Iran whereby, in exchange for lifting the sanctions, Iran promised to dismantle its uranium enrichment and plutonium projects, to the point at which Iran would likely require a year or more to reconstitute its nuclear programs and assemble a bomb.[4]

The raw numbers are impressive: five cases of containment (Soviet Union and China during the Cold War; Libya, Iraq, and Iran during the post–Cold War era), each of which lasted at least two decades. In three cases (China, Libya, and Iraq), containment ultimately led to regime change.[5] Reasonable people can disagree about exactly when the United States first tried and then stopped trying to contain the Soviet Union and China. Extensive cooperation between the United States and the Soviet Union after Iraq invaded Kuwait in 1990 strongly suggests that containment of the Soviet Union ended sometime around 1989–90. Henry Kissinger's trip to Beijing in 1971, followed by President Nixon's own visit in 1972, likewise offered incontrovertible evidence that the United States and the People's Republic of China were no longer enemies. If, however, the historical record achieved by containment has proven so stellar, how do we account for claims put forward by containment pessimists that there are two kinds of containment policies at work in the post–Cold War world: those that have already failed and those that are about to fail? Two explanations come readily to mind.

First, containment, as practiced by the United States during the Cold War, often tried to slow the pace of events in order to reduce the risk of being swept up into an unwanted conflict spiral referred to as the Sarajevo Syndrome. The goal of the policy was to lessen the risk of repeating the errors that preceded the outbreak of the First World War.[6] In contrast to the Bush Doctrine's emphasis on swift action, taking the initiative, and so on, US policy makers during the Cold War were arguably more concerned with avoiding escalatory spirals, meaning that the parties to a crisis might move too quickly, events might then get out of hand, diplomats would lose control, and the end result would be catastrophe. The longer these Cold War crises—such as those over the Taiwan Strait or Berlin—dragged on, the greater the temptation to conclude that containment must be failing, and thus the greater the concern on the US side that sheer frustration might cause one of these crises to blow up in policy makers' faces. Alternatively, when one of these crises fizzled out with nothing much settled in return, US policy makers feared that this too might be a pathway to frustration and war. In retrospect, claims that Cold War crises were failures are surprising in view of the time and effort invested by the leaderships on both sides of the Atlantic to ensure that they remained firmly in control from start to finish.

To escape some of these problems and the fears that they inspired, US policy makers tried to shift to the Soviet Union (or one of its surrogates) the onus of firing the first shot in any confrontation between them. Relinquishing the initiative, as we saw in earlier chapters, was itself a prescription for slowing down the pace of events, even as the United States and its adversaries maneuvered for better position vis-à-vis one another. The length of these bargaining contests made them seem very dangerous (and they often were). From this, pundits and other commentators often drew the conclusion that US policy was failing. Indeed, it was taken almost as a given that a democracy could not engage in this kind of secret maneuvering the way an authoritarian state could.

Is that really true? Could a democracy like the United States reasonably be asked to sustain a containment policy against multiple opponents for a period of years, if not decades? These questions suggest a second explanation for the gap between claims that containment was failing and the results actually obtained by persistence and determination.

During the Cold War, containment as practiced by the United States was almost always about more than just assembling large and capable armed forces and then using those forces to deter or defend against Soviet military action, should some occur. During the Cold War, "if Europe was to be defended, it was important that nuclear forces do more than simply cancel each other out."[7] These requirements put a premium on ingenuity and innovation—finding new ways to get some leverage from weapons that were widely thought to be unusable. Here was an obvious challenge. Did the United States meet the standard being proposed? Was the requisite ingenuity actually forthcoming? A strong case can be made that the answer to these questions is yes.

As the Cold War began, adoption of a containment policy by the Truman and Eisenhower administrations was a way of saying that time was on our side, and that "the Soviet Union would eventually collapse or mellow from internal stresses and strains."[8] Even so, "the steady growth of Soviet power and the expansion of Communist influence in Asia were facts of life during the Cold War. American military policy confronted not a condition but a trend."[9] A containment policy required much more than just flipping a switch from off to on. Containment required a more or less continual set of adjustments, sized and shaped to respond to whatever the Communist side was doing now. This made containment seem very burdensome, but hindsight suggests there are multiple reasons why a superpower that was also a democracy would be very well-suited to sustaining a containment policy for four decades or longer.

First, United States was so blessed with resources, both material and intellectual, that only one other state (the Soviet Union) could hope to match within a reasonable time frame. George Kennan provided a cogent explanation for why the Soviets acted as they did, initially in his famous "Long Telegram" from Moscow in January 1946 and then in his even more influential article, "The Sources of Soviet Conduct," which appeared in the journal *Foreign Affairs* in July 1947.[10] Also prominent here would be the secretary of the navy and future secretary of defense James Forrestal, who provided the intellectual foundation for US policy in a private letter dated December 8, 1947, and included in Forrestal's published diaries.

"At the present time," Forrestal wrote,

> we are keeping our military expenditures below the levels which our military leaders must in good conscience estimate as the minimum which would in themselves ensure national security. By doing so, we are able to assist in European economic recovery. . . . In other words we're taking a calculated risk in order to follow a course which offers a prospect of eventually achieving national security and also long-term world stability. . . . As long as we can out-produce the world, can control the sea, and can strike inland with the atomic bomb, we can assume certain risks otherwise unacceptable in an effort to restore world trade, to restore the balance of

power—military power—and to eliminate some of the conditions that breed war. The years before any possible power can achieve the capability effectively to attack us with weapons of mass destruction are our years of opportunity.[11]

Second, the United States benefited greatly from the presence of shrewd leaders who weren't afraid to make changes. G. John Ikenberry notes that "the secret of the United States' long brilliant run as the world's leading state was its ability and willingness to exercise power within alliances and multinational frameworks, which made its power and agenda more acceptable to allies and other key states around the world."[12]

Third, the United States was able to sustain for decades a policy of containment. Saddam Hussein built an army with dozens of divisions and thousands of tanks, and what he got in return was a stalemated war with Iran during the 1980s and two wars lost to US presidents who were both named Bush. It wasn't just a coincidence that these outcomes were achieved. During the Cold War and the post–Cold War era, the American side was constantly tinkering with policies that were intended to be revised and renewed, for decades, if need be. On the US side in particular, new ideas were always bubbling up toward the surface as the competitors for elective and appointive office strove to make their voices heard and their ideas understood. In addition, incumbents in the United States were and still are constantly on the lookout for innovations that might improve their own chances for reelection (or reappointment and maybe a promotion too). In the United States, policy innovation is a never-ending process. In the Soviet Union (Stalin), Iraq (Saddam Hussein), and Libya (Colonel Qaddafi), in contrast, policy innovation was something to be taken seriously only after the demise of the current supreme leader.

This is not to suggest that containment was perfect. Samuel Huntington, for example, was sharply critical of US military policy after the Second World War. "Budgetary policy gave domestic needs priority and left the country without the military forces needed to implement the foreign policy of the diplomats or the strategy of the soldiers. The Army did not get [Universal Military Training]. The Air Force did not get the 70 wings it wanted. The State Department did not get its limited war divisions. The two great constraints on effective military planning, the doctrinal heritage from the past and the pressure of domestic needs, combined to produce a serious gap between military policy and foreign policy."[13]

This is not a suggestion that US policy makers got it all wrong. Sometimes waiting really is the best option available. Francis Gavin points out that "the threat posed by a nuclear-armed China under Mao Zedong was far more terrifying than anything Iraq's Saddam Hussein or current 'rogue' rulers could muster. China, with a population of more than 700 million in 1964, had already fought the United States in Korea; attacked India; and threatened Indochina, Indonesia, and Taiwan. . . . [China's leader, Mao Zedong,] had already declared that nuclear war with the United States was not to be feared."[14] US policy makers "increasingly viewed Mao's regime as both irrational and extremist. . . . The U.S. strategy of containment and nuclear deterrence, which had kept the Soviet Union at bay for so many years, appeared inapplicable to the Chinese."[15] Was China really impervious to pressures from other states, especially the United States?

As described by Francis Gavin, Mao's regime in China was neither irrational nor undeterrable. The Johnson administration was left to contemplate but ultimately to reject a preventive attack on Chinese nuclear facilities. "After thoughtful consideration, the Gilpatric Committee and the Johnson administration wisely rejected pre-emption for China and in general." In this case, there was a payoff for being patient. China did not precipitate nuclear war, and neither did it prove to be reckless or undeterrable.[16] "The Chinese nuclear test did not bring about the foreign policy or military debacle that President Kennedy feared, but it may have accelerated Sino-American rapprochement." The next US president, Richard Nixon, "believed that China's nuclear potential made a fresh approach, not preventive action, mandatory."[17] As a result, "by 1969 China and the U.S. had begun a dialogue that flourished into a tacit anti-Soviet alliance by 1972, a mere eight years after the PRC acquired a nuclear capability. That relationship played an important role in ending the Cold War on terms favorable to the United States"[18]

Although the fact was not appreciated as the Cold War began, the United States was in a dominant position with regard to both security issues and political economy. The US economy had been left untouched and unscathed during the Second World War. US industrial capability was unmatched during the Cold War. Memories (especially in Moscow) of how much the United States had produced and then given away inspired caution on the part of prospective challengers to US hegemony.[19] The United States was also technologically superior to every other state, with the exception of Britain. The United States also had a growing stockpile of nuclear weapons, plus long-range aircraft to deliver them. Last but not least, the United States had a vibrant political system that was the source of repeated innovations, like the formulation of containment in the 1940s and the 1950s, or the Republicans' turn to a strategy based on a rapprochement with Communist China during the 1970s.

In sum, the United States had more cards to play than any other state, and the administrations of Franklin D. Roosevelt, Harry S. Truman, and Dwight D. Eisenhower were not afraid to use them. For every card the Soviets played, the United States had at least one card that could trump it. When the Soviets meddled in the Greek civil war, the United States responded with aid programs to Greece and Turkey. When the Soviets staged a coup in Czechoslovakia, the United States sent B-29s to Britain (the kind of airplane that had carried the atomic bombs to Hiroshima and Nagasaki). When the Soviets tried to intimidate Europe by blockading Berlin, the United States responded with the Berlin airlift and the European Recovery Program (the Marshall Plan). When the Soviets kept the Berlin blockade in place for months, the United States responded by negotiating a formal alliance with the states of western Europe—one that carried no expiration date.[20]

The Cold War ended roughly twenty-five years ago, but there are still grounds for questioning how much has really changed. In view of the size and strength of the US armed forces and the US economy relative to the rest of the world, there is no reason to believe that the United States is in any danger of losing its position of preeminence. The United States continues to have more cards than any potential rival. Provided that future administrations play those cards wisely, containment (if called upon) should continue to work, as it has in the past.

Deterrence Is Not Enough

As explained by George Kennan in a memorable metaphor, the Soviet Union ruled by Stalin was, for all practical purposes, insatiable. Like a "fluid stream," he wrote, "its main concern is to make sure that it has filled every nook and cranny available to it in the basin of world power."[21] In effect, Kennan was saying, the US-Soviet rivalry would be played out not in a cataclysmic struggle like the Second World War but rather in a series of challenges, thrust and parry, move and countermove. Such a contest would put a premium on ingenuity, adaptability, and resourcefulness, to thwart whatever moves the Soviets or their surrogates might make.

Seen this way, containment was about more than merely assembling large and capable armed forces and then using them to thwart whatever scheme Stalin and his henchmen might be hatching. Containment put a premium on ingenuity and innovation, and on finding ways to leverage weapons that were widely believed to be unusable. Once again, there are strong grounds for believing that the requisite ingenuity was, is, and will continue to be available to the United States.

First, as the Cold War began, the United States had already proved that it could raise armed forces numbering in the millions to fight global wars against Germany (First World War) and Japan and Germany (Second World War). In both cases, the armed forces needed to win those two wars were demobilized almost immediately after the fighting stopped. "The rapid demobilization," Samuel Huntington subsequently wrote, "did weaken the support for American diplomacy in the first eighteen months after the end of the [Second World War]. It is a mistake, however, to think that any other course was possible. Demobilization was the last phase of World War II.

181

As such, it was not the alternative to a wiser and more effective policy but rather a prerequisite to it. The citizen-armies mobilized to fight World War II were ill-adapted to the requirements of the Cold War. . . . The decks had to be cleared, the World War II force dissolved, before new armies could be brought into existence shaped and trained for the radically new needs of the Cold War."[22]

Second, democracies, especially the United States, have often been disparaged—wrongly—as defective in the formulation and execution of foreign policy. As Kenneth Waltz notes, regarding US foreign policy during the Cold War, "To maintain large foreign aid programs, to sustain heavy defense spending in years of peace, to garrison odd corners of the world, to fight on occasion in distant lands without prospect of tangible gains—these tasks were thought to exceed the political capacity of the nation. They have all been steadily accomplished."[23]

Third, unlike authoritarian states (Qaddafi's Libya, Saddam's Iraq, and the Kim family's North Korea), democracies have an affinity for "real intellectual openness [and] an absence of doctrinal rigidities."[24] The inventor of a new idea (e.g., Kennan and containment) will get the first word in the argument that follows, but it is almost impossible to determine who will get the last word, because these arguments, fought out on the pages of various scholarly journals, seem to go on forever. Nonetheless, democracies innovate effectively, replacing a truly fearsome pair of opponents (Joseph Stalin and Mao Zedong) with a lesser pair (Kim Jong Il and Mahmoud Ahmadinejad).

Fourth and finally, the case studies covered in the earlier chapters suggest that deterrence has become very much a one-way street. When a superpower like the United States confronts a regional power like Libya, Iraq, or Iran, the superpower can make very credible threats to take military action against the regional power, but not vice versa.

Time Is Not on Our Side

Americans have often assumed that hesitation and delay could be politically and even militarily fatal for whatever course of action the United States is following. "It should be noted," Walt Rostow, in a draft paper titled "Basic National Security Policy," wrote "that we have generally been at a disadvantage in crises, since the Communists command a more flexible set of tools for imposing strain on the Free World—and a greater freedom to use them—than we normally command. . . . This asymmetry makes it attractive for the Communists to apply limited debilitation pressures upon us in situations where we find it difficult to impose on them an equivalent price for their intrusions."[25] Similarly, it was taken almost as a given that this sort of asymmetry meant that greater opportunities to cause trouble would inevitably redound to the Communists' benefit because their political position was almost always more flexible than the United States could afford.

Was this really true? One answer came from the State Department. In 1963, State Department analysts concluded that a nuclear-armed China would "eschew rash military actions" or even "nuclear blackmail." China was instead expected to use its nuclear capability as a "political weapon . . . to earn respect, to promote neutralism, to encourage revolutionaries."[26] In effect China—which had a huge population base, a continent-size state, and large armed forces—was expected to behave more circumspectly than Saddam Hussein's Iraq, even though Iraq had almost no margin of error vis-à-vis the United States. Israel and China both crossed the nuclear threshold in the 1960s, but in neither case did proliferation lead to an immediate cascade of new weapons. Israel did not emerge as a declared nuclear power, and other Middle East states did not rush to acquire nuclear weapons of their own. In Asia, Japan continued to rely on US nuclear protection. In South Asia the Indian and Pakistani nuclear programs remained both discreet and opaque until the 1998 nuclear tests by India and Pakistan.[27]

What, if anything, does all this mean? In brief, it suggests that there were opportunities available if only someone would seize them. Israel sought to deflect attention from its own nuclear program by adopting as declaratory policy that "the Iranians are always five to seven years from the bomb. Time passes but they're always five to seven years from the bomb."[28] More important, five to seven years was the time required for the United States and China to complete their rapprochement, culminating in Richard Nixon's 1972 visit to Beijing. These cases suggest that time may not always be on our side, but this is not necessarily bad, as it allows the parties to a new political initiative the time and the political incentives necessary to resolve most of or all the issues at stake between them.

These cases are one way to illustrate the West's ability to show resilience and strength in the face of multiple opponents, but not the only way. The Bush Doctrine was outwardly pessimistic about the West's ability to undertake a prolonged attempt to thwart an adversary's designs, for reasons we have already explored: containment can't hold forever, deterrence is not enough, time is not on our side, and so on. Containment, on the other hand, counseled patience, caution, self-confidence—precisely the qualities that the second Bush administration had already convinced itself were not enough. This is why the Bush Doctrine preferred action to waiting. Containment called for greater preparedness by the Western democracies. The Bush Doctrine called for seizing the initiative at the first possible moment. Because it did so, there was no need to maneuver the Libyans, the Iraqis, and the Iranians into positions that might not have required the need to fight at all. The second Bush administration also had little to say about states that didn't conform to its expectations regarding rogue states, especially Iraq.

In retrospect it is at least mildly surprising that this belief in seizing the initiative should have been so widely held during the run-up to the second Persian Gulf War in 2003. The experience of the United States during both the Cold War and the post–Cold War world was very different from what was claimed by the second Bush administration. The cases of the Soviet Union and China during the Cold War and Libya, Iran, and Iraq after the Cold War all suggest that the United States was quite capable of waging multi-decade struggles against all sorts of opponents, including a superpower (the Soviet Union), a minor power (Libya), and three regional powers (China, Iraq, and Iran). "Has containment worked?" Writing in 1972, Chalmers Roberts answered his own question: "In Europe there is more stability than at any time since World War II. . . . Berlin is defused. In Asia a new live-and-let-live arrangement is already visible although its form remains shadowy."[29] If containment worked so well, why didn't it attract more support among policy makers in both the United States and Europe?

As Samuel Huntington explains, almost from the start of the Cold War, containment as US policy was not without rivals. These included adopting a policy of negotiations and concessions, restricting US concerns to the Western Hemisphere and the oceans surrounding it, and precipitating a showdown with the Communist powers. Knowing what we know about how the Second World War ended and the Cold War began, it is not surprising that the United States would reject the first and second options so soon after having fought a global war against foes with seemingly insatiable appetites, who treated agreements with other states with about as much reverence as that given to a paper towel.[30] The question was, What should the United States do about the third alternative?

This was an especially interesting issue, because the proponents of the third option often described such a showdown as one in which the United States would bring down the full weight of its air power and sea power on Communist China, thereby suggesting that victory in such a one-sided war could be cheap and easy. This view also assumed that the United States could fight and defeat China without stirring intervention by the Soviet Union.

Like the Bush Doctrine in the early 2000s, much of the appeal of the third option was based on the assumption "that time was on the Soviet side and that the United States should use its superior strength before it was dissipated or neutralized."[31] Showdown proposals generally took one of three forms. "First, some advocated outright preventive war." After the Soviets had successfully tested their first atomic device in August 1949, war between the United States and the Soviet Union was seen as inevitable sooner or later; hence, from the US point of view, "it could be desirable to precipitate a showdown while the United States still possessed a monopoly of operational nuclear weapons." Nonetheless, "preventive war policies never received substantial support with the [US] government."[32]

A second version of the showdown proposal was to bring the full weight of US air and sea power to bear on the Chinese, thereby forcing the ruling Chinese Communist Party to withdraw from Korea and maybe even from portions of mainland China. The target of this second version of the show-down was China, not the Soviet Union.[33]

The third version of the showdown scenario was the liberation of the mainland, which had relatively little support both outside and within the US government.[34]

Why was American democracy thought not to be up to issues of strategy and their implementation? Like the second Bush administration, Republicans during the Cold War were skeptical and even derisive of containment, which was "not designed to win victory conclusively." Containment's aim was not to solve the problem posed by the Soviet Union and China but rather to live with it "presumably forever." In other words, "ours are tread-mill policies," John Foster Dulles declared, "which, at best, might perhaps keep us in the same place until we drop exhausted."[35]

Dulles's metaphor was a nifty play on words, but he neglected to point out that competition requires two, not just one. Contrary to Dulles's claims about who was exhausting whom, containment as practiced during the Cold War counseled careful deliberation prior to taking action of almost any kind. "In these circumstances," Kennan wrote in his *Foreign Affairs* article in 1947, "it is clear that the main element of any United States policy toward the Soviet Union must be that of a long-term patient but firm and vigilant containment of Russian expansive tendencies." This approach, Kennan continued, "has nothing to do with outward histrionics: with threats or blustering or superfluous gestures of outward 'toughness.'"[36]

Indeed, what stands out in retrospect about Kennan's writings on containment is the absence of any suggestion that haste is essential if disaster is to be avoided. Quite the contrary, Kennan's writings were suffused with an almost sublime optimism that the United States could and would prevail in a lengthy Cold War with the Soviets, provided the United States kept its cool and avoided misguided and unnecessary schemes, such as preventive war against the Soviet Union. As Kennan himself put it, "The West could win this cold war."[37]

Marxism-Leninism, Kennan noted in *Foreign Affairs*, had endowed the Soviets with their own sublime confidence in the inevitability of their victory over capitalism, which had the fortunate effect of convincing Soviet leaders "that there is no hurry about it. The forces of progress can take their time in preparing the final *coup de grâce*."[38]

In effect, success in the Cold War was overdetermined. Both sides could and did believe they could outlast their opponent if only they could hang on longer. We live, however, not in the past but in the post–Cold War world. And in the post–Cold War world, policies based on patience and careful preparation should work even more effectively than during the Cold War, because noted troublemakers such as Stalin, Khrushchev, and Mao, with their control over the enormous resources of the Soviet Union and the People's Republic of China, are no longer around to cause difficulties.

Acting Is Better Than Waiting

Does waiting always, or at least often, lead to a bad outcome? The case studies suggest four reasons why the answer to this question is often "not necessarily."

First, events can take a turn for the better as well as for the worse. Within a few years of recommendations for preventive war against Stalin, the threat that he posed had changed: he was dead. The threat of preventive war against China in the 1960s was washed away when President Nixon's secret diplomacy produced the rapprochement of the early 1970s. "Overnight Mao went from being a dire threat to a tacit ally against the Soviet Union. . . . The surprisingly peaceful end of the Cold War [demonstrated] the wisdom of waiting the adversary out and relying on containment and deterrence rather than precipitating a showdown that turned out to be unnecessary."[39]

Second, as the Cold War began, US officials believed they were facing, in the form of Stalin's Soviet Union, an opponent that would seek to "expand its influence through every possible means and attempt to fill every power vacuum."[40] Stalin's Soviet Union and Mao's People's Republic of China were the original rogue states. Each posed a threat to US interests far graver than Saddam Hussein's Iraq. Yet as each approached and then achieved nuclear weapon status, the US government's reaction was very different from the one formulated by the second Bush administration toward Iraq. Stalin, Mao, Colonel Qaddafi, and Saddam Hussein all thought they could outlast the United States. They were all wrong.

Third, containment isn't passive or narrowly focused. A superpower has many options open to it. "In general," George Breslauer wrote regarding the Cold War, "Dulles' rhetoric tended to cancel out Eisenhower's occasional olive branches during 1953–1954. Psychological warfare against the USSR was intensified, with an eye toward reducing the morale of the Soviet leadership, stirring conflicts within it, and stirring discontent within the USSR and Eastern Europe. The rhetoric of 'liberation' was in the air."[41]

Fourth, an additional claim that does not seem to have stood up well over time is the second President Bush's assertion that "the only path to peace and security is the path of action."[42] In wartime, flexibility is often highly valued because it allows policy makers to adapt to changing circumstances. Having the initiative in foreign policy, Schelling conceded, is good "if it means imaginativeness, boldness, [and] new ideas."[43] On the other hand, deterrence of anything but an assault on the United States itself "often depends on getting into a position where the initiative is up to the enemy and it is he who has to make the awful decision to proceed to a clash." In general, "when both sides abhor collision the advantage often goes to the one who can arrange the status quo in his favor and leaves to the other the 'last clear chance' to stop or turn aside."[44]

Khrushchev and his Soviet colleagues appear to have understood quite well the logic behind this kind of reasoning. According to the US statesman Averell Harriman, Khrushchev said to him in a 1959 meeting, "Your generals . . . talk of maintaining your position in Berlin with force. That is bluff. . . . If you send in tanks, they will burn and make no mistake about it. If you want war, you can have it, but remember, it will be your war. Our rockets will fly automatically." According to Harriman's account, Khrushchev's colleagues echoed his statement by chorusing "automatically."[45] In effect, Khrushchev was trying to arrange the status quo in and around Berlin in a way that undermined the Allied military presence in that city. At a summit meeting, Khrushchev was allegedly reminded that Berlin was not worth a war to him either. "No," he replied, "but you are the ones that have to cross a frontier."[46] In this case, at least, the alleged arranging was not entirely convincing. Since the three Allied powers had repeatedly made clear their satisfaction with the territorial arrangements in Berlin and Germany too, the only way to change the status quo in Europe would have required Soviet forces to cross a frontier—either into West Berlin or into West Germany itself.

Deterrence and containment are often used as if they are two sides of the same coin. This is not surprising. Deterrence and containment share an important similarity: shifting to an adversary the responsibility for taking the first step down the path to war. "Deterrence involves setting the stage— by announcement, by rigging the trip wire, by incurring the obligation— and *waiting*. The overt act is up to the opponent."[47] For coercive threats to work, our side must not change whatever threats it has issued, even as our side works assiduously to achieve a situation in which only our adversary can avert disaster by adjusting its position, situation, or stance on whatever is in dispute.[48]

In similar fashion, one of the reasons why containment proved doable during the Cold War is that, aside from the initial act that transfers the initiative from the state doing the containing to the state being contained, it asks very little of the former. Once US forces were on the ground in Berlin and West Germany, the United States did not have to do much more except participate in routine training and maintenance.[49] For containment to work, the crucial requirement was that United States and its allies be there on the ground in Berlin and Germany and positioned where Soviet forces would have to bump into or in some way make contact with US forces if there ever should be a war.

Offense Is Better Than Defense

These points are important to recall, because they help us understand why containment during the Cold War worked so well even as it lasted such a long time. What stands out in retrospect about the conduct of the Cold War by US officials is the way their actions effectively repudiated many of the components of what would become the Bush Doctrine. In contrast to the Bush Doctrine's emphasis on acting rather than waiting, or speeding things up because there is no time to spare, or taking the offensive, and so on, US officials during the Cold War consistently and persistently sought to slow events down, to gain time and to think clearly about what their next move should be. In contrast to the Bush Doctrine, US officials during the international crises of the 1950s and 1960s (e.g., Taiwan Straits, Berlin, Cuban Missile Crisis) were haunted by memories of how the participants in previous international crises (such as Sarajevo 1914; Munich 1938, the outbreak of the Korean War) had often advocated hasty actions before they had a good grasp of what was going on, got caught up in events, lost confidence in their ability to cope, and so on.

What Schelling called the "art of commitment" likewise often asked very little of the United States (a congressional resolution, a treaty of alliance). But since commitments are more liable to be weakened or undermined as circumstances change, relinquishing the initiative seems a surer way to pursue containment.[50]

Preventive Action Works Better Than Alternatives

"Preventive war thinking," the historian Marc Trachtenberg has written, "was quite common in the early atomic age."[51] Bernard Brodie, among others, shared this view. In the late 1940s and early 1950s, "preventive war thinking was surprisingly common on the American side. Brodie, for example, frequently came into contact with it while he was at RAND and during his visits to the Air War College, where it was, as he put it, for several years the "prevailing philosophy.""[52] On at least two occasions, US policy makers considered, and rejected, the option of waging preventive war: one during the early 1950s, against the Soviet Union; and a second in the mid-1960s, versus China. China's decrepit air and naval forces may have offered tempting targets for a US military establishment that was intent on preventing a future Pearl Harbor, but this begs the question whether preventive strikes were the cure for what ailed us. In the cases of both the Soviet Union and China, proponents of preventive war argued that action had to be taken immediately if disaster was to be avoided, essentially the same position that would later be included within the Bush Doctrine. Yet in every case, US officials quite deliberately rejected haste in favor of watchful waiting. China under Mao Zedong was particularly feared as a state that might catalyze war on its own, aimed at wiping out capitalism while allowing the surviving Communists to inherit the world. China, however, did not use its nuclear weapons to wage indiscriminate war on the capitalist world. "Nor has [China] been reckless or undeterrable. By 1969 China and the United States had begun a dialogue that flourished into a tacit anti-Soviet alliance by 1972, a mere eight years after the PRC [People's Republic of China] acquired a nuclear capability. This relationship played an important role in ending the Cold War on terms favorable to the United States."[53]

In effect, the containment strategy, as practiced by the United States during both the Cold War and the post–Cold War worlds, was notable both for what it included (the Marshall Plan, NATO, and the Korean War rearmament effort) and for what it omitted (preventive war against the Soviet Union in the late 1940s and preventive war against China during the mid-to-late 1960s). The Cold War is long since over and done, but the Bush Doctrine continues to urge a quick resort to force in the event that deterrence or containment might be about to fail. Deterrence, in contrast, aimed for a long-term political relation and military competition with the target state. The Bush Doctrine urged seizing the initiative, to keep an adversary off balance and unable to fight effectively. Containment, in contrast, urged relinquishing the initiative, in order to place on the target state the responsibility for starting a war that might otherwise be avoided. The Bush Doctrine advocated unilateral action against the target state. Containment, in contrast, aimed at building a coalition within which strategy and supporting policies could be evaluated and within which the weaker ideas could be weeded out. The Bush Doctrine reflected the fear that democracies might not be up to a long-term struggle against a vicious and determined opponent, such as Saddam Hussein, or the Islamic State movements in Iraqi and Syria, and across the Middle East. The historical record, on the other hand, suggests that democracies can and indeed have waged multi-decade struggles against Colonel Qaddafi, Saddam Hussein, Iranian mullahs, and the religious fanatics running ISIS. On the whole, patience, which was often scorned as the province of the weak and wimpy, in effect led to partial reconciliation with both China during the 1970s and the Soviet Union during the 1980s (SALT, the INF treaty).

Why Containment Worked

1. MOVE AND COUNTERMOVE

One of the advantages of being a democracy and a superpower is that these conditions offer the United States multiple options for thwarting or blocking actions being taken by one or more of its rivals. Consider in this regard the "resolution of the 1946 crisis in Iran," which one scholar claims "proved to be one of the most successful tests of the American strategy of containment." Beyond checking the Soviet advance, Kuross Samii writes, "what distinguishes the whole affair was the method by which the Truman administration confronted the Soviets. . . . Unlike later examples of containment, the United States did not dispatch troops to do the fighting for the native inhabitants, nor was there covert interference. . . . Instead, the United States provided moral support and permitted the indigenous forces in Iran to defend the territorial integrity of their homeland."[54]

2. RELINQUISHING THE INITIATIVE

What stands out to an observer blessed with hindsight is the contrast between the Bush Doctrine's urging of preventive action, and the way in which US policy makers and others involved in shaping containment sought to avoid hasty or unexpected actions that might trigger the very war they were trying to prevent.

During the Cold War as well as during the post–Cold War world too, there were always plenty of doubts regarding how long containment might last and whether deterrence could hold, but this did not mean military action was imminent or ever near-term. Military action, it was widely believed, might well lead to an outcome much worse than the status quo; hence US statesmen sought to slow down events, so as to keep them under control, and above all to shift to the Soviets, the Chinese, Colonel Qaddafi, and the Iraqis and Iranians responsibility for crossing the threshold of violence first. The United States would not initiate a conflict, but it would be ready to retaliate if need be.

3. OTHERS WILL HELP

Politics makes for strange bedfellows, sometimes surprisingly so, like the United States and Iran in the aftermath of the 9/11 terrorist attacks on the United States. In response to a US request, the Iranian government agreed to the use of its territory for search-and-rescue operations for downed coalition aircrews in Afghanistan as well as the transshipment of US food supplies to Afghanistan through Bandar Abbas. More recently, Tehran announced that any US personnel downed in Iranian territory during a possible US war with Iraq would be promptly repatriated. Members of the US Congress had already met with senior Iranian officials to discuss the way ahead.[55]

More important was the positioning of the United States during the post–Cold War world. During the Cold War, the United States was the most powerful state, but it did face potential enemies against which even the United States would have to fight hard, if war should ever come. In the post–Cold War world, "The U.S. heads a remarkable and historic system of alliances. Never before has a great power elicited such support from the world's other powers and provoked so little direct opposition." States that once instinctively responded to what they saw as US imperialism now seem more willing to cooperate with the United States rather than balance against it. "Even powers outside the Western alliance system—Russia, China, India, Indonesia—generally choose to cooperate with the United States." As Michael O'Hanlon observes, "[what] is most impressive about the Western Alliance system is how strong and durable it has become. The United States does not have to fear war against another Great Power."[56] The stronger the US position internationally, the more credible its threats to impose a containment regime on a recalcitrant rival.

4. THE STRENGTHS OF DEMOCRACIES

To the participants who lived through the Cold War, containment as it was then practiced by the Truman, Eisenhower, Kennedy-Johnson, and Nixon administrations often *seemed* very onerous and burdensome. Unlike the Bush Doctrine, containment often sought to slow things down, to prevent events from slipping out of control, as they had done in Europe during July 1914. Slowing things down for the sake of maintaining control over events, however, raised questions of credibility and effectiveness, sometimes in surprising ways. This was not an easy task. Michael Krepon has written very insightfully that during the Cold War, "America's primary competitors were two nuclear-armed, megalomaniacal mass murderers, Josef Stalin and Mao Zedong." As Krepon points out, "dealing with North Korea and Iran is not easy, but managing relations with the Soviet Union and 'Red' China was even more challenging. As worrisome as Kim Jong Il and Mahmoud Ahmadinejad are, they are no match for Stalin and Mao." He concludes that "with patience, persistence, and wise policies, previous American leaders managed to contain and reduce nuclear dangers. With better leadership, relentless effort, and sound strategies, today's leaders can succeed too."[57]

The case studies that make up most of this book leave no doubt that America's leaders can and have learned from their successes as well as their failings. Can they be counted on to continue to do the same? An insightful anecdote can often make a point better than dozens of pages of dry academic prose. A good example would be the prediction offered by the former secretary of defense James Schlesinger. The future, Schlesinger opined, would likely be more difficult than the past. "The prospects are increased turbulence and instability for the balance of the century. The basic reason is . . . the relative decline of American power and . . . the reduced will of the American people to play a combined role as international guardian and self-appointed moral preceptor—in short, the end of *Pax Americana*."[58]

Within a decade, of course, the Berlin Wall was crumbling, Communist governments were resigning, and declinism was being replaced by triumphalism as the principal theme of contemporary analyses of international relations. By the time Schlesinger offered his gloomy assessment, a strong case could be made that there was indeed a declining superpower casting about anxiously for a new role internationally, but it was not the United States. Nonetheless, from the vantage point of January 1981—with US diplomats held hostage in Iran, the Soviets bogged down in Afghanistan, and antinuclear protests forming on the horizon—recent events might well have left the impression that containment was not working as hoped and couldn't be effective any time soon.

Therein lies the core of the problem. Will the United States find the requisite patience and persistence now that it needs them more than ever? Writing in 1971, Andrew Pierre argued that containment became more difficult from the 1940s and 1950s to the 1970s, because "in the past we had a conceptual basis to guide our actions. This is far less true today." As he saw it, then, "we were relatively clear about our objectives in Korea [or Western Europe] . . . we are now uncertain what our role should be in many areas of the world."[59] Pierre claimed that "former American instincts for the containment of communism are being diminished." Likewise, he saw the United States losing its willingness to contain, at the very time the Soviet Union was stepping up its competitive behavior.[60]

Kenneth Waltz offers a second explanation for why US democracy has so often been thought to be inadequate compared to the challenges that it faced. "Weaknesses," Waltz wrote, "were thought to inhere in the structure of American politics; strengths were much underestimated." Among the strengths that were often underestimated, those that Richard Neustadt famously called "separated institutions sharing power" were prominent. "The American system," as Waltz put it, "is one of contention among strong institutions whose cutting edges have been honed in recurrent conflict" with each other.[61]

Still a third perspective is that offered by Samuel Huntington. Strategic programs, Huntington wrote in his classic study of American defense policy, "are not the product of expert planners, who rationally determine the actions necessary to achieve desired goals. They are the result of controversy, negotiation, and bargaining among officials and groups with different interests and perspectives."[62] The development of a consensus for a strategic program, such as containment, involves elaborate processes of bargaining as complex and subtle as those required for either domestic or foreign policy.[63]

A "modern dictatorship," Walter Laqueur once wrote, "has powerful instruments with which . . . to postpone the day of reckoning for a very long time."[64] If that assessment is correct, then why was it the United States, with its tendentious debates, endless bickering, and flawed policies, that won the Cold War and not the Soviet Union?[65] One answer to this question comes from an unexpected source.

Democracy, Alexis de Tocqueville wrote in his classic treatment of government in the United States, "appears to me better adapted for the peaceful conduct of society, or for an occasional effort of remarkable vigor, than for the hardy and prolonged endurance of the great storms which beset the political existence of nations. . . . [A] democracy can only with great difficulty regulate the details of an important undertaking, persevere in a fixed design, and work out its execution in spite of serious obstacles."[66]

As the Cold War began, there was widespread interest in the question of how a democracy like the United States might stand up to a foe like the Soviet Union. In Walter Lippmann's view, "The genius of American policy does not lie in holding positions indefinitely. . . . It is, therefore, not an efficient instrument for a foreign policy like containment."[67]

The first fifteen years of the Cold War, however, suggested to Samuel Huntington, Kenneth Waltz, and hardly anyone else, that the United States had unforeseen powers of endurance in foreign policy. Huntington's classic assessment is worth quoting at length. "In a constitutional democracy, the forces of pluralism correct and counterbalance the instabilities, enthusiasms, and irrationalities of the prevailing mood. Indeed, . . . a constitutional democracy appears peculiarly suited *for* [emphasis added] the "prolonged endurance" of the storms of international politics. . . . It lacks not staying power but acting power. Yet the government which does have the capacity for sudden spectacular success usually also has the capacity for sudden spectacular failure. The American government may well be incapable of both."[68]

The record of US defense policy between 1945 and 1960, which is when Huntington wrote *The Common Defense* and especially its eloquent concluding paragraphs, suggested to Huntington that it was not Tocqueville but Fisher Ames who provided the more accurate picture of a constitutional democracy seeking to make its way in foreign affairs. "A monarchy or a despotism, Ames suggested, is like a full-rigged sailing ship. . . . It is beautiful to behold. It responds sharply to the helm. But in troubled waters, when it strikes a rock, its shell is pierced and it quickly sinks to the bottom. A republic, however, is like a raft: slow, ungainly, impossible to steer, no place from which to control events, and yet endurable and safe. It will not sink, but one's feet are always wet."[69]

Notes

1. Preventive War and Containment

1. Michael Hirsh, "Bush and the World," *Foreign Affairs* 81, no. 5 (September–October 2002): 18–43. See also Adam Roberts, "The 'War on Terror' in Historical Perspective," *Survival* 47, no. 2 (Summer 2005): 101–30, and Steven Miller's review essay, "Terrifying Thoughts: Power, Order, and Terror after 9/11," *Global Governance* 11, no. 2 (2005): 247–71.

2. *The National Security Strategy of the United States of America* (Washington, DC: White House, September 2002), 15. See also Kenneth Pollack's characterization of the Soviet leadership as "fundamentally conservative decision-makers." Kenneth Pollack, "Next Stop Baghdad?," *Foreign Affairs* 81, no. 2 (March–April 2002): 37.

3. *The National Security Strategy of the United States of America* (Washington, DC: White House, March 2006), 18. This sentence appears in a section intended to summarize the 2002 version.

4. Quoted in Mike Allen and Karen DeYoung, "Bush: U.S. Will Strike First at Enemies," *Washington Post*, June 2, 2002.

5. The president made these remarks at a Texans for Rick Perry reception. *Public Papers of the Presidents of the United States, George W. Bush* (Washington, DC: National Archives and Records Administration, 2005), 994.

6. During the early Cold War, the Chinese Communist regime led by Mao Zedong regularly staged "Hate America" days to rouse the populace and garner support for the regime.

7. "Facing 'Common Enemy,' Terrorism and Weapons of Mass Destruction," *New York Times*, February 1, 2003.

8. Ibid. Concerning the impact of the September 11 terrorist attacks on the Bush administration's worldview see Melvyn Leffler, "Bush's Foreign Policy," *Foreign Policy*, no. 144 (September–October 2004): 24–25.

9. Quoted in Ivo Daalder, "Beyond Preemption: An Overview," in *Beyond Preemption*, ed. Ivo Daalder (Washington, DC: Brookings Institution Press, 2007), 5.

10. *National Security Strategy*, 2002, 15.

11. White House, "The President's State of the Union Address," Washington, DC, January 28, 2003.

12. "Questions for John Bolton," *New York Times Magazine*, November 4, 2007, https://www.nytimes.com/2007/11/04/magazine/04wwln-Q4-t.html?adxnnl=1&adxnnlx=1.

13. *National Security Strategy*, 2002, 15. See also US Department of Defense, *Quadrennial Defense Review Report*, February 6, 2006, 24.

14. *National Security Strategy*, 2002, 15. See also Karen DeYoung and Mike Allen, "Bush Shifts Strategy from Deterrence to Dominance," *Washington Post*, September 21, 2002.

15. White House, "President Bush Delivers Graduation Speech at West Point," West Point, New York, June 1, 2002, https://georgewbush-whitehouse.archives.gov/news/releases/2002/06/20020601-3.html.

16. DeYoung and Allen, "Bush Shifts Strategy from Deterrence to Dominance."

17. *National Security Strategy*, 2002, 14.

18. Robert Kagan, "The September 12 Paradigm," *Foreign Affairs* 87, no. 5 (September–October 2008): 34.

19. US Department of Defense, *Quadrennial Defense Review Report*, 4.

20. M. Elaine Bunn, "Preemptive Action: When, How, and to What Effect," *Strategic Forum*, no. 200 (July 2003): 2–3. For more on the Bush administration's view that deterrence is not enough see Robert Jervis, "Understanding the Bush Doctrine," *Political Science Quarterly* 118, no. 3 (Fall 2003): 365–88.

21. *National Security Strategy*, 2002, 15.

22. White House, "President Bush Delivers Graduation Speech at West Point."

23. *National Security Strategy*, 2002, 15.

24. Karl P. Mueller, Jasen J. Castillo, Forrest E. Morgan, Negeen Pegahi, and Brian Rosen, *Striking First: Preemptive and Preventive Attack in U.S. National Security Policy* (Santa Monica, CA: RAND, 2006), 194.

25. Quoted in Michael Wines, "Aspin Orders Pentagon Overhaul of Strategy on Nuclear Weapons," *New York Times*, October 30, 1993.

26. Quoted in Lawrence Freedman, "War in Iraq: Selling the Threat," *Survival* 46, no. 2 (Summer 2004): 17.

27. Ashton Carter and William Perry, "If Necessary, Strike and Destroy," *Washington Post*, June 22, 2006. This article was published roughly a decade after Perry left the Defense Department. He was succeeded by William Cohen as secretary of defense.

28. Condoleezza Rice, "Campaign 2000: Promoting the National Interest," *Foreign Affairs* 79, no. 1 (January–February 2000), quoted in Freedman, "War in Iraq," 15.

29. US Department of Defense, *Quadrennial Defense Review Report*, 18.

30. White House, "President Delivers State of the Union Address," Washington, DC, January 29, 2002, https://georgewbush-whitehouse.archives.gov/news/releases/2002/01/20020129-11.html. See also Mueller et al., *Striking First*, 44.

31. Michael Krepon, "Nuclear Pessimism Is Not the Answer," in *Breaking the Nuclear Impasse: New Prospects for Security against Weapons Threats*, ed. Jeffrey Laurenti and Carl Robichaud (New York: Century Foundation, 2007), 38.

32. White House, "President Bush Delivers Graduation Speech at West Point."

33. Condoleezza Rice, "CNN Late Edition with Wolf Blitzer," interview with Wolf Blitzer, CNN, September 8, 2002.

34. White House, "President Bush Delivers Graduation Speech at West Point."

35. Suggested by Jervis, "Understanding the Bush Doctrine," 371.

36. White House, "President Bush Delivers Graduation Speech at West Point."

37. White House, "President Bush Outlines Iraq Threat," Cincinnati, October 7, 2002, https://georgewbush-whitehouse.archives.gov/news/releases/2002/10/20021007-8.html.

38. *National Security Strategy*, 2002, 15. See also *National Security Strategy*, 2006, 23.

39. Central Intelligence Agency, *National Strategy for Combating Terrorism*, February 2003, 21.

40. Jeffrey Laurenti, "Introduction: Clearing the Nuclear Clouds," in Laurenti and Robichaud, *Breaking the Nuclear Impasse*, 2.

41. White House, "President Bush Delivers Graduation Speech at West Point."

42. *National Security Strategy*, 2006, 8. The excerpt quoted here was intended as a summary of the 2002 version.

43. Quoted in Bunn, "Preemptive Action," 3.

44. Krepon, "Nuclear Pessimism Is Not the Answer," 39.

45. *The National Security Strategy of the United States of America* (Washington, DC: White House, September 2002), 15.

46. *National Security Strategy*, 2002, 14.

47. Ibid.

48. Letter from President George W. Bush, *National Security Strategy*, 2002, ii. See also Jervis, "Understanding the Bush Doctrine," 369.

49. Colin Dueck and Ray Takeyh, "Iran's Nuclear Challenge," *Political Science Quarterly* 122, no. 2 (2007): 198.

50. G. John Ikenberry, "America's Imperial Ambition," *Foreign Affairs* 81, no. 5 (September–October 2002): 45.

51. For example, the so-called axis of evil (Iraq, Iran, North Korea).

52. See, for example, Etel Solingen, *Nuclear Logics: Contrasting Paths in East Asia and the Middle East* (Princeton, NJ: Princeton University Press, 2007), 160.

53. Joseph Cirincione, *Bomb Scare: The History and Future of Nuclear Weapons* (New York: Columbia University Press, 2007), 75.

54. Pollack, "Next Stop Baghdad?," 33.

55. Ibid., 40. See also George Lopez and David Cortright, "Containing Iraq: Sanctions Worked," *Foreign Affairs* 83, no. 4 (July–August 2004): 90–103.

56. In 2014, Iran offered to return some of these aircraft to Iraq, so that they could be used by the largely Shiite government and armed forces of Iraq against ISIS (Islamic State in Iraq and Syria), a largely Sunni movement.

57. Solingen, *Nuclear Logics*, 153–54.

58. Cirincione, *Bomb Scare*, 117.

59. Ibid., 117–18.

60. Solingen, *Nuclear Logics*, 153–54; Cirincione, *Bomb Scare*, 75. See also Hans Blix, "Restoring Faith in the Double Bargain," in Laurenti and Robichaud, *Breaking the Nuclear Impasse*, 70.

61. On this point see Dueck and Takeyh, who describe containment as a strategy with "considerable variety in its operationalization," in "Iran's Nuclear Challenge," 198. For a specific example see the description of containment by Anthony Lake, "Confronting Backlash States," *Foreign Affairs* 73, no. 2 (March–April 1994): 46.

62. F. Gregory Gause III, "Getting It Backward on Iraq," *Foreign Affairs* 78, no. 3 (May–June 1999): 54. The distinction between a safe haven and a no-fly zone is explained in Robert Litwak, *Rogue States and U.S. Foreign Policy* (Washington, DC: Woodrow Wilson Center Press, 2000), 125.

63. Raymond Tanter, with Matthew Fogarty, "Baghdad's Resilient Rogue," *Journal of International Affairs* 54, no. 2 (Spring 2001): 524.

64. Suggested by Leffler, "Bush's Foreign Policy," 23.

65. Rodney W. Jones and Mark G. McDonough, with Toby F. Dalton and Gregory D. Koblentz, *Tracking Nuclear Proliferation: A Guide in Maps and Charts* (Washington, DC: Carnegie Endowment for International Peace, 1998), 224.

66. The Kim family in North Korea is the obvious exception, along with the Assad family in Syria.

67. Suggested by Shai Feldman, "The Bombing of Osirak Revisited," *International Security* 7, no. 2 (Autumn 1982): 123–27.

68. For example, President Richard Nixon and Henry Kissinger rethought US policy toward the People's Republic of China during President Nixon's first term in office.

69. The quoted phrase is from President Bush's 2002 commencement address at West Point: White House, "President Bush Delivers Graduation Speech at West Point." See also Michael Krepon, who labels Stalin and Mao "two nuclear-armed, megalomaniacal mass murderers," in "Nuclear Pessimism Is Not the Answer," 33.

70. Mueller et al., *Striking First*, 26. See also Richard Betts, "Suicide from Fear of Death?," *Foreign Affairs* 82, no. 1 (January–February 2003): 39.

71. John Lewis Gaddis, "A Grand Strategy," *Foreign Policy*, no. 133 (November–December 2002): 54.

72. Richard Betts, *American Force: Dangers, Delusions, and Dilemmas in National Security* (New York: Columbia University Press, 2011), 142–43; see also Betts, "Striking First: A History of Thankfully Lost Opportunities," *Ethics and International Affairs* 17 (Winter 2003): 23.

73. Betts, "Suicide from Fear of Death?," 39. See also Tanter and Fogarty, "Baghdad's Resilient Rogue," 522.

74. Betts, *American Force*, 136. See also Betts, "Striking First," 22.

75. Joseph Cirincione and Carl Robichaud, "Into the Breach: The Drive for a New Global Nuclear Strategy," in Laurenti and Robichaud, *Breaking the Nuclear Impasse*, 10.

76. Cirincione counts thirteen countries as having given up nuclear weapons, weapons-related research, or active discussions of pursuit of nuclear weapons. *Bomb Scare*, 43.

77. Ibid., 62–63.

78. Betts, *American Force*, 132.

79. *National Security Strategy*, 2002, 14.

80. DeYoung and Allen, "Bush Shifts Strategy from Deterrence to Dominance."

81. Quoted in ibid.

82. Saki Ruth Dockrill, "Dealing with Fear: Implementing the Bush Doctrine of Preemptive Attack," *Politics & Policy* 34, no. 2: 352.

83. Ibid., 351.

84. White House, "Vice President Speaks at VFW 103rd National Convention," Nashville, August 26, 2002, https://georgewbush-whitehouse.archives.gov/news/releases/2002/08/20020826.html. See also Walt Slocombe, "Force, Pre-emption and Legitimacy," *Survival* 45, no. 1 (Spring 2003): 125.

85. Thomas Schelling, *The Strategy of Conflict* (Cambridge, MA: Harvard University Press, 1960), 37; Thomas Schelling, *Arms and Influence* (New Haven, CT: Yale University Press, 1966), 43–49.

86. See, for example, President Dwight Eisenhower's views on regaining the initiative in the Cold War and forcing the Soviets into taking a more defensive position, in Kenneth Osgood, "Form before Substance: Eisenhower's Commitment to Psychological Warfare and Negotiations with the Enemy," *Diplomatic History* 24, no. 3 (Summer 2000): 418.

87. Mueller et al., *Striking First*, 96.

88. Ibid., 181.

89. The Soviets had hoped to sneak their medium-range and intermediate-range missiles into Cuba, but the Americans were a step ahead of them too.

90. Mueller et al., *Striking First*, 152.

91. The article that changed the way we think about alliances was Thomas Christensen and Jack Snyder, "Chain Gangs and Passed Bucks: Predicting Alliance Patterns in Multipolarity," *International Organization* 44, no. 2 (Spring 1990): 137–68. See also Thomas Christensen, "Perceptions and Alliances in Europe, 1865–1940," *International Organization* 51, no. 1 (Winter 1997): 65–97.

92. Stanley Renshon, *National Security in the Obama Administration* (New York: Routledge, 2010), 109.

93. For more on this point see Michael Brown et al., eds., *Do Democracies Win Their Wars?* (Cambridge, MA: MIT Press, 2011).

94. This is a theme developed at greater length by Samuel Huntington, *The Common Defense* (New York: Columbia University Press, 1961), especially chap. 3, and Kenneth Waltz, *Foreign Policy and Democratic Politics* (Boston: Little, Brown, 1967).

95. Richard Neustadt, *Presidential Power* (New York: John Wiley and Sons, 1960), 28.

96. Powell quoted in Bunn, "Preemptive Action," 7. Rice quotation in White House, "Dr. Condoleezza Rice Discusses President's National Security Strategy," New York, October 1, 2002, https://georgewbush-whitehouse.archives.gov/news/releases/2002/10/20021001-6.html.

97. Lake, "Confronting Backlash States," 50–51.

98. Ibid., 55.

99. Suggested by Robert Jervis, "Deterrence Theory Revisited," *World Politics* 31, no. 2 (January 1979): 312.

2. Containing Qaddafi's Libya

1. Etel Solingen, *Nuclear Logics: Contrasting Paths in East Asia and the Middle East* (Princeton, NJ: Princeton University Press, 2007), 214. See also Carl Robichaud, "Reversing the Spread of Nuclear Weapons," in *Breaking the Nuclear Impasse: New Prospects for Security against Weapons Threats*, ed. Jeffrey Laurenti and Carl Robichaud (New York: Century Foundation, 2007), 105.

2. See, for example, Flynt Leverett, "Why Libya Gave Up on the Bomb," *New York Times*, January 13, 2004; Martin Indyk, "The Iraq War Did Not Force Gadaffi's Hand," *Financial Times*, March 9, 2004; Robert Litwak, "Living with Nuclear Outliers," *New York Times*, June 25, 2012. See also the explanations offered by President George W. Bush and Vice President Dick Cheney, regarding why Libya surrendered its WMD programs, quoted in Bruce Jentleson and Christopher Whytock, "Who 'Won' Libya?" *International Security* 30, no. 3 (Winter 2005–6): 48.

3. Solingen, *Nuclear Logics*, 219.

4. Quoted in Bernard Gwertzman, "U.S. Pledges to Aid African Countries That Resist Libyans," *New York Times*, June 3, 1981.

5. David Ottaway, "Qaddafi Overtures Rejected by U.S.," *Washington Post*, April 2, 1986.

6. Don Oberdorfer and David Ottaway, "U.S. Engages Libya in a War of Nerves," *Washington Post*, January 14, 1986. See also Bob Woodward and Don Oberdorfer, "State Dept. Acted to Block U.S.-Egypt Attack on Libya," *Washington Post*, February 20, 1987.

7. Daniel Byman, Kenneth Pollack, and Gideon Rose, "The Rollback Fantasy," *Foreign Affairs* 78, no. 1 (January–February 1999): 33. For more on Libya's dysfunctional economy see Dirk Vandewalle, "Qadhafi's 'Perestroika': Economic and Political Liberalization in Libya," *Middle East Journal* 45, no. 2 (Spring 1991): 228.

8. Lisa Anderson, "Libya and American Foreign Policy," *Middle East Journal* 36, no. 4 (Autumn 1982): 519.

9. The coup that overthrew King Idris is described more fully by Ronald Bruce St John, *Libya and the United States: Two Centuries of Strife* (Philadelphia: University of Pennsylvania Press, 2002), 83–85.

10. James Markham, "Libya's Islamic Visions Are a Real Nightmare in Africa," *New York Times*, December 28, 1980. Six years later, Edward Schumacher offered a very similar assessment, that Qaddafi had "at one time or another backed subversive groups in almost every other North African country." Edward Schumacher, "The United States and Libya," *Foreign Affairs* 65, no. 2 (Winter 1986–87): 332.

11. Suggested by "The Duce of Libya," *Economist*, January 31, 1981, and George Russell, "A Nasty Reality of Our Times," *Time*, October 19, 1981. See also Christopher Wren, who discusses Qaddafi's support for Idi Amin in Uganda and Emperor Bokassa of the Central African Empire. Christopher Wren, "Libya's Identity Blurred by Ties with East, West, and Terrorism," *New York Times*, October 14, 1979. In 1984, to cite one more example, the US State Department's counterterrorism unit identified fifteen Libyan-sponsored terrorist schemes. Regarding this last point see George Shultz, *Turmoil and Triumph: My Years as Secretary of State* (New York: Charles Scribner's Sons, 1993), 677. Shultz was President Reagan's second secretary of state. He succeeded Alexander Haig in 1982.

12. For more on Qaddafi's multiple schemes and his ability to provoke the United States see "Targeting Qaddafi," *Time*, April 21, 1986.

13. "Dedicated Troublemaker," *Time*, August 31, 1981. See also "Master of Mischief," *Time*, April 7, 1986; Russell, "Nasty Reality of Our Times"; Henry Schuler, "Beyond Billy: The Importance of Investigating Libya's Treacheries," *Washington Post*, July 27, 1980.

14. For example, the 1985 attacks on the El Al ticket counters in the Rome and Vienna airports. Qaddafi's Libya was widely believed to have sheltered the terrorists who carried out these attacks.

15. Shultz, *Turmoil and Triumph*, 677.

16. Bob Woodward and Lou Cannon, "Moscow Rebuffs Protest over Libyan Missiles," *Washington Post*, December 20, 1985.

17. George C. Wilson, "Qaddafi was a Target of U.S. Raids," *Washington Post*, April 18, 1986. See also Ottaway, "Qaddafi Overtures Rejected by U.S." The US raid on Tripoli and Benghazi is discussed more fully in St John, *Libya and the United States*, 135–46.

18. Except, of course, oil.

19. Robert Woodward, *Veil: The Secret Wars of the CIA, 1981–1987* (New York: Simon & Schuster, 1987), 409.

20. Oye Ogunbadejo, "Qaddafi's North African Design," *International Security* 8, no. 1 (Summer 1983): 154.

21. Wren is skeptical of the Soviet rapid deployment force claim. "Libya's Identity Blurred," 1, 16. See also John Cooley, "Soviets in Libya: A New Mediterranean Power," *Washington Post*, March 10, 1981; Claire Sterling, "Qaddafi Spells Chaos," *New Republic*, March 7, 1981; Russell, "Nasty Reality of Our Times"; Anderson, "Libya and American Foreign Policy," 526.

22. President Reagan's first secretary of state, Alexander Haig, quotes an "important Soviet diplomat" as telling a US official that Qaddafi was a "madman." Alexander M. Haig Jr., *Caveat: Realism, Reagan, and Foreign Policy* (New York: Macmillan, 1984), 109.

23. As of December 1985, much of the Soviet weaponry delivered to Libya years earlier remained unused and in storage. Woodward and Cannon, "Moscow Rebuffs Protest." See also Christopher Dickey, "Libya Says It May Allow Soviet Bases," *Washington Post*, April 19, 1986.

24. Only one police officer was on duty in front of the embassy when a mob of approximately two thousand people—carrying pro-Iran banners and urged on by sound trucks—attacked the embassy. For more on the attack on the embassy see "Embassy of the United States in Libya Is Stormed by a Crowd of 2,000," *New York Times*, December 3, 1979; John Maclean, "U.S. May Break Off Relations with Libya," *Chicago Tribune*, December 2, 1979; Don Oberdorfer and J. P. Smith, "U.S. Suspends Most Diplomatic Ties with Libya," *Washington Post*, December 6, 1979; Youssef Ibrahim, "Americans in Libya Walk Warily after Embassy Assault," *New York Times*, December 14, 1979.

25. Youssef Ibrahim, "Libyan Leader Sets Aside Threats to Curtail Oil Exports to the U.S.," *New York Times*, December 11, 1979.

26. Jonathan C. Randal, "Qaddafi Says Carter Promised New Mideast Policy if Re-elected," *Washington Post*, January 10, 1980.

27. Dusko Doder, "U.S. Expels Two for Harassment of Libya's Foes," *Washington Post*, April 18, 1980.

28. Joe Ritchie, "U.S. Expels Four More Libyan Diplomats," *Washington Post*, May 4, 1980.

29. Quoted in David Hoffman, "Qaddafi's Isolation Urged," *Washington Post*, January 8, 1986.

30. Quoted in George C. Wilson, "U.S. Releases Photos of Libyan Jets," *Washington Post*, January 6, 1989.

31. See, for example, John Cooley's list of Qaddafi's plots and schemes in "The Libyan Menace," *Foreign Policy*, no. 42 (Spring 1981): 75–76.

32. Haig, *Caveat*, 30.

33. Ibid., 172.

34. Ibid., 137.

35. Ibid., 137.

36. Quoted in Woodward, *Veil*, 97.

37. The phrase "on a roll" was attributed to a senior State Department official, quoted in Bernard Gwertzman, "U.S. Plans to Seek Actions by Allies to Deter Qaddafi," *New York Times*, April 30, 1984.

38. Markham, "Libya's Islamic Visions." See also the comments by Assistant Secretary of State Chester Crocker, quoted in Gwertzman, "U.S. Pledges to Aid African Countries."

39. Quoted in Russell, "Nasty Reality of Our Times," 28.

40. William Safire, "Looking for Trouble," *New York Times*, September 25, 1980.

41. Quoted in Hoffman, "Qaddafi's Isolation Urged."

42. "Dedicated Troublemaker," 26.

43. Quoted in Christopher Dickey, "Qaddafi Uses Oil Money to Seek a 'Concrete Utopia,'" *Washington Post*, January 15, 1986.

44. Ariel Merari, from Tel Aviv University's Jaffee Center for Strategic Studies, quoted in William Claiborne, "Raid Called Example of Israeli Method," *Washington Post*, April 17, 1986.

45. Christopher Dickey, "Qaddafi Seen Reining In His Army," *Washington Post*, January 14, 1986.

46. Qaddafi asked the Soviets for an alliance a few months after the US bombing raids on Tripoli and Benghazi. Facing a United States that had recently tried to assassinate him, Qaddafi turned to the Soviets on the grounds that "the nonaligned movement" was "not enough." It would, however, have to do, because the Soviets turned him down. Loren Jenkins, "Gadhafi Skips Appearance," *Washington Post*, June 12, 1986.

47. See, for example, the discussion of the Moroccan-Libyan union as little more than a "frail marriage of convenience," in Lisa Anderson, "Don't Play into Qaddafi's Hands," *New York Times*, September 18, 1984. See also "Libyan Leader Calls for Union with Syria," *Los Angeles Times*, September 2, 1980.

48. Russell, "Nasty Reality of Our Times," 28.

49. Mary-Jane Deeb, "Qaddafi's Calculated Risks," *SAIS Review* 6, no. 2 (Summer–Fall 1986): 152.

50. Quoted in Ogunbadejo, "Qaddafi's North African Design," 164.

51. See, for example, Alan Cowell, "Amid Hi-Fis and AK-47s, a Libyan Identity Crisis," *New York Times*, September 14, 1982.

52. Cowell, "Amid Hi-Fis and AK-47s."

53. Bernard Nossiter, "Qaddafi Opposition Getting Stronger," *New York Times*, May 27, 1981.

54. Cooley, "Soviets in Libya." See also Joseph Fitchet, "Libya Denies Reports of Mutiny by Army Unit," *Washington Post*, August 19, 1980.

55. William E. Smith, "Havoc at Home, Too, for Qaddafi," *Time*, May 14, 1984.

56. Lisa Anderson, "A Coup Will Topple Qaddafi If We Just Keep Our Hands Off," *Washington Post*, June 13, 1986. See also Caryle Murphy, "Some Libyan Troops Reportedly in Mutiny," *Washington Post*, October 28, 1993.

57. There were several confrontations between US and Libyan forces regarding the Gulf of Sidra. These are discussed more fully in the rest of this chapter.

58. Christopher Dickey, "Qaddafi Faces Pressure from Neighboring States," *Washington Post*, November 17, 1985.

59. Richard Halloran, "Libyans Are Challenging U.S. Forces in a War of Nerves," *New York Times*, October 24, 1980. See also St John, *Libya and the United States*, 115.

60. "U.S. AWACS Planes Sent to Egypt amid Reports of Moves by Libya," *New York Times*, February 17, 1983; Bernard Gwertzman, "U.S. Officials Say Libyan Threat Led to AWACS Dispatch," *New York Times*, February 18, 1983.

61. Trevor Rowe, "Tripoli Embassy Sacked; U.S. Denounces Libya," *Washington Post*, April 3, 1992.

62. See, for example, the list of activities that Qaddafi was pursuing in Woodward, *Veil*, 409–11. Concerns about Libyan hit squads were also widespread during the Carter administration, fueled by, among other things, Qaddafi's campaign of terror that resulted in the murder of Libyan citizens in London, Rome, and Valletta, Malta. See, for example, Richard Lyons, "Suspected Libyan Terrorists Were Watched by F.B.I.," *New York Times*, May 9, 1980. For the Reagan administration's concerns see Bernard Gwertzman, "U.S. Plans to Seek Actions by Allies to Deter Qaddafi," *New York Times*, April 30, 1984.

63. Quoted in Gwertzman, "U.S. Plans to Seek Actions by Allies."

64. See, for example, "Targeting Qaddafi." Carter's response to Libyan provocations was indeed weak. On this point see St John's account of Carter's meeting with the Libyan chargé d'affaires, *Libya and the United States*, 112.

65. Halloran, "Libyans Are Challenging U.S. Forces." See also Safire, "Looking for Trouble."

66. Halloran, "Libyans Are Challenging U.S. Forces."

67. Cooley, "Soviets in Libya."

68. "To the Shores of Tripoli," *Newsweek*, August 31, 1981.

69. The pilots who flew Libyan fighter aircraft were known to disregard the instructions passed to them by their controllers on the ground. This point is developed further in the rest of this chapter.

70. Safire, "Looking for Trouble." See also Halloran, "Libyans Are Challenging U.S. Forces."

71. Vice Admiral William Rowden, commander of the Sixth Fleet, quoted in "News Conference aboard the *Nimitz*," *New York Times*, August 25, 1981.

72. "News Conference aboard the *Nimitz*." Other sources give slightly different numbers regarding when and how often these exercises were held in the Gulf of Sidra, but all agree that contesting Libya's claim was something the United States could and should be doing. See, for example, "To the Shores of Tripoli"; "Shootout over the Med," *Time*, August 31, 1981; Bernard Gwertzman, "U.S. Reports Shooting Down 2 Libya Jets That Attacked F-14s over Mediterranean," *New York Times*, August 20, 1981; St John, *Libya and the United States*, 114–15.

73. Bernard Gwertzman, "U.S. Action: Sign to Libya," *New York Times*, August 21, 1981. See also "To the Shores of Tripoli."

74. Gwertzman, "U.S. Action."

75. "To the Shores of Tripoli"; "Shootout over the Med."

76. "To the Shores of Tripoli."

77. Thomas Schelling, *The Strategy of Conflict* (Cambridge, MA: Harvard University Press, 1960), 137–39; Thomas Schelling, *Arms and Influence* (New Haven, CT: Yale University Press, 1966), 43–49.

78. For more on this line of reasoning see Stephen Van Evera, "The Cult of the Offensive and the Origins of the First World War," *International Security* 9 (Summer 1984): 58–107; Stephen Van Evera, "Offense, Defense, and the Causes of War," *International Security* 22 (Spring 1998): 5–43.

79. Schelling, *Arms and Influence*, 44.

80. Other concepts invented by Schelling would include the diplomacy of violence, the manipulation of risk, the art of commitment, and the idiom of military action, to name a few. All these are developed more fully in *Strategy of Conflict* and *Arms and Influence*.

81. Schelling, *Strategy of Conflict*, 137–38.

82. For example, garrisoning West Berlin, or proclaiming Cuba under quarantine in 1962.

83. Schelling, *Arms and Influence*, 44–45.

84. For example, the arrangements that settled the various Cold War crises over Berlin (1948, 1959, 1961), the Taiwan Strait (1954–55, 1957–58), or Cuba (1962).

85. The evaluation is from a senior State Department official, quoted in "Shootout over the Med."

86. Quoted in Halloran, "Libyans Are Challenging U.S. Forces."

87. "Shootout over the Med."

88. A sortie is one flight by one airplane. For more on these estimates see "To the Shores of Tripoli" and "Shootout over the Med."

89. Quoted in Gwertzman, "U.S. Reports Shooting Down 2 Libya Jets."

90. "News Conference aboard the *Nimitz*"; Alan Cowell, "45 Libya Incidents Reported by Navy," *New York Times*, August 25, 1981.

91. Schelling, *Arms and Influence*, 44–45.

92. See, for example, Robert Tucker, "The Middle East: Carterism without Carter?," *Commentary* 72 (September 1981): 25–36.

93. "To the Shores of Tripoli." This incident is also discussed in St John, *Libya and the United States*, 125–26.

94. Quoted in "Cat and Mouse with Qaddafi," *Time*, February 3, 1986.

95. George Wilson, "U.S. Naval Force to Cross Qaddafi's 'Line of Death' Soon."

96. See, for example, "Targeting Qaddafi," 30.

97. Quoted in Christopher Dickey, "Libya Seeks to Divide U.S., Allies," *Washington Post*, January 10, 1986.

98. The April 1986 attacks on Tripoli and Benghazi were in retaliation for a terrorist bombing of a West German discotheque in which two US military personnel died.

99. Quoted in Kevin Costelloe (Associated Press), "Qaddafi Warns U.S.," *Washington Post*, April 10, 1986.

100. Schumacher, "United States and Libya," 339.

101. See, for example, Joshua Sinai, "Libya's Pursuit of Weapons of Mass Destruction," *Nonproliferation Review* 4 (Spring–Summer 1997): 92–100. See also Joshua Sinai, "Gaddafi and Saddam in Cahoots," *Washington Post*, January 29, 1998. Sinai's *Nonproliferation Review* article is filled with useful information on the origins and progress of the Libyan CW program.

102. See, for example, David Ottaway, "U.S. Says Libya near Chemical Weapon Production," *Washington Post*, September 15, 1988; Don Oberdorfer, "U.S. Voices Concern over Japanese Firm's Role in Libyan Factory," *Washington Post*, September 16, 1988; David Ottaway, "CIA Chief Says Libya Builds Massive Chemical Arms Plant," *Washington Post*, October 26, 1988; St John, *Libya and the United States*, 159.

103. For more on Libya's CW program see St John, *Libya and the United States*, 146–48. For more about the fire at the Rabta factory see ibid., 159–62.

104. Oberdorfer, "U.S. Voices Concern," and Ottaway, "U.S. Says Libya Near Chemical Weapon Production."

105. Lou Cannon and David Ottaway, "New Attack on Libya Discussed," *Washington Post*, December 22, 1988.

106. Quoted in R. Jeffrey Smith and David Ottaway, "U.S. Aims to Pressure Qaddafi on Plant," *Washington Post*, January 7, 1989.

107. R. Jeffrey Smith and Edward Cody, "U.S. Drive to Censure Libya Lags," *Washington Post*, January 7, 1989.

108. Cannon and Ottaway, "New Attack on Libya Discussed."

109. Jennifer Parmelee, "U.S. Navy Jets Shoot Down 2 Libyan Fighters," *Washington Post*, January 5, 1989, and Molly Moore and George C. Wilson, "U.S. Navy Jets Shoot Down 2 Libyan Fighters: 'Hostile Intent' of MiGs Is Cited," *Washington Post*, January 5, 1989.

110. See, for example, "Libya Asks Security Council for Protection against the United States," *Washington Post*, January 6, 1989.

111. Moore and Wilson, "U.S. Navy Jets Shoot Down 2." For more on the MiG shootdown see St John, *Libya and the United States*, 148–49.

112. Quoted in Wilson, "U.S. Releases Photos of Libyan Jets."

113. Quoted in Moore and Wilson, "'Hostile Intent' of MiGs Is Cited."

114. Ibid.

115. Ibid.

116. Ibid.

117. Fred Hiatt, "U.S. Attack on Libya: A Raid That Went Right," *Washington Post*, April 20, 1986; Christopher Dickey, "Response to Raid to Be Evaluated," *Washington Post*, April 27, 1986.

118. Hiatt, "U.S. Attack on Libya," and David Ignatius, "Bombing Gadhafi Worked," *Washington Post*, July 13, 1986.

119. Leverett, "Why Libya Gave Up on the Bomb." See also Indyk, "Iraq War Did Not Force Gaddafi's Hand." Joseph Cirincione likewise sees a "desire to get out from sanctions and become integrated in the international community" as the "primary driver" behind Qaddafi's decision to end his clandestine nuclear program. Joseph Cirincione, *Bomb Scare: The History and the Future of Nuclear Weapons* (New York: Columbia University Press, 2007), 78.

120. Cirincione, *Bomb Scare*, 115.

121. Jonathan Schwartz, "Dealing with a 'Rogue State': The Libya Precedent," *American Journal of International Law* 101, no. 3 (July 2007): 553–54.

122. Lally Weymouth, "The Business of Terrorism in Libya," *Washington Post*, November 14, 1991.

123. For example, Jim Hoagland, "Algeria Pulls Back from Union with Libya," *Washington Post*, November 2, 1987.

124. Quoted in Edward Walsh, "U.S. Hints Readiness to End Confrontation," *Washington Post*, April 14, 1986. See also "Libyan Restraint," *Newsweek*, June 23, 1986.

125. Schwartz, "Dealing with a 'Rogue State,'" 554.

126. Ibid., 554.

127. See, for example, Jo Warrick, "U.S. Displays Nuclear Parts Given by Libya," *Washington Post*, March 16, 2004.

128. Schwartz, "Dealing with a 'Rogue State,'" 574.

129. Anderson, "Coup Will Topple Qaddafi If We Just Keep Our Hands Off," *Washington Post*, April 13, 1986. These problems were hardly new to Qaddafi's Libya. On this latter point see Youssef Ibrahim, "Qaddafi's Changes Are Said to Put Libya in Turmoil," *New York Times*, May 16, 1980.

130. Quoted in Jennifer Parmelee, "Journalists' Visit to Libyan Plant Leaves Its Purpose Unclear," *Washington Post*, January 8, 1989.

131. Regarding Libya's ruined economy see Vandewalle, "Qaddafi's 'Perestroika,'" 228. See also Patrick Tyler, "Gadhafi Rule Seen in Peril Following Military Setbacks," *Washington Post*, March 27, 1987.

132. Dickey, "Qaddafi Seen Reining In His Army."

133. Bruce Jentleson, "The Reagan Administration and Coercive Diplomacy: Restraining More Than Remaking Governments," *Political Science Quarterly* 106 (Spring 1991): 73.

134. George C. Wilson and David Hoffman, "U.S. Ends Naval Exercises off Libya," *Washington Post*, March 28, 1986.

135. Hiatt, "U.S. Attack on Libya."

136. Hoagland, "Algeria Pulls Back from Union with Libya."

137. Quoted in Richard Bernstein, "The Libyans Are Exporting Their Revolutionary Ardor," *New York Times*, April 29, 1984. See also St John, *Libya and the United States*, 144–45.

138. Mary-Jane Deeb, "New Thinking in Libya," *Current Affairs* 89 (April 1990): 152–77; Lisa Anderson, "Rogue Libya's Long Road," *Middle East Report*, no. 24 (Winter 2006): 42–47.

139. "Thriving on Trouble," 30.

140. See, for example, Clement Henry Moore, who notes that "by 1986 virtually all development projects in Libya had ground to a halt for lack of oil revenues." Clement Henry Moore, "The Northeastern Triangle: Libya, Egypt, and the Sudan," *Annals of the American Academy of Political and Social Science* 489, no. 1 (January 1987): 31.

141. Geoffrey Kemp, "An Insider's View of Our Frustrating Joust with Qaddafi," *Washington Post*, January 12, 1986.

142. Ibid. See also "Duce of Libya," 11.

143. Richard Halloran, "U.S. Aide Says AWACS Will Quit Egypt," *New York Times*, February 22, 1983. See also Eric Margolis, "The Libyan Bogeyman," *New York Times*, March 3, 1983.

144. Dickey, "Qaddafi Faces Pressure."

145. The East Asian tigers come readily to mind.

146. Robert Litwak, *Rogue States and U.S. Foreign Policy* (Washington, DC: Woodrow Wilson Center Press, 2000), 97.

147. "Duce of Libya," 11.

148. Gwertzman, "U.S. Pledges to Aid African Countries."

3. Dual Containment of Iraq and Iran

1. So was Libya's Colonel Qaddafi, discussed in chapter 2.

2. The story of how Saddam clawed his way to national and international prominence, frequently over the dead bodies of his political opponents, is well told by Judith Miller and Laurie Mylroie, in *Saddam Hussein and the Crisis in the Gulf* (New York: Random House, 1990).

3. See, for example, John Esposito's description of how Ayatollah Khomeini made his way to the peak of Shia Islam, in *The Islamic Threat* (New York: Oxford University Press, 1992), 112.

4. For more on Khomeini as an Iranian nationalist see Tarek Massoud, "Misreading Iran," *Current History* 97, no. 615 (January 1998): 39.

5. Nita Renfrew claims that Iran started the war by attempting to export the ayatollah's revolution to Iraq and by subverting Saddam Hussein's government from within: "Who

Started the War?," *Foreign Policy*, no. 66 (Spring 1987): 98–108. Efraim Karsh takes a similar position, that the "war began because the weaker state, Iraq, attempted to resist the hegemonic aspirations of its strong neighbor, Iran": "Geopolitical Determinism: The Origins of the Iran-Iraq War," *Middle East Journal* 44, no. 2 (Spring 1990): 257.

6. Miller and Mylroie, *Saddam Hussein and the Crisis in the Gulf*, 109.

7. George Shultz, *Turmoil and Triumph: My Years as Secretary of State* (New York: Charles Scribner's Sons, 1993), 236.

8. For more on the ayatollah as "the man many Americans loved to hate" see Esposito, *Islamic Threat*, 105.

9. Mohammad E. Ahrari, "Iran and the Superpowers in the Gulf," *SAIS Review* 7, no. 1 (Winter–Spring 1987): 162–63.

10. Quoted in Robert Woodward, *Veil: The Secret Wars of the CIA, 1981–1987* (New York: Simon & Schuster, 1987), 407.

11. For more on dual containment see Robert Litwak, *Rogue States and U.S. Foreign Policy* (Washington, DC: Woodrow Wilson Center Press, 2000), 56–70. See also Michael Klare, *Rogue States and Nuclear Outlaws* (New York: Hill & Wang, 1995).

12. See, for example, Alexander Joffe, "After Saddam Is Gone," *Middle East Quarterly* 7, no. 2: 33–41.

13. For more on the Reagan administration's approach to containment see Fareed Zakaria, "The Reagan Strategy of Containment," *Political Science Quarterly* 105, no. 3 (Autumn 1990): 373–95; Bruce Jentleson, "The Reagan Administration and Coercive Diplomacy: Restraining More Than Remaking Governments," *Political Science Quarterly* 106, no. 1 (Spring 1991): 57–82.

14. See, for example, Martin Indyk, speaking on behalf of the Clinton administration, who described the government of Iraq as a "criminal regime" that was "irredeemable." Quoted in F. Gregory Gause III, "The Illogic of Dual Containment," *Foreign Affairs* 73, no. 2 (March–April 1994): 57. George Shultz's predecessor as secretary of state within the Reagan administration, Alexander Haig, called the Iranian government a "theocratic regime in Tehran that seemed to have abandoned reason." Alexander M. Haig Jr., *Caveat: Realism, Reagan and Foreign Policy* (New York: Macmillan, 1984), 30.

15. Shultz, *Turmoil and Triumph*, 236. Shultz was President Reagan's second secretary of state, succeeding Alexander Haig in 1982.

16. For more on Iraq and Iran as natural rivals see Karsh, "Geopolitical Determinism," 267–68. See also R. K. Ramazani, *Revolutionary Iran* (Baltimore: Johns Hopkins University Press, 1986), 4–5.

17. Milton Viorst, "Iraq at War," *Foreign Affairs* 65, no. 2 (Winter 1986): 359. See also Ramazani, *Revolutionary Iran*, 24–27.

18. Judith Yaphe, "Challenges to Persian Gulf Security: How Should the U.S. Respond?," *Strategic Forum*, no. 237 (November 2008): 4.

19. The US reaction is described in Shultz, *Turmoil and Triumph*, 926.

20. Ibid. See also Shahram Chubin, "U.S. Security Interests in the Persian Gulf in the 1980s," *Daedalus* 109, no. 4 (Fall 1980): 31.

21. For more on the US reaction to the events of 1979 see Walter Levy, "Oil and the Decline of the West," *Foreign Affairs* 58, no. 5 (Summer 1980): 999–1000.

22. R. Jeffrey Smith and Daniel Williams, "White House to Step Up Plans to Isolate Iran, Iraq," *Washington Post*, May 23, 1993, A26. Carter's administration used the term "regional influentials," to no great effect on US foreign policy. For President Reagan's policy toward Iraq and Iran see James A. Baker III, *The Politics of Diplomacy: Revolution, War and Peace, 1989–1992* (New York: G. P. Putnam's Sons, 1995), 262. The Clinton administration appears to have pioneered the term *a strategy of dual containment*, which emerged from a comprehensive policy review ordered by President Clinton.

23. Viorst, "Iraq at War," 361. See also Elie Kedouri, "The Illusions of Powerlessness," *New Republic*, November 29, 1980, 18; Anthony Lake, "Confronting Backlash States," *Foreign Affairs* 73, no. 2 (March–April 1994): 48.

24. Trita Parsi, *Treacherous Alliance: The Secret Dealings of Israel, Iran, and the U.S.* (New Haven, CT: Yale University Press, 2007), 170–71.

25. Richard Sokolsky, *Beyond Containment: Defending U.S. Interests in the Persian Gulf*, INSS Special Report (Washington, DC: National Defense University, Institute for National Strategic Studies, September 2002), 1.

26. Miller and Mylroie, *Saddam Hussein and the Crisis in the Gulf*, 199–200.

27. Chubin, "U.S. Security Interests," 41. For a similar assessment of Britain's role see James A. Bill, "Resurgent Islam in the Persian Gulf," *Foreign Affairs* 63, no. 1 (Fall 1984): 115.

28. Chubin, "U.S. Security Interests," 39. See also Bruce Jentleson, *With Friends Like These: Reagan, Bush, and Saddam, 1982–1990* (New York: W. W. Norton, 1994), 32.

29. For more on the twin pillars approach see Parsi, *Treacherous Alliance*, 36–37.

30. Concerning the twin pillars approach see also Barry Rubin, *Paved with Good Intentions: The American Experience and Iran* (New York: Oxford University Press, 1980), chapter 5. Burden shifting as a political strategy for the NATO countries is discussed more fully in Wallace J. Thies, *Friendly Rivals: Bargaining and Burden-Shifting in NATO* (Armonk, NY: M. E. Sharpe, 2003).

31. Chubin, "U.S. Security Interests," 42.

32. Kenneth Pollack, "Securing the Gulf," *Foreign Affairs* 82, no. 4 (July–August 2003): 2, 4.

33. Chubin, "U.S. Security Interests," 52. See also Miller and Mylroie, *Saddam Hussein and the Crisis in the Gulf*, 187.

34. Miller and Mylroie, *Saddam Hussein and the Crisis in the Gulf*, 189.

35. Odom, "Cold War Origins of the U.S. Central Command," 52.

36. Ibid., 57–58.

37. Ibid., 52. See also Jack Fuller, "Dateline Diego: Paved-Over Paradise," *Foreign Policy*, no. 28 (Fall 1977): 175–86, and Olav Njolstad, "Shifting Priorities: The Persian Gulf in US Strategic Planning in the Carter Years," *Cold War History* 4, no. 3 (April 2004): 21–55.

38. Odom, "Cold War Origins of the U.S. Central Command," 59.

39. Ibid., 54–55.

40. "I sit here all day," Harry Truman commented, "trying to persuade people to do the things they ought to have sense enough to do without my persuading them. . . . That's all the powers of the President amount to." Truman's assessment is quoted approvingly in Richard Neustadt, *Presidential Power* (New York: John Wiley and Sons, 1960), 9–10.

41. See, for example, Robert Tucker's critique of Carter's indecisiveness in "Oil and American Power—Six Years Later," *Commentary* 68, no. 3 (September 1979): 38. See also Robert Tucker, "The Purposes of American Power," *Foreign Affairs* 59, no. 2 (Winter 1980–81): 251.

42. Odom, "Cold War Origins of the U.S. Central Command," 70, 82. For a more critical appraisal of what the Carter administration did and did not do see Robert Legvold, "Containment without Confrontation," *Foreign Policy*, no. 40 (Autumn 1980): 83.

43. Odom, "Cold War Origins of the U.S. Central Command," 52.

44. Ibid., 53.

45. Ibid., 56.

46. Roger D. Hansen, "The Reagan Doctrine and Global Containment: Revival or Recessional," *SAIS Review* 7, no. 1 (Winter–Spring 1987): 39. Regarding the Reagan administration's preference for focusing on the *Soviet* threat to the Persian Gulf see Shai Feldman, "The Bombing of Osirak Revisited," *International Security* 7, no. 2 (Autumn 1982): 128–29.

47. Robert Osgood, "The Revitalization of Containment," *Foreign Affairs* 60, no. 3 (1981): 465–502.

48. George Kennan used similar phrasing to describe the rivalry between the United States and the Soviet Union in a letter to Walter Lippmann, quoted in Wallace Thies, "Learning in U.S. Policy toward Europe," in *Learning in U.S. and Soviet Foreign Policy*, ed. George Breslauer and Philip Tetlock (Boulder, CO: Westview, 1991), 164.

49. Concerning Ayatollah Khomeini's determination to export Iran's revolution to nearby states see Esposito, *Islamic Threat*, 118.

50. Shireen Hunter, "Post-Khomeini Iran," *Foreign Affairs* 68, no. 5 (Winter 1989–90), 133–34.

51. Sullivan's dispatches are discussed in Jimmy Carter, *Keeping Faith* (New York: Bantam Books, 1982), 449.

52. Baker, *Politics of Diplomacy*, 261. Concerning Iraq's weaknesses see Klare, *Rogue States*, 44–48.

53. Ibid., 261.

54. For a sharply worded critique of the Reagan administration's "strategy of worldwide war" see Jeffrey Record, "Jousting with Unreality: Reagan's Military Strategy," *International Security* 8, no. 3 (Winter 1983–84): 3–18. See also Barry Posen and Stephen Van Evera, "Reagan Administration Defense Policy: Departure from Containment," in *Eagle Resurgent*, ed. Kenneth Oye et al. (Boston: Little, Brown, 1987), 73–114, and Hansen, "Reagan Doctrine and Global Containment," 43–48.

55. Odom, "Cold War Origins of the U.S. Central Command," 78.

56. Ibid.

57. Lake, "Confronting Backlash States," 48.

58. Joseph McMillan, "U.S. Interests and Objectives," in *The United States and the Persian Gulf*, ed. Richard Sokolsky (Washington, DC: National Defense University Press, 2003), 21–22.

59. Lake, "Confronting Backlash States."

60. The details of each of these cases are presented in chapter 2.

61. Lake, "Confronting Backlash States," 47.

62. Ibid. At the time this article was published, Lake was President Clinton's first national security adviser.

63. Ibid.

64. Ibid., 48.

65. Ibid., 55.

66. Ibid., 49.

67. Viorst, "Iraq at War," 361. Concerning the Carter administration's reaching out to Iraq see Jentleson, *With Friends Like These*, 34.

68. Viorst, "Iraq at War," 361. James A. Bill dates the US tilt toward Iraq to late 1983: "Resurgent Islam in the Persian Gulf," 118.

69. Klare, *Rogue States*, 37. Regarding the Reagan administration's 1982 tilt toward Iraq see Litwak, *Rogue States*, 53–54.

70. George H. W. Bush and Brent Scowcroft, *A World Transformed* (New York: Vintage Books, 1998), 305.

71. Shultz, *Turmoil and Triumph*, 237.

72. Janice Gross Stein, "The Wrong Strategy in the Right Place," *International Security* 13, no. 3 (Winter 1988–89): 147.

73. See, for example, the account of Donald Rumsfeld's visit to Baghdad in Parsi, *Treacherous Alliance*, 113.

74. Harold Saunders, "The Iran-Iraq War: Implications for U.S. Policy," in *Gulf Security and the Iran-Iraq War*, ed. Thomas Naff (Washington, DC: National Defense University Press, 1985), 72.

75. Stein, "Wrong Strategy in the Right Place," 149–50. Regarding the so-called tanker war see Ramazani, *Revolutionary Iran*, 224–25.

76. Claudia Wright, "Iraq—New Power in the Middle East," *Foreign Affairs* 58, no. 2 (Winter 1979–80): 260.

77. Shultz, *Turmoil and Triumph*, 243.

78. The profits realized from selling arms to the Iranians were used to fund purchases of weapons that were then given to the Contras in Nicaragua.

79. Shultz, *Turmoil and Triumph*, 926.

80. Saunders, "Iraq-Iran War," 73.

81. Shultz, *Turmoil and Triumph*, 926.

82. Ibid., 933.

83. Ibid.

84. Stein, "Wrong Strategy in the Right Place," 149–50.

85. Shultz, *Turmoil and Triumph*, 934.

86. Ibid.

87. Jentleson, "Reagan Administration," 62.

88. Perhaps because of the time required to mobilize resources before launching another strike like Iraq's invasions of Iran and Kuwait.

89. Bandwagoning and buck-passing are the other two possibilities.

90. Stein, "Wrong Strategy in the Right Place," 158–60.

91. Ibid., 160.

92. Shultz, *Turmoil and Triumph*, 933.

93. Ibid., 934–35.

94. Richard Russell, "Iran in Iraq's Shadow: Dealing with Tehran's Nuclear Weapons Bid," *Parameters* 34 (Autumn 2004): 33.

95. Pollack, "Securing the Gulf," 3.

96. Shultz, *Turmoil and Triumph*, 935.

97. See, for example, W. Seth Carus, "Iran as a Military Threat," *Strategic Forum*, no. 113 (May 1997). See also Paula DeSutter, "Deterring Iranian NBC Use," *Strategic Forum*, no. 110 (April 1997).

98. Chubin, "U.S. Security Interests," 43. Iran's desire to export its Islamic revolution (both during Khomeini's rule and then under Khomeini's successors) is discussed more fully by Ahrari, "Iran and the Superpowers," 157–68.

99. Shultz, *Turmoil and Triumph*, 926.

100. Ibid. See also Miller and Mylroie, *Saddam Hussein and the Crisis in the Gulf*, 208–9.

101. Shultz, *Turmoil and Triumph*, 926.

102. Ibid.

103. Ibid., 926.

104. Gause, "Illogic of Dual Containment," 57.

105. Baker, *Politics of Diplomacy*, 261.

106. Pollack, "Securing the Gulf," 9.

107. Ibid., 2.

108. Stein, "The Wrong Strategy in the Right Place," 142.

109. McMillan, "U.S. Interests and Objectives," 23.

110. Sokolsky, *Beyond Containment*, 1.

111. Gause, "Illogic of Dual Containment," 56–66.

112. Odom, "Cold War Origins of the U.S. Central Command," 80. Even Gause would seem likely to agree: "If there is one part of the world where the Clinton administration cannot be accused of lacking a clear foreign policy, it is the Persian Gulf." Gause, "Illogic of Dual Containment," 56.

113. McMillan, "U.S. Interests and Objectives," 23.

114. Gause, "Illogic of Dual Containment," 56–66.

115. McMillan, "U.S. Interests and Objectives," 23.

116. Ibid.

117. Ibid.

118. Ibid.

119. Gause, "Illogic of Dual Containment," 62. During the 1960s the Johnson administration likewise accepted the view that military actions and diplomatic initiatives could be "orchestrated" in such a way as to maximize the pressure on the North Vietnamese government. For more on "orchestrating" words and deeds see Wallace Thies, *When Governments Collide: Coercion and Diplomacy in the Vietnam Conflict, 1964–1968* (Berkeley: University of California Press, 1980), especially chapters 1 and 6.

120. Gause, "Illogic of Dual Containment," 60.

121. Ibid., 60.

122. Paul Jabber, "U.S. Interests and Regional Security in the Middle East," *Daedalus* 109, no. 4 (Fall 1980): 68.

123. Gause, "Illogic of Dual Containment," 57.

124. Ibid., 57.

125. Stein, "Wrong Strategy in the Right Place," 142.

126. Odom, "Cold War Origins of the U.S. Central Command," 79.

127. Ibid.

128. Russell, "Iran in Iraq's Shadow," 33.

129. For more on naval warfare in the Persian Gulf see ibid.

130. Jentleson, *With Friends Like These*, 66.

131. McMillan, "U.S. Interests and Objectives," 23.

132. Lake, "Confronting Backlash States," 48.

133. Ibid., 78.

4. Containing Iraq

1. Daniel Byman, Kenneth Pollack, and Matthew Waxman, "Coercing Saddam Hussein: Lessons from the Past," *Survival* 40, no. 3 (Autumn 1998): 127.

2. Amatzia Baram, "Deterrence Lessons from Iraq," *Foreign Affairs* 91, no. 4 (July–August 2012): 76, 78.

3. The quotation is from a note to himself penned by Secretary of State James A. Baker III, on October 20, 1990, and reprinted in Baker's memoir, *The Politics of Diplomacy: Revolution, War and Peace, 1989–1992* (New York: G. P. Putnam's Sons, 1995), 303 (emphasis in original).

4. Robert Jervis, "The Confrontation between Iraq and the US: Implications for the Theory and Practice of Deterrence," *European Journal of International Relations* 9, no. 2 (2003): 322–23.

5. Ibid., 323.

6. Baker, *Politics of Diplomacy*, 262.

7. Amatzia Baram, "The Iraqi Invasion of Kuwait: Decision-Making in Baghdad," in *Iraq's Road to War*, ed. Amatzia Baram and Barry Rubin (New York: St. Martin's, 1993), 6.

8. Baker, *Politics of Diplomacy*, 261.

9. For another estimate of Iraqi losses during Desert Storm see Michael Klare, *Rogue States and Nuclear Outlaws* (New York: Hill and Wang, 1995), 145.

10. Baram, "Iraqi Invasion of Kuwait," 7.

11. Judith Miller and Laurie Mylroie, *Saddam Hussein and the Crisis in the Gulf* (New York: Random House, 1990), 135. See also Michael Gordon and Bernard Trainor, *The Generals' War* (Boston: Little, Brown, 1995), 12.

12. George H. W. Bush and Brent Scowcroft, *A World Transformed* (New York: Vintage Books, 1998), 305.

13. Ibid.

14. Mark Heller, "Iraq's Army: Military Weakness, Political Utility," in Baram and Rubin, *Iraq's Road to War*, 39.

15. For more on Saddam's decision to attack Iran in 1980 see Baram, "Deterrence Lessons from Iraq," 79–80.

16. Grudging loyalty, but loyalty nonetheless.

17. Baker, *Politics of Diplomacy*, 263–64.

18. This point is suggested ibid., 437.

19. F. Gregory Gause III, "Iraq's Decisions to Go to War, 1980 and 1990," *Middle East Journal* 56, no. 1 (Winter 2002): 69–70.

20. Efraim Karsh, "Geopolitical Determinism: The Origins of the Iran-Iraq War," *Middle East Journal* 44, no. 2 (Spring 1990): 257.

21. Ibid., 267.

22. Miller and Mylroie, *Saddam Hussein and the Crisis in the Gulf*, 54.

23. Miller and Mylroie estimate that Iraq suffered 120,000 killed and 300,000 wounded and took on an "astronomical foreign debt" as a result of its participation in the Iraq-Iran War. Ibid., 127.

24. This description of Saddam is by the French president François Mitterrand, quoted in Baker, *Politics of Diplomacy*, 314. Mitterrand also referred to Saddam as "intelligent, smart, and more dangerous" than other Arab leaders. "Saddam Hussein," Mitterrand continued, "is not harmless. He is dangerous. He needs to be contained."

25. Zachary Karabell, "Backfire: U.S. Policy toward Iraq, 1988–2 August 1990," *Middle East Journal* 49, no. 1 (Winter 1995): 31, 33. There was a third choice—namely, recasting Saddam's image to make him a more acceptable partner. On this see Richard Herrmann, "The Middle East and the New World Order: Rethinking U.S. Political Strategy after the Gulf War," *International Security* 16, no. 2 (Fall 1991): 48–49.

26. Avner Yaniv, "Israel Faces Iraq: The Politics of Confrontation," in Baram and Rubin, *Iraq's Road to War*, 244.

27. Baker, *Politics of Diplomacy*, 262–63.

28. Yaniv, "Israel Faces Iraq," 244.

29. Ibid., 245.

30. Ibid., 244–45.

31. Quoted in Barry Rubin, "The United States and Iraq: From Appeasement to War," in Baram and Rubin, *Iraq's Road to War*, 256.

32. Yaniv, "Israel Faces Iraq," 244.

33. Ibid., 245.

34. Rubin, "United States and Iraq," 256.

35. George Shultz, *Turmoil and Triumph: My Years as Secretary of State* (New York: Charles Scribner's Sons, 1993), 243.

36. Ibid., 240–41.

37. Ibid., 243.

38. Ibid.

39. Baker, *Politics of Diplomacy*, 263. See also Bush and Scowcroft, *World Transformed*, 306.

40. Baker, *Politics of Diplomacy*, 263–64.

41. Karabell, "Backfire," 37.

42. Yaniv, "Israel Faces Iraq," 245.

43. The differences between compellence and brute force are developed more fully in Thomas Schelling, *Arms and Influence* (New Haven, CT: Yale University Press, 1966), chapter 1.

44. Karabell, "Backfire," 39.

45. Bush and Scowcroft, *World Transformed*, 307.

46. Rubin, "United States and Iraq," 261–62.

47. Ibid., 260.

48. Bush and Scowcroft, *World Transformed*, 306.

49. Karabell, "Backfire," 28–29.

50. Anthony Lake, "Confronting Backlash States," *Foreign Affairs* 73, no. 2 (March–April 1994): 48, 52.

51. Bush and Scowcroft, *World Transformed*, 305.

52. Baker, *Politics of Diplomacy*, 269.

53. Ibid.

54. Rubin, "United States and Iraq," 260.

55. Ibid., 261–62.

56. Klare, *Rogue States*, 31.

57. Baker, *Politics of Diplomacy*, 268.

58. Ibid., 271.

59. Bush and Scowcroft, *World Transformed*, 313.

60. Baker, *Politics of Diplomacy*, 331.

61. Ibid., 268.

62. Ibid., 441.

63. Ibid.

64. Daniel Byman, "After the Storm: U.S. Policy toward Iraq since 1991," *Political Science Quarterly* 115, no. 4 (Winter 2000–2001): 494–95.

65. For more on the first President Bush's reasoning see Colin Powell, *My American Journey* (New York: Random House, 1995), 500. See also Barry R. Posen, "U.S. Security Policy in a Nuclear Armed World, or, What If Iraq Had Had Nuclear Weapons?," *Security Studies* 6 (Spring 1997): 1–31; Byman, "After the Storm," 494–95.

66. Baker, *Politics of Diplomacy*, 334.

67. F. Gregory Gause III, "Getting It Backward on Iraq," *Foreign Affairs* 78, no. 3 (May–June 1999): 54.

68. Marc Weller, "The U.S., Iraq and the Use of Force in a Unipolar World," *Survival* 41, no. 4 (Winter 1999–2000): 88–89.

69. Byman, "After the Storm," 494.

70. Ibid., 503. See also Herrmann, "Middle East and the New World Order," 56.

71. Byman, "After the Storm," 504.

72. Ibid., 505.

73. Ibid., 493.

74. Rubin, "United States and Iraq," 269.

75. Baker, *Politics of Diplomacy*, 267.

76. Baram, "Iraqi Invasion of Kuwait," 11.

77. See, for example, the comments by Secretary of State James Baker and April Glaspie, US ambassador to Iraq, about improving relations between the United States and Iraq, quoted in Bob Woodward, *The Commanders* (New York: Simon & Schuster, 1991): 211–12.

78. Baker, *Politics of Diplomacy*, 301.

79. Ibid.

80. Bush and Scowcroft, *World Transformed*, 341.

81. Suggested in Byman, Pollack, and Waxman, "Coercing Saddam Hussein," 134.

82. Bush and Scowcroft, *World Transformed*, 335.

83. Byman, Pollack, and Waxman, "Coercing Saddam Hussein," 135.

84. Baram, "Deterrence Lessons from Iraq," 86–87.

85. Byman, Pollack, and Waxman, "Coercing Saddam Hussein," 134–37. This was Operation Vigilant Warrior.

86. Baram, "Deterrence Lessons from Iraq," 86.

87. Ibid. See also Byman, "After the Storm," 506.

88. Byman, Pollack, and Waxman, "Coercing Saddam Hussein," 140. For an insightful account of how move and countermove influenced the composition of the UNSCOM and IAEA inspection teams see Weller, "U.S., Iraq and the Use of Force," 83–97.

89. Byman, "After the Storm," 506–7.

90. Raymond Tanter, with Matthew Fogarty, "Baghdad's Resilient Rogue," *Journal of International Affairs* 54, no. 2 (Spring 2001): 524.

91. Gause, "Getting It Backward on Iraq," 55.

92. The 1979 attacks on three US embassies—Iran, Pakistan, and Libya—set a terrible precedent in this regard.

93. Gause, "Getting It Backward on Iraq," 54. For more on damages and casualties caused by Operation Desert Fox see Weller, "U.S., Iraq and the Use of Force," 87.

94. Richard Burt, "U.S. Buildup Urged in the Persian Gulf," *New York Times*, June 28, 1979, A6.

95. Michael Getler, "Pentagon Trumpets 'Tripwire,' A-Arms," *Washington Post*, February 2, 1980, A1.

96. In Iraq, Saddam's was the only mind that mattered on issues of war and peace.

97. Bush and Scowcroft, *World Transformed*, 392–93.

98. Ibid.

99. Ibid.

100. On this point see the map reproduced in Press, "Myth of Air Power," 15.

101. A good example here would be the Western outpost in Berlin, which confronted the Soviets with a choice between tolerating this Western enclave, or taking some kind of military action against it, with all the attendant risks and unknowns of conflict between two nuclear-armed superpowers. The Berlin airlift of 1948–49 is another good example of how the West confronted the Soviets with a similar choice—either accept the airlift or do something very foolish to bring it to a halt.

102. The best discussion of division counts and the military balance in Europe remains Alain Enthoven and K. Wayne Smith, *How Much Is Enough?* (New York: Harper & Row, 1971).

5. Invading Iraq

1. Lawrence Freedman, "War in Iraq: Selling the Threat," *Survival* 46 (Summer 2004): 21.

2. Joseph McMillan, "U.S. Interests and Objectives," in *The United States and the Persian Gulf*, ed. Richard Sokolsky (Washington, DC: National Defense University Press, 2003), 23.

3. Daniel Byman, Kenneth Pollack, and Gideon Rose, "The Rollback Fantasy," *Foreign Affairs* 78 (January–February 1999): 37.

4. Kenneth Pollack, "Next Stop Baghdad?," *Foreign Affairs* 81, no. 2 (March–April 2002): 33–34.

5. Kenneth Pollack, "Spies, Lies, and Weapons: What Went Wrong?," *Atlantic Monthly*, January–February 2004, http://www.theatlantic.com/issues/2004/01/media-preview/pollack.htm.

6. Jackson Diehl, "Is Iraq the Model for the Mideast after All?," *Washington Post*, October 9, 2011.

7. Daniel Byman, "After the Storm: U.S. Policy toward Iraq since 1991," *Political Science Quarterly* 115, no. 4 (Winter 2000–2001): 494–95.

8. Adeed Dawisha, "The Long and Winding Road to Iraqi Democracy," *Perspectives on Politics* 8, no. 3 (September 2010): 880. For more on this controversy see Larry Diamond, "What Went Wrong in Iraq," *Foreign Affairs* 83 (September–October 2004): 43–44.

9. See chapter 1.

10. Barry Rubin, "The United States and Iraq: From Appeasement to War," in *Iraq's Road to War*, ed. Amatzia Baram and Barry Rubin (New York: St. Martin's, 1993), 269.

11. Amatzia Baram, "Deterrence Lessons from Iraq," *Foreign Affairs* 91 (July–August 2012): 83. See also Barry Blechman and Tamara Wittes, "Defining Moment: The Threat and Use of Force in American Foreign Policy," *Political Science Quarterly* 114, no. 1 (Spring 1999): 14; Lawrence Freedman and Efraim Karsh, *The Gulf Conflict, 1990–1991* (Princeton, NJ: Princeton University Press, 1993), 194–98.

12. For more on Saddam's enemies and their impact on his actions see Freedman and Karsh, *Gulf Conflict*, 28–31.

13. For more on the Reagan administration's goals see Bruce Jentleson, *With Friends Like These: Reagan, Bush, and Saddam, 1982–1990* (New York: W. W. Norton, 1994), 20, 33, 42–48. See also Freedman and Karsh, *Gulf Conflict*, 23–28.

14. Freedman and Karsh, *Gulf Conflict*, 24.

15. Jentleson, *With Friends Like These*, 15–27.

16. The first agricultural credits—which were to become the mainstay of the US-Iraqi relationship—were agreed in 1982. Freedman and Karsh, *Gulf Conflict*, 25.

17. Michael Gordon and Bernard Trainor, *The Generals' War* (Boston: Little, Brown, 1995), 8.

18. For more on the so-called Iran-Contra Affair see Jentleson, *With Friends Like These*, 56–59.

19. Ibid., 101–3, 127–38. In a realpolitik world, reversals of alliances are common rather than rare. The reasons why are discussed more fully in Wallace J. Thies, *Why NATO Endures* (New York: Cambridge University Press, 2009), chapter 2.

20. Jentleson, *With Friends Like These*, 105–27. The Iraqis also created a worldwide network of dummy corporations to buy components needed to assemble a nuclear weapon. For more on Saddam's purchasing network see Freedman and Karsh, *Gulf Conflict*, 33–37.

21. Freedman and Karsh, *Gulf Conflict*, 58.

22. Jentleson, *With Friends Like These*, 198.

23. For example, the United States in Vietnam, and the Soviet Union in Afghanistan.

24. See, for example, Freedman, "War in Iraq," 11–12, and Pollack, "Next Stop Baghdad?," 32–47.

25. Byman, "After the Storm," 494–95; George Lopez and David Cortright, "Containing Iraq: Sanctions Worked," *Foreign Affairs* 83 (July–August 2004): 90–103, especially 91.

26. Byman, "After the Storm," 493–516. Byman includes in his account a fifth instrument that could be used to weaken Saddam Hussein's grip on Iraq: support for the Iraqi opposition, which I do not use. I omit the Iraqi opposition in part because hindsight reveals just how

inconsequential opposition groups such as the Iraqi National Congress would prove to be, and in part because I wish to focus on the military and diplomatic aspects of containment.

27. Lopez and Cortright, "Containing Iraq," 94.

28. For more on how the Desert Shield build-up stretched across several months see Freedman and Karsh, *Gulf Conflict*, 201–3.

29. For the reasons why Iraq did not strike preemptively at coalition forces as they were deploying in Saudi Arabia and preparing to invade Iraq see Freedman and Karsh, *Gulf Conflict*, 276.

30. Gordon and Trainor, *Generals' War*, 267–88.

31. For a more detailed description of the ground, sea, and air forces maintained by the United States in the vicinity of the Persian Gulf in the aftermath of the first Gulf War see Richard Kugler, "U.S. Defense Strategy and Force Planning," in Sokolsky, *United States and the Persian Gulf*, 91–93. Pre-positioning US forces in the Indian Ocean was a policy first advocated by the Carter administration in response to the Soviet invasion of Afghanistan at the end of 1979. The Reagan administration accelerated the pre-positioning timetable as part of its response to Soviet military superiority.

32. Byman, "After the Storm," 507. See also Stuart Archer, "No-Fly Zones Are Complex and Dangerous," *Washington Post*, April 11, 2013, A11.

33. Kenneth Pollack, "The Regional Military Balance," in Sokolsky, *United States and the Persian Gulf*, 63.

34. F. Gregory Gause III, "Getting It Backward on Iraq," *Foreign Affairs* 78, no. 3 (May–June 1999): 54.

35. Rubin, "United States and Iraq," 269. See also Pollack, "Regional Military Balance," 69.

36. Etel Solingen, *Nuclear Logics: Contrasting Paths in East Asia and the Middle East* (Princeton, NJ: Princeton University Press, 2007), 150.

37. Ibid., 153–54.

38. Freedman and Karsh, *Gulf Conflict*, 191–92.

39. Ibid., 190.

40. Ibid., 189.

41. Daniel Byman, Kenneth Pollack, and Matthew Waxman, "Coercing Saddam Hussein," *Survival* 40, no. 3 (Autumn 1998): 137–40. See also the summary of the views of containment pessimists, above, and Pollack, "Spies, Lies, and Weapons."

42. More detailed accounts of these eight episodes are available in three superbly crafted journal articles: Byman, "After the Storm," 508–12; Byman, Pollack, and Waxman, "Coercing Saddam Hussein," 136–40; Blechman and Wittes, "Defining Moment," 1–30.

43. Blechman and Wittes, "Defining Moment," 15.

44. Archer, "No-Fly Zones Are Complex and Dangerous," A11.

45. Byman, "After the Storm," 508. See also Byman, Pollack, and Waxman, "Coercing Saddam Hussein," 137.

46. Blechman and Wittes, "Defining Moment," 16.

47. Byman, "After the Storm," 506.

48. Blechman and Wittes, "Defining Moment," 16. See also Byman, Pollack, and Waxman, "Coercing Saddam Hussein," 137–38.

49. Byman, "After the Storm," 506.

50. Blechman and Wittes, "Defining Moment," 16. See also Byman, "After the Storm," 506; Byman, Pollack, and Waxman, "Coercing Saddam Hussein," 137–38.

51. Byman, "After the Storm," 509.

52. Byman, Pollack, and Waxman, "Coercing Saddam Hussein," 138–39.

53. Byman, "After the Storm," 506–7.

54. Ibid., 507.

55. The targets struck included those selected as part of Operation Desert Fox in December 1998, intended to degrade Iraq's programs to acquire WMDs. There were other targets struck too; for example, as retaliation for the launch of an Iraqi surface-to-air missile at a US or British airplane enforcing the no-fly zones over northern and southern Iraq. Byman, "After the Storm," 510.

56. Byman, "After the Storm," 510.

57. McMillan, "U.S. Interests and Objectives," 24.

58. "Iraq: Road to the Current Crisis," *Washington Post*, February 15, 1998, A34. These palaces and presidential sites included approximately one thousand buildings.

59. Blechman and Wittes, "Defining Moment," 15.

60. Ibid., 16.

61. Freedman, "War in Iraq," 22.

62. For more on this point see Kenneth Pollack's assessment of Iraq's armed forces as of March 2003 (just before the United States invaded Iraq), "Regional Military Balance," 62–71.

63. Freedman and Karsh, *Gulf Conflict*, 85.

64. For more on NSD-26 see Jentleson, *With Friends Like These*, 94–105.

65. Ibid., 144.

66. Pollack, "Next Stop Baghdad?," 33.

67. Pollack, "Spies, Lies, and Weapons." See also the arguments made by containment pessimists, summarized above.

68. Freedman, "War in Iraq," 37–38.

69. Ibid., 15.

70. Ibid.

71. Pollack, "Next Stop Baghdad?," 36.

72. Byman, "After the Storm," 495–96.

73. Robin Wright, "Iraq Occupation Erodes Bush Doctrine," *Washington Post*, June 28, 2004, A1.

74. Byman, "After the Storm," 513.

75. For a more skeptical view of the inspectors' accomplishments see Kenneth Pollack, "A Last Chance to Stop Iraq," *New York Times*, February 21, 2003, A27.

76. Fred Halliday, "The Gulf War and Its Aftermath: First Reflections," *International Affairs* 67, no. 2 (April 1991): 225.

77. For more on chain-ganging see Thomas Christensen and Jack Snyder, "Chain Gangs and Passed Bucks: Predicting Alliance Patterns in Multipolarity," *International Organization* 44, no. 2 (Spring 1990): 137–68.

78. Freedman and Karsh, *Gulf Conflict*, 293.

79. The classic works here would be Mancur Olson, *The Logic of Collective Action* (Cambridge, MA: Harvard University Press, 1965), and Mancur Olson and Richard Zeckhauser, "An Economic Theory of Alliances," *Review of Economics and Statistics* 48, no. 3 (August 1966): 266–79.

80. Suggested by Diamond, "What Went Wrong in Iraq," 46.

81. Freedman, "War in Iraq," 15.

82. Freedman and Karsh, *Gulf Conflict*, 150.

6. Containing Iran

1. "The Gathering Storm," *Economist*, January 9, 2010, 25.

2. Benjamin Netanyahu, quoted in ibid., 26.

3. Ephraim Sneh, quoted in Trita Parsi, *Treacherous Alliance: The Secret Dealings of Israel, Iran, and the U.S.* (New Haven, CT: Yale University Press, 2007), 15.

4. "Gathering Storm," 25.

5. Danielle Pletka, "Why Iran Can't Be Contained," *Washington Post*, December 15, 2009, A29.

6. Highly enriched uranium, also known as U-235, and plutonium.

7. Greg Jaffe and Steven Mufson, "Iran Hit with New Sanctions," *Washington Post*, January 18, 2016, A8. Iranian compliance with the terms of this agreement is also discussed in Joby Warrick, "Inspectors 'Stretched,' but Iran Nuclear Deal Is Working, Watchdog Says," *Washington Post*, June 5, 2016, A10.

8. Michael Eisenstadt, "Living with a Nuclear Iran?," *Survival* 41 (Autumn 1999): 138.

9. Charles Krauthammer, "Iran: Orchestrator of Disorder," *Washington Post*, January 1, 1993, A19.

10. Rowland Evans and Robert Novak, "Iran Is Making Satellite of Sudan," *Chicago Sun-Times*, August 19, 1993. See also Jeffrey Lefebvre, "Iran in the Horn of Africa: Outflanking U.S. Allies," *Middle East Policy* 19 (Summer 2012): 117–33.

11. Quoted in John Mintz, "Sweating Out the 'Sunburn,'" *Washington Post*, June 13, 1993, H6. Martin Indyk was at the time senior director for the Middle East for the US National Security Council.

12. Ibid. Christopher was secretary of state during President Clinton's first term (1993–97).

13. *National Strategy for Combating Terrorism*, September 2006, 15, http://www.globalsecu rity.org/security/library/policy/national/nsct_sep2006.pdf.

14. For more on the Iranian military buildup see R. Jeffrey Smith, "Projected Iranian Buildup Scaled Back, Analysts Say," *Washington Post*, November 18, 1995, A22.

15. Gordon Oehler, director of the CIA's Nonproliferation Center, quoted in R. Jeffrey Smith, "Chinese Firms Supply Iran with Gas Factories, U.S. Says," *Washington Post*, March 8, 1996, A26.

16. Charles Krauthammer, "Defy America, Pay No Price," *Washington Post*, January 8, 2016, A19. See also Carol Morello, "Iran to Build More Missiles," *Washington Post*, January 1, 2016, A6.

17. Patrick Knapp, "The Gulf States in the Shadow of Iran," *Middle East Quarterly* (Winter 2010): 50.

18. Vali Nasr and Ray Takeyh, "The Costs of Containing Iran," *Foreign Affairs* 87, no. 1 (January–February 2008): 88.

19. Colin Dueck and Ray Takeyh, "Iran's Nuclear Challenge," *Political Science Quarterly* 122, no. 2 (2007): 192.

20. For more on Iran's positioning internationally see chapters 3 and 7.

21. Cf. James Lindsay and Ray Takeyh, "After Iran Gets the Bomb: Containment and Its Complications," *Foreign Affairs* 89, no. 2 (March–April 2010): 34.

22. Pletka, "Why Iran Can't Be Contained," A29.

23. Nasr and Takeyh, "Costs of Containing Iran," 88.

24. Quoted in Joseph Cirincione, *Bomb Scare: The History and the Future of Nuclear Weapons* (New York: Columbia University Press, 2007), 168.

25. Quoted in ibid.

26. Kenneth Pollack and Ray Takeyh, "Taking on Tehran," *Foreign Affairs* 84, no. 2 (March–April 2005): 25.

27. Ayatollah Mahmood Hashemi Shahroudi, quoted in ibid., 22.

28. Ted Koppel, "30 Years Later, Iran Still Holds Us Hostage," *Washington Post*, January 23, 2011, B1, B4.

29. Zeev Raz, quoted in "Gathering Storm," 25.

30. Richard Russell, "Iran in Iraq's Shadow: Dealing with Tehran's Nuclear Weapons Bid," *Parameters* 34 (Autumn 2004): 37.

31. Dueck and Takeyh, "Iran's Nuclear Challenge," 190.

32. Farideh Farhi, "'Atomic Energy Is Our Assured Right': Nuclear Policy and the Shaping of Iranian Public Opinion," in *Nuclear Politics in Iran*, ed. Judith Yaphe (Washington, DC: National Defense University, 2010), 11–12.

33. But see Kenneth Waltz, "Why Iran Should Get the Bomb," *Foreign Affairs* 91 (July–August 2012): 2–5.

34. Farhi, "'Atomic Energy Is Our Assured Right,'" 11–12. See also Robert Litwak, *Rogue States and U.S. Foreign Policy* (Washington, DC: Woodrow Wilson Center, 2000), 82–87.

35. Glenn Kessler, "IAEA Cites Iran on Uranium Work," *Washington Post*, September 9, 2003, A9.

36. Glenn Frankel and Keith Richburg, "Euros Seek Arms Accord in Tehran," *Washington Post*, October 21, 2003, A1, A22; Glenn Frankel, "Iran Vows to Curb Nuclear Activities," *Washington Post*, October 22, 2003, A1; Joby Warrick, "Iran Still Has Nuke Deadline, U.S. Says," *Washington Post*, October 23, 2003, A17.

37. Fareed Zakaria, "The Stealth Nuclear Threat," *Newsweek*, August 16, 2004, 33.

38. Ray Takeyh, "Time for Détente with Iran," *Foreign Affairs* 86, no. 2 (March–April 2007): 17–32, especially 17, 19.

39. Quoted in Cirincione, *Bomb Scare*, 167. See also Warrick, "Inspectors 'Stretched,'" A10.

40. Farhi, "Atomic Energy Is Our Assured Right," 11–12.

41. Pollack and Takeyh, "Taking on Tehran," 24.

42. See, for example, Steven Mufson and Marc Kaufman, "Longtime Foes U.S., Iran Explore Improved Relations," *Washington Post*, October 29, 2002, A9.

43. Peter Slevin, "U.S. Met with Iranians on War," *Washington Post*, February 8, 2003, A1. The Iranian foreign minister, Kamal Kharazi, promised that Iran would be prepared to resettle, albeit temporarily, refugees who tried to cross into Iran. He also promised that Iran would participate in search-and-rescue missions. See also Michael Dobbs, "Pressure Builds for President to Declare Strategy on Iran," *Washington Post*, June 15, 2003, A20.

44. Glenn Kessler, "U.S. Ready to Resume Talks with Iran, Armitage Says," *Washington Post*, October 23, 2003, A21. See also Slevin, "U.S. Met with Iranians on War," A1, A15; Robin Wright, "U.S. Warms to Prospect of New Talks with Iran," *Washington Post*, December 30, 2003, A13.

45. Nasr and Takeyh, "Costs of Containing Iran," 88.

46. Takeyh, "Time for Détente with Iran," especially 17, 22.

47. Richard Bonney, *False Prophets: The "Clash of Civilizations" and the Global War on Terror* (Oxford: Peter Lang, 2008), 115.

48. Eisenstadt, "Living with a Nuclear Iran?," 135.

49. Pollack and Takeyh, "Taking on Tehran," 20–21. The following two articles were written mostly with Iraq in mind, but their analysis of deterrence theory carries over to Iran as well: Posen, "U.S. Security Policy in a Nuclear-Armed World"; Robert Jervis, "The Confrontation between Iraq and the US: Implications for the Theory and Practice of Deterrence," *European Journal of International Relations* 9, no. 2 (2003): 315–37.

50. National Intelligence Estimate, November 2007, quoted in Cirincione, *Bomb Scare*, 169.

51. Eisenstadt, "Living with a Nuclear Iran?," 135. See also Dalia Dassa Kaye and Eric Lorber, "Containing Iran: What Does It Mean?," *Middle East Policy* 19 (Spring 2012): 57.

52. Russell, "Iran in Iraq's Shadow," 33.

53. Pollack and Takeyh, "Taking on Tehran," 34.

54. Joseph Cirincione and Carl Robichaud, "Into the Breach: The Drive for a New Global Nuclear Strategy," in *Breaking the Nuclear Impasse: New Prospects for Security against Weapons Threats*, ed. Jeffrey Laurenti and Carl Robichaud (New York: Century Foundation, 2007), 10.

55. Nasr and Takeyh, "Costs of Containing Iran," 92–93.

56. For example, Krauthammer, "Defy America, Pay No Price," A19.

57. Nasr and Takeyh, "Costs of Containing Iran," 86, 88.

58. Lindsay and Takeyh, "After Iran Gets the Bomb," 34 (emphasis added).

59. Charles Krauthammer, "The 'Deterrence Works' Fantasy," *Washington Post*, August 31, 2012, A25. See also Pletka, "Why Iran Can't Be Contained," A29.

60. Matthew Kroenig, "Time to Attack Iran," *Foreign Affairs* 91, no. 1 (January–February 2012): 76.

61. Carol Morello, "Iran Takes Last Key Step to Gain Sanctions Relief," *Washington Post*, January 12, 2016, A9.

62. Anoushiravan Ehteshami, "Iran's Tenth Presidential Election: Implications for Iran and the Region," in Yaphe, *Nuclear Politics in Iran*, 53.

63. Bruno Tertrais, "A Nuclear Iran and NATO," *Survival* 52, no. 6 (December 2010–January 2011): 50.

64. Eric Edelman, Andrew Krepinevich, and Evan Braden Montgomery, "The Dangers of a Nuclear Iran: The Limits of Containment," *Foreign Affairs* 90, no. 1 (January–February 2011): 67.

65. Takeyh, "Time for Détente with Iran," 20. See also Frederic Wehrey, "The Saudi Thermidor," *Current History* 113 (December 2014): 348.

66. Lindsay and Takeyh, "After Iran Gets the Bomb," 34. See also Edelman, Krepinevich, and Montgomery, "Dangers of a Nuclear Iran," 67.

67. Kroenig, "Time to Attack Iran," 77.

68. Tertrais, "Nuclear Iran and NATO," 50.

69. For more on Shia-Sunni relations and their influence on containment see Parsi, *Treacherous Alliance*, 93.

70. Still very useful here would be Barry Rubin, *Paved with Good Intentions: The American Experience with Iran* (New York: Oxford University Books, 1980).

71. Shahram Chubin and Robert Litwak, "Debating Iran's Nuclear Aspirations," *Washington Quarterly* 26, no. 4 (Autumn 2003): 101.

72. Dafna Linzer, "Iran Is Judged 10 Years from Nuclear Bomb," *Washington Post*, August 2, 2005, A1, A10.

73. Dima Adamsky et al., "The War over Containing Iran," *Foreign Affairs* 90, no. 2 (March–April 2011): 167. See also Warrick, "Inspectors 'Stretched,'" A10.

74. Lindsay and Takeyh, "After Iran Gets the Bomb," 39.

75. Dueck and Takeyh, "Iran's Nuclear Challenge," 190.

76. Regarding the size of the US nuclear stockpile see US Department of State, *Transparency in the U.S. Nuclear Weapons Stockpile*, April 27, 2015.

77. Dueck and Takeyh, "Iran's Nuclear Challenge," 190.

78. Shahram Chubin, "Iran's Power in Context," *Survival* 51, no. 1 (February–March 2009): 179–80.

79. Takeyh, "Time for Détente with Iran," 17, 19.

80. Barack Obama, "The Next Steps in Nuclear Security," *Washington Post*, March 31, 2016, A17.

81. Takeyh, "Time for Détente with Iran," 17.

82. Chubin, "Iran's Power in Context," 181–82.

83. Kessler, "IAEA Cites Iran on Uranium Work," A9.

84. Dueck and Takeyh, "Iran's Nuclear Challenge," 190.

85. Steve Coll, "U.S. Halted Nuclear Bid by Iran," *Washington Post*, November 17, 1992, A1, A30.

86. Dueck and Takeyh, "Iran's Nuclear Challenge," 190.

87. David Hoffman, "Ukraine Bows to U.S. Pressure," *Washington Post*, March 7, 1998, A16.

88. Stan Crock and Carol Matlack, "What a Deal with Iraq Won't Fix: The Weapons Buildup in Iran," *Business Week*, March 9, 1998, 55.

89. Mohsen M. Milani, "Tehran's Take: Understanding Iran's U.S. Policy," *Foreign Affairs* 88, no. 4 (July–August 2009): 52.

90. For more on this episode see John M. Goshko, "China Drops Reactor Deal with Iran," *Washington Post*, September 28, 1995, A22.

91. Barton Gellman and John Pomfret, "U.S. Action Stymied China Sale to Iran," *Washington Post*, March 13, 1998, A1, A20.

92. Robert Burns, "Centrifuges Pose Bigger Nuclear Weapons Risk Than Reactors," Associated Press, May 10, 1995.

93. Smith, "Projected Iranian Buildup Scaled Back," A22.

94. See, for example, the articles by Ray Takeyh and Charles Krauthammer cited earlier in this chapter.

95. See Nasr and Takeyh's discussion of the second Bush administration, "Costs of Containing Iran," 88.

96. Ibid.

97. Jessica Tuchman Mathews, "Nuclear Weapons: The Iran Question," *Washington Post*, January 22, 1995, C7.

7. Containment Reappraised

1. Thomas Schelling, *Arms and Influence* (New Haven, CT: Yale University Press, 1966), 81.

2. Symington's views are described in Marc Trachtenberg, "A 'Wasting Asset': American Strategy and the Shifting Nuclear Balance, 1949–1954," *International Security* 13, no. 3 (Winter

1988–89): 25. See also Robert Osgood's discussion of "the view that military containment is obsolete in the Third World," in *Limited War Revisited* (Boulder, CO: Westview, 1979), 76; Robert Tucker, "The Purposes of American Power," *Foreign Affairs* 59, no. 2 (Winter 1980): 265; "Should We Bomb Red China's Bomb?," *National Review*, January 12, 1965, 8–9, cited by Gordon Chang, "JFK, China and the Bomb," *Journal of American History* 74, no. 4 (March 1988): 1287.

3. Walter Lippmann, quoted in John Lewis Gaddis, "Containment: A Reassessment," *Foreign Affairs* 55, no. 4 (July 1977): 875. See also Charles Gati, "What Containment Meant," *Foreign Policy*, no. 7 (Summer 1972): 31.

4. Greg Jaffe and Stephen Mufson, "Iran Hit with New Sanctions," *Washington Post*, January 18, 2016, A8.

5. In China, the ineffective Hua Guofeng was replaced by Deng Xiaoping. Saddam Hussein in Iraq was at first replaced by the US-imposed Coalition Provisional Authority, then by an appointed Iraqi government, and then by an elected parliament led by Nouri al-Maliki. Libya ousted Qaddafi, but his replacement had control over the capital, Tripoli, but very little other than Tripoli. To this day, Libya remains a failed state more than anything else.

6. Oran Young, *The Politics of Force: Bargaining during International Crises* (Princeton, NJ: Princeton University Press, 1968).

7. Marc Trachtenberg, "Strategic Thought in America, 1952–1966," *Political Science Quarterly* 104, no. 2 (Summer 1989): 318.

8. Samuel Huntington, *The Common Defense* (New York: Columbia University Press, 1961), 32.

9. Ibid.

10. Mr. X [George Kennan], "The Sources of Soviet Conduct," *Foreign Affairs* 25, no. 4 (July 1947): 566–82.

11. Walter Millis, ed., *The Forrestal Diaries* (New York: Viking, 1951), 351–52.

12. G. John Ikenberry, "America's Imperial Ambition," *Foreign Affairs* 81, no. 5 (September–October 2002): 56. For more on relations among and between the NATO allies see Wallace J. Thies, *Friendly Rivals: Bargaining and Burden-Shifting in NATO* (Armonk, NY: M. E. Sharpe, 2003).

13. Huntington, *Common Defense*, 47.

14. Francis Gavin, "Blasts from the Past," *International Security* 29, no. 3 (Winter 2004–5): 100–101.

15. Ibid., 104.

16. The CIA got it right. See Gordon Chang's citation of a CIA paper dated July 1963 that called attention to moderation in the Chinese public statements and predicted further moderation in the future. "JFK, China, and the Bomb," 1309.

17. William Burr and Jeffrey Richelson, "Whether to 'Strangle the Baby in the Cradle': The United States and the Chinese Nuclear Program, 1960–1964," *International Security* 25, no. 3 (Winter 2000–2001): 97. Roswell Gilpatric was deputy secretary of defense during the Kennedy and Johnson administrations.

18. Gavin, "Blasts from the Past," 135.

19. For more on this point see Adam Ulam, *The Rivals: America and Russia since World War II* (New York: Viking, 1971), 3–27.

20. The creation of the NATO alliance is discussed more fully in Wallace J. Thies, *Why NATO Endures* (New York: Cambridge University Press, 2009), chapter 3.

21. Mr. X, "Sources of Soviet Conduct," 575. See also Huntington, *Common Defense*, 34.

22. Huntington, *Common Defense*, 38.

23. Kenneth Waltz, "The Politics of Peace," *International Studies Quarterly* 11, no. 3 (September 1967): 207.

24. Marc Trachtenberg, "Strategic Thought in America," 319.

25. Walt Rostow, draft "Basic National Security Policy," March 26, 1962, 173–74, quoted in John Lewis Gaddis, *Strategies of Containment: A Critical Appraisal of American National Security Policy during the Cold War* (New York: Oxford University Press, 1982), 214.

26. Quoted in Burr and Richelson, "Whether to 'Strangle the Baby in the Cradle,'" 77.

27. David McDonough, *Nuclear Superiority: The "New Triad" and the Evolution of Nuclear Strategy* (London: International Institute of Strategic Studies, Adelphi Papers 383, 2006), 30–31.

28. Trita Parsi, *Treacherous Alliance: The Secret Dealings of Israel, Iran, and the U.S.* (New Haven, CT: Yale University Press, 2007), 167.

29. Chalmers Roberts, "How Containment Worked," *Foreign Policy*, no. 7 (Summer 1972): 51.

30. Huntington, *Common Defense*, 15–18.

31. Ibid., 17.

32. Ibid. For more on the preventive war option see Chang, "JFK, China, and the Bomb," 1207–309.

33. Huntington, *Common Defense*, 17–18.

34. Ibid., 18.

35. John Foster Dulles, quoted in ibid. Dulles served as secretary of state from 1953 to 1959.

36. Mr. X, "Sources of Soviet Conduct," 575.

37. Quoted in Wallace Thies, "Learning in U.S. Policy toward Europe," in *Learning in U.S. and Soviet Foreign Policy*, ed. George Breslauer and Philip Tetlock (Boulder, CO: Westview, 1991), 164.

38. Mr. X, " Sources of Soviet Conduct," 572–73.

39. Richard Betts, *American Force: Dangers, Delusions, and Dilemmas in National Security* (New York: Columbia University Press, 2013), 136.

40. Huntington, *Common Defense*, 34.

41. George Breslauer, "Do Soviet Leaders Test New Presidents?," *International Security* 8, no. 3 (1983–84): 86.

42. Quoted in Robert Jervis, "Confrontation between Iraq and the US: Implications for the Theory and Practice of Deterrence," *European Journal of International Relations* 9, no. 2 (2003): 318.

43. Schelling, *Arms and Influence*, 44.

44. Ibid., 44–45.

45. Quoted in ibid., 39. Schelling saw this maneuver as adding automaticity to a Soviet deterrent threat, even as it placed the onus for starting a war on the West.

46. Quoted in Schelling, *Arms and Influence*, 46–47.

47. Ibid., 71.

48. Suggested by David Auerswald's discussion of policy flexibility in *Disarmed Democracies: Domestic Institutions and the Use of Force* (Ann Arbor: University of Michigan Press, 2000), 1. Auerswald, in turn, drew on Schelling, *Arms and Influence*, 44.

49. Schelling, *Arms and Influence*, 47–48.

50. Suggested ibid., 48–49.

51. Trachtenberg, "'Wasting Asset,'" 7.

52. Quoted in Trachtenberg, "Strategic Thought in America," 314.

53. Gavin, "Blasts from the Past," 135.

54. Kuross Samii, "Truman against Stalin in Iran: A Tale of Three Messages," *Middle Eastern Studies* 23, no. 1 (January 1987): 106.

55. Joseph McMillan, "U.S. Interests and Objectives," in *The United States and the Persian Gulf*, ed. Richard Sokolsky (Washington, DC: National Defense University Press, 2003), 26. For the Iranians' offer of help after 9/11 see Parsi, *Treacherous Alliance*, 227–29.

56. Michael O'Hanlon, *Defense Strategy for the Post-Saddam Era* (Washington, DC: Brookings Institution Press, 2005), 3.

57. Michael Krepon, "Nuclear Pessimism Is Not the Answer," in *Breaking the Nuclear Impasse*, ed. Jeffrey Laurenti and Carl Robichaud (New York: Century Foundation, 2007), 33–34.

58. James Schlesinger, "The International Implications of Third-World Conflict: An American Perspective," in *Third-World Conflict and International Security: Part I; Papers from the IISS 22nd Annual Conference*, Adelphi Papers 166 (International Institute for Strategic Studies, 1981), 5.

59. Andrew Pierre, "America Down, Russia Up," *Foreign Policy*, no. 4 (Fall 1971): 166.

60. Ibid., 185.

61. Waltz, "Politics of Peace," 207. See also Richard Neustadt, *Presidential Power* (New York: John Wiley and Sons, 1960); Kenneth Waltz, *Foreign Policy and Democratic Politics* (Boston: Little, Brown, 1967).

62. Huntington, *Common Defense*, 146.

63. Kennan himself believed that Soviet hostility toward the outside world would not last forever, and thus it was in the interests of the United States to be prepared to benefit from changes in the Soviet position. Gaddis, "Containment: A Reassessment," 881.

64. Walter Laqueur, "What Do We Know about the Soviet Union?," *Commentary* 75, no. 2 (February 1983): 16.

65. In the remaining pages of this chapter I draw very heavily on the book that in my judgment is the single best book ever written on the subject of American defense policy. Huntington, *Common Defense*, 446–47.

66. Alexis de Tocqueville, *Democracy in America*, vol. 1 (New York: Vintage Books, 1954), 237, 243–44. Suggested by Huntington, *Common Defense*, 446.

67. Walter Lippmann, *The Cold War* (New York: Harper, 1947), 20. Suggested by Huntington, *Common Defense*, 446.

68. Huntington, *Common Defense*, 446.

69. Fisher Ames, address to the US House of Representatives, 1795, quoted in Huntington, *Common Defense*, 447.

Index

9/11 attacks, 2, 3

Afghanistan, 9, 31, 64, 111, 142, 190
agricultural credits, 71, 73, 84, 93, 97, 98,
  106, 124, 141, 212n16
air battles and showdowns
  with Iraq, 69, 133–36; Desert Storm, 64,
    89–90, 102–3, 105, 108, 115, 126–27;
    no-fly zones, 9, 103, 104, 109–10,
    127–29, 131–32, 134, 135–36,
    137–44, 148
  with Libya, 22, 40, 43, 44, 45, 46–47, 49,
    69, 202n52, 202n98
al-Qaeda, 9, 64, 151–52, 159
Ames, Fisher, 193
Anderson, Lisa, 28, 48–49
Annan, Kofi, 135
appeasement, 99
Argentina, 10, 12, 161, 168
Aspin, Les, 4
assassinations, 22, 132–33
axis of evil, 11, 13, 159

Bahrain, 77, 163–64
Baker, James A, III, on Iraq
  after Iran-Iraq War, 67, 88
  concerns about, 101, 102
  importance of relations, 97
  potential for war with, 80, 88
  sanctions, 106–7
  settling for containment, 104
  WMDs, 103
balancing, 69, 80, 114
bandwagoning, 76, 114, 145, 163–64

Belgium, 53, 75, 77, 78
Benghazi
  bombing raid on, 22, 40, 43, 44, 45, 46–47,
    49, 69, 202n52, 202n98
  chemical weapons factories near, 41
  mutiny in, 28
Ben-Gurion, David, 4
Berlin airlift, 15, 211n101
Betts, Richard, 11–12
bin Laden, Osama, 9
Blair, Tony, 2, 4, 13
Blechman, Barry, 133, 137
Blix, Hans, 8
Bolton, John, 3, 154
Brazil, 12, 161
Breslauer, George, 186
Bridgeton (ship), 74, 77
Brodie, Bernard, 188
Brown, Harold, 111
Brzezinski, Zbigniew, 95
buck passing, 16, 75–76, 115, 169
burden shifting, 61, 69–70, 146
Bush 41 (George H.W.), administration.
  See also First Gulf War
  dual containment by, 57–58, 60, 67, 69, 93,
    96, 97, 99
  Iran and, 93–94, 100, 153, 168, 170
  Iraq, favorable stance towards,
    91–92, 93–94, 96, 97–102, 106, 123–24,
    141
  Iraq's plans to assassinate, 132–33
  Libya and, 21, 42
Bush 41 (George H.W.), on Iran-Iraq war,
  71–72, 99–100

Bush 43 (George W.) administration.
See also Second Gulf War
Bush doctrine, 6–18, 14, 188, 189
containment supporters in, 4, 17–18
Iran and, 13–14, 151–52, 153, 159
Iraq and, 13–14, 16–18, 121, 142, 148–49
Libya and, 21
Byman, Daniel, 104–5, 120, 125–26, 133, 135, 142

Carlucci, Frank, 44
Carter administration
Iran and, 56, 62, 71, 93, 94, 99
Iran-Iraq War and: dual containment, 56, 60, 82, 84, 94, 95–96; relinquishing initiative, 73–75
Iraq and, 56, 59–60, 71, 94, 95
Libya and, 21, 23, 24–25, 28–29, 31–32, 35, 37, 46, 51–52, 201n62
Middle East policy overall, 59, 62–65, 71, 82, 84, 111, 213n31
Soviet Union and, 65, 213n31
CENTCOM, 63, 64, 68, 84, 85
Chad, 21, 25, 53
chain-ganging, 16, 76
chemical weapons. *See* WMD; *specific country*
Chemical Weapons Convention, 152
Cheney, Dick, 3, 14
China
containment of, 2–3, 11, 12, 153, 175–89, 180, 183, 186, 189
Iran and, 169
Cirincione, Joseph, 8, 12, 46
Clinton administration
China, Iran, and, 169
containment of Iraq by, 81, 92, 121, 133–35, 136
dual containment by, 57–58, 60, 69–71, 81–82, 83, 84–85, 93
Libya and, 21, 47
preventative war, support of by, 4
Cold War, containment during, 65–68
effectiveness of, 2–3, 6, 11, 12, 153, 161–62, 170, 176, 184, 188
end of, 70, 76, 176–77
military imbalance, 117–18
options, wide range of, 180–81
other countries helping, 191
pessimism about, 175–89
relinquishing initiative, 5, 15–16, 17, 33, 177, 187–88
time on our side, 12, 123, 175, 177–80, 185–86
collective action theory, 76–77
compellence, 104
constructive engagement, 97, 99, 102

containment strategies. *See also specific country or conflict*
Bush (43) admin. supporters of, 4, 17–18
during Cold War, appraisal of, 177–89
criticisms of, 2–6
democracies: as disadvantageous for, 18, 51, 57, 177, 182, 189, 192–93; as suited to, 17, 52, 179, 182, 191–92
optimism about, 119, 120, 121, 126–27, 160–62
options, wide range of, 10–11, 18, 115, 186, 190
other countries helping, 16–17, 82, 114–15, 190–91
pessimism about: Cold War, 175–89; Iraq, 119–21, 125, 141–42; Iran, 151, 153–60, 162–63, 167, 171–73
power imbalances, 14–15, 180, 182
relinquishing initiative, 14–15, 33–34, 190
success of, *viii*, 12, 176–77; criteria for, *vii*, 46–47, 84, 172
theory of, *vii*, 6–7, 18–19
time on our side, *vii*, 7, 10–14
Cortright, David, 125–26, 128
Crocker, Chester, 21
Cuban Missile Crisis, 2, 15–16, 175, 188, 198n89

Dawisha, Adeed, 121
democracies
as disadvantageous for containment, 18, 51, 57, 177, 182, 189, 192–93
as suited to containment, 17, 52, 179, 182, 191–92
Desert Storm, 64, 89–90, 102–3, 105, 108, 115, 126–27
Desert Strike, 133–34
deterrence
containment and, 187–88
criticisms of, 2–6
failures of, 104
relinquishing initiatve and, 33–34, 174–75, 187
successes of, 162
de Tocqueville, Alexis, 193
dictatorships, and rationality
Bush 43 admin. on, 2–3, 4, 11, 12–13
during Cold War, 11, 12, 180
Iran and, 154, 155–56, 157, 159, 160–61, 162, 191
Qaddafi and, 26–27, 30
Diehl, Jackson, 121
dual containment
Bush 41 admin., 57–58, 60, 67, 69, 93, 96, 97, 99

Carter admin., 56, 60, 82, 84, 94, 95–96
Clinton admin., 57–58, 60, 69–71, 81–82,
    83, 84–85, 93
Reagan admin., 56–57, 67–69, 71–75,
    79–80, 83–84, 85–86, 91, 93, 96–97, 99
Dueck, Colin, 152, 165
Dulles, John Foster, 185, 186

Egypt, 52–53
Eisenhower administration, 178, 185, 186
Europe, 155–58, 160, 166, 168, 170–71
    See also specific country

Fifth Fleet, 84
First Gulf War
    context, 89, 91–92, 106, 116, 121–24
    Desert Shield, 64, 104, 115
    Desert Storm, 64, 89–90, 102–3, 105, 108,
        115, 126–27
    as failure of containment, 88, 101–2
    moves and countermoves, 108–10
    other countries helping, 70, 114–16
    power imbalance, 108, 113, 117–18
    relinquishing initiative, 112–15
Ford administration, 51–52, 62, 64, 84, 99
Forrestal, James, 178–79
France
    Gulf Wars and, 146
    Iran and, 75, 77, 156, 157, 168–69, 170–71
    Iraq and, 108, 132
    Libya and, 53
Freedman, Lawrence, 120, 135, 140, 141
free riders, 114–15

Gaddis, John Lewis, 11
Gause, F. Gregory, III, 81, 82
Gavin, Francis, 179–80
Germany
    Gulf Wars and, 146
    Iran and, 78, 156, 157, 168–69, 170–71
    tanker war and, 77
Glaspie, April, 124
Gorbachev, Mikhail, 49
Gross Stein, Janice, 76–77, 80–81, 82–83
Gulf Wars. See First Gulf War; Second
    Gulf War

Haig, Alexander, 25–26
Harriman, Averell, 187
hostage taking (by Iran), 24, 55, 56, 93
    as general tactic, 152, 154, 169
    impact on US-Libyan relations, 25, 31, 32
    trading for arms, 72–73, 85–86, 93, 94–95,
        99
Howard, Dan, 43–44
Huntington, Samuel, 17, 179, 181, 184,
    192–93

Hussein, Saddam, analysis of, 55–57, 87,
    121–23, 209n24
    See also Iraq

IAEA (International Atomic Energy
    Authority)
    Iran and, 154, 156, 157, 168–69
    Iraq and, 109, 110, 130, 141, 143, 145, 147
Ikenberry, G. John, 179
India, 169, 171, 183
Indian Ocean, 62–63, 82, 84, 109, 111, 127,
    134–35, 145–46, 213n31
Indyk, Martin, 151
intelligence sharing (with Iraq), 68, 73, 78,
    84, 85, 93, 106, 117, 124
Iran. See also dual containment;
    Iran-Iraq War
    containment of: difficulties, 55–57;
        effectiveness, 158–59, 162–65, 169–72,
        176; optimism about, 160–62;
        pessimism about, 151, 153–60, 162–63,
        167, 171–73
    cooperation from, post-9/11, 190–91,
        216n43
    Europe and, 155–58, 160, 166, 168,
        170–71
    hostage taking by, 24, 55, 56, 93, 152, 154,
        169; impact on US-Libyan relations, 25,
        31, 32; trading for arms, 72–73, 85–86,
        93, 94–95, 99
    Israel and, 150, 152–53, 154
    Khomeini, 55–57, 58, 62, 66–67, 77
    moves and countermoves, 78–80,
        165–67
    Obama and, 150
    options, wide range of, 165–67
    other countries helping, 74–78, 168–71
    power imbalance with, 78–79, 161
    religious extremism in, 152; irrationality
        and, 154, 155–56, 157, 159, 160–61, 162,
        191
    relinquishing initiative to, 73–75
    sanctions against, 150, 156, 157, 158–59,
        176
    Shah of, 57, 61–62, 66, 99, 155
    terrorism, support of by, 151–52, 159
    threat presented by, 151–53
    time on our side, 66–67, 158
    WMD of, 150, 151, 155, 156, 160, 168;
        abandonment of, 158, 164–65; cheating
        of inspectors, 154, 156, 157, 168; limits
        accepted, 150, 158, 163, 167, 170–71,
        176; negotiating tactics, 156–58, 168,
        169, 172
Iran-Contra Affair, 72–73, 85–85
Iran-Iraq War
    context, 56, 91, 94

Iran-Iraq War (*continued*)
  dual containment during, 57–60, 67–73,
    91–99; criticisms of, 55–57, 80–83, 85,
    104, 141–42; effectiveness of, 80–86 86
  moves and countermoves, 69, 78–80, 85,
    136–37
  options, wide range of, 72, 81, 83–84
  other countries helping, 59, 67–68,
    75–78
  power imbalance, 83–84
  pro-Iraq orientation during, 91–99;
    agricultural credits, 71, 73, 84, 93, 97,
    98, 106, 124, 141, 212n16; intelligence
    sharing, 68, 73, 78, 84, 85, 93, 106, 117,
    124; military aid, 71, 97
  reduction of Iraq's power after, 9, 88, 93,
    143
  tanker war, 73–75, 78, 79–80, 82–83, 84,
    85–86, 124
Iraq, containment of (1991–2003).
    See also First Gulf War; Second Gulf
    War: Iran-Iraq War
  effectiveness of, 104–5, 133, 140–45
  failure of, 120, 131–36
  moves and countermoves, 108–10,
    136–37
  no-fly zones, 9, 103, 104, 109–10, 127–29,
    131–32, 134, 135–36, 137–44, 148
  optimism about, 119, 120, 121, 126–27
  options, wide range of, 105
  other countries helping, 16, 108, 145–49
  pessimism about, 119–21, 125, 141–42
  power imbalance, 9, 143
  relinquishing initiative to, 111–14,
    137–40
  Saddam, analysis of, 55–57, 87, 121–23,
    209n24
  time on our side, 105, 139–40
  WMD and: abandonment of, 7–9, 12, 20,
    46, 48, 105, 138, 162, 176; Desert Fox, 81,
    85, 110, 128, 135–36, 213n55;
    development of, 40–45, 78, 87, 90, 98,
    103; effectiveness of inspections
    regime, 105; inspections abandoned, 7,
    110, 135, 141, 145; invasion because of,
    2, 6, 7, 144; requirement to eliminate,
    103, 108, 125; resistance to inspections,
    7, 105, 109, 110, 128, 130–31, 132,
    134–35, 136, 138, 147; sanctions, 7, 103,
    105, 106–7, 108, 123, 125, 126, 130–31,
    142, 148
Islamabad, attack on embassy in, 24
Israel, 94, 95, 96, 97, 150, 152–53, 154, 183
Italy, 77, 78

Jentleson, Bruce, 84
Johnson (Lyndon B.) administration, 180,
    208n119

Karsh, Efraim, 92, 140
Kemp, Geoffrey, 52
Kennan, George, 178, 181, 185
Kennedy, John F., 175, 180
Khomeini (Ayatollah), 55–57, 58, 62, 66–67,
    77
Khrushchev, Nikita, 11, 187
Kimmitt, Robert, 100
Krauthammer, Charles, 151, 154, 162
Krepon, Michael, 191
Kroenig, Matthew, 10, 162, 163
Kurds, 90, 93, 103, 129, 131, 133–34
Kuwait. *See also* First Gulf War
  Reagan admin. and, 73, 75, 77, 78, 79,
    82–83
  Soviet Union and, 59, 85
Kuwait pre-Gulf War, 59

Lake, Anthony, 69–70
Laqueur, Walter, 193
Laurenti, Jeffrey, 5
Lehman, John, 36
Libya
  context, 20–26, 30–32, 48–51
  effectiveness of policy on, 12, 27, 45–48,
    52, 176
  Gulf of Sidra clashes, 27, 28, 31–32, 35–40,
    44–45
  moves and countermoves, 29, 30–33, 34,
    35–45, 47, 51–52
  options, wide range of, 29, 42, 47–48
  other countries helping, 42, 43, 52–53
  power imbalance, 23, 27–29, 50–51
  Qaddafi, analysis of, 12–13, 26–27, 30,
    199n10, 200n22
  relinquishing initiative to, 28, 33–42, 45,
    52, 113
  sanctions against, 29
  Soviets and, 49
  Tripoli bombing raid, 22, 40, 43, 44, 45,
    46–47, 49, 52, 69, 202n98
  Tripoli embassy attack, 24, 29, 176
  WMD development by, 40–45, 78, 87, 88,
    90, 103; abandonment of, 12, 20, 46, 48,
    138, 176
Lindsay, James, 162, 163
Lippmann, Walter, 176
Litwak, Robert, 53
Long Telegram, 178
Lopez, George, 125–26, 128

Mao Zedong
  analysis of, 11, 12, 86, 180
  containment of, 186
  threat presented by, 179–80, 186, 189,
    191
McMillan, Joseph, 81, 84–85, 120, 135–36
Miller, Judith, 89, 92

mines (under sea), 74, 77
Mirza, Suroor Mahmoud, 130
Mitchell, George, 146
Mitterrand, François, 209n24
moves and countermoves
    during First Gulf War, 108–10
    with Iran, 78–80, 165–67
    during Iran-Iraq War, 69, 78–80, 85,
        136–37
    with Iraq (1991–2003), 108–10, 136–37
    with Libya, 29, 30–33, 34, 35–45, 47,
        51–52
Mueller, Karl, 14–15
Mylroie, Laurie, 89, 92

Nasr, Vali, 152, 162
naval battles and showdowns
    Iran and, 73–75, 78, 79–80, 82–83, 84,
        85–86, 124
    Libya and, 27, 28, 31–32, 35–40, 36, 44–45
Netherlands, 75, 77, 78
Nicaragua, 25, 65, 207n78
Nidal, Abu, 48, 49
Nixon administration
    China and, 177, 180, 183, 186
    Middle East and, 61, 69, 99
no-fly zones (Iraq), 9, 103, 104, 109–10,
    127–29, 131–32, 134, 135–36, 137–44,
    148
North Korea
    advisers to Qaddafi from, 28
    Bush 43 admin. and, 11, 13–14, 17
    cheating of WMD inspectors by, 154
    Clinton admin. and, 4
    deterrence of, 60
    nuclear weapons of, 159, 161
    pilots from, 30–31, 45, 113
    Soviet Union and, 65
    threat level presented by, 191
NPT, 156–57, 172
NSD-26, 97, 99, 141
nuclear reversal, 12

Obama, Barack, 150
Odom, William, 63–64, 68, 81
O'Hanlon, Michael, 191
options, wide range of
    during Cold War, 180–81
    containment strategies and, 10–11, 18,
        115, 186, 190
    with Iran, 165–67
    during Iran-Iraq War, 72, 81, 83–84
    with Iraq, 105
    with Libya, 29, 42, 47–48
Osirak nuclear reactor, 154

Pakistan, 171, 183
Pan Am 103 bombing, 46, 48, 53

Perry, William, 4
Pierre, Andrew, 192
Pollack, Kenneth, 8, 61, 77, 80, 120–21, 125,
    128, 141
Powell, Colin, 17–18, 104
power imbalances
    containment strategies and, 14–15, 180,
        182
    First Gulf War and, 108, 113, 117–18
    with Iran, 78–79, 161
    Iran-Iraq War and, 83–84
    Iraq and (1991–2003), 9, 143
    Libya and, 23, 27–29, 50–51
    Second Gulf War, 119, 123
Presidential Directive 18 (PD-18), 63, 84
preventative war
    Bush doctrine, 6–18, 14, 188, 189
    Clinton admin. support of, 4
    proactiveness and, 3–6, 13–14, 104, 142,
        174, 183–84, 188–89
    rationales for, vii–viii, 121, 184–85
    timescales and, vii–viii, 4–5, 7, 14, 174,
        183, 184–85
provocation, 34

Qaddafi, Muammar, analysis of, 12–13,
    26–27, 30, 199n10, 200n22
    See also Libya
Qatar, 77, 163–64

Rabta facility, 41, 42, 44
Rapid Deployment Force (RDF), 63–65, 82,
    84
Reagan administration. See also Iran-Iraq
    War
    dual containment by, 56–57, 67–69,
        71–75, 79–80, 83–84, 85–86, 91, 93,
        96–97, 99
    global containment by, 65–68
    Iran and, 71–75, 78–80, 83–84, 153, 166,
        168; hostages and, 32, 72–73, 85–86, 93,
        94–95, 99
    Iraq, favorable stance towards, 83, 91,
        94–97, 100–101, 123–24, 140–41;
        agricultural credits, 71, 73, 84, 93, 97,
        98, 106, 124, 141, 212n16; intelligence
        sharing, 68, 73, 78, 84, 85, 93, 106, 117,
        124; military aid, 71, 97
    Libya and, 21, 22, 25–27, 30, 32, 33, 48, 50,
        52–53, 113
    Middle East overall policy, 64–65, 66,
        213n31
Regan, Donald, 30
relinquishing the initiative
    during Cold War, 5, 15–16, 17, 33, 177,
        187–88
    containment strategies and, 14–15, 33–34,
        190

relinquishing the initiative (*continued*)
  deterrence and, 33–34, 174–75, 187
  during First Gulf War, 112–15
  during Iran-Iraq War, 73–75
  to Iraq (1991–2003), 111–14, 137–40
  to Libya, 28, 33–42, 45, 52, 113
  preventative war and, 3–4
  to Soviet Union, 15, 33, 175, 177, 187–88
Renshon, Stanley, 17
Rice, Condoleezza, 4, 5, 18, 46, 148–49
Roberts, Chalmers, 184
Robichaud, Carl, 12
rogue states, 13
Rose, Gideon, 120
Ross, Dennis, 100
Rostow, Walt, 182
Rowden, William, 36
Rubin, Barry, 99, 101, 129
Rumsfeld, Donald, 2, 6
Russia, 100–7091, 163, 166, 168, 169
  See also Soviet Union

Samii, Kuross, 190
sanctions
  against Iran, 150, 156, 157, 158–59, 176
  against Iraq, 7–9, 18, 81, 103, 105, 106–7,
    108, 123, 125, 126, 130–31, 142, 148
  against Libya, 29, 43, 46
Saudi Arabia, 61, 77
Schelling, Thomas, 14, 33–34, 187
Schlesinger, James, 192
Schumacher, Edward, 40
Schwartz, Jonathan, 47
Scowcroft, Brent, 71–72, 90, 98, 99–100, 112
Sea Isle City (tanker), 78
Sebha facilities, 41
Second Gulf War (2003 invasion of Iraq)
  containment as alternative to, 119,
    121–23, 136, 142–49
  containment before, 103, 124–25
  context, 121–23
  as failure of containment, 120, 131–36
  success of, 121
  WMD fears as trigger to, 2, 6, 7, 144
Shah of Iran, 57, 61–62, 66, 99, 155
Shiites
  Iran and, 55–56, 58, 152, 154, 164
  Iraq and, 8, 90, 103, 129, 131, 147
Shultz, George, 22, 30, 42
Sidra, Gulf of, clashes in, 27, 28, 31–32,
  35–40, 44–45
Sokolsky, Richard, 81
Solingen, Etel, 20, 130
South Africa, 12, 161, 171
South Korea, 161
Soviet Union. *See also* Russia
  containment pessimism about, 175–89

effectiveness of containment of, 2–3, 6, 11,
    12, 153, 176, 185–86
  ending of Cold War and, 70, 176–77
  Iran and, 166, 168, 169, 170–71
  Kuwait and, 59, 85
  Libya and, 49
  overall international aggression of, 65
  relinquishing initiative to, 15, 33, 175, 177,
    187–88
  time on our side, 12, 175, 177–80
Stalin, Joseph, 11, 12, 86, 181, 186, 191,
  197n69
Stark, attack on, 69
Sudan, 25, 29, 52, 53, 151
Sullivan, William, 67
Symington, Stuart, 176
Syrian pilots, 30–31, 45, 49, 113

Taiwan, 161
Takeyh, Ray, 152, 157–58, 162, 163, 165,
  166–67
Talbott, Strobe, 26
tanker war (with Iran), 73–75, 78, 79–80,
  82–83, 84, 85–86, 124
Tanter, Raymond, 109–10
Tarhuna facility, 41
terrorism designation, 46
Tertrais, Bruno, 163
time (on our side)
  during Cold War, 12, 123, 175, 177–80,
    185–86
  containment strategies and, *vii*, 7, 10–14
  Iran and, 66–67, 158
  Iraq and (1991–2003), 105, 139–40
  preventative war and, *vii–viii*, 4–5, 7, 14,
    174, 183, 184–85
  Second Gulf War and, 122–23, 148
  Soviet Union and, 12, 175, 177–80
Trachtenberg, Marc, 188
Tripoli
  attack on embassy in, 24, 29, 176
  bombing raid on, 22, 40, 43, 44, 45, 46–47,
    49, 52, 69, 202n98
Truman administration, 178
Twin Pillars policy, 61–62, 66, 155

Ukraine, 12, 168
United Kingdom
  Cold War and, 15
  Iran and, 74–75, 77, 155–56, 157, 168–69,
    170–71
  Iraq and, 9, 89, 104, 108, 109–10, 127–29,
    131–32, 137–38, 144
  Libya and, 48
  Middle East dominance of, 61
United Nations
  Iran and, 156, 157, 168–69

Iraq and, 103, 105, 108–9, 110, 121, 123,
    128, 130–31, 133, 135, 137, 141
  Libya and, 29, 53
UNMOVIC, 130, 135
UNSCOM, 105, 109, 110, 128, 130, 135, 141,
    147
  Iraq and, 105, 109, 110, 128, 130, 135, 141
UTA 772 bombing, 46, 48, 53

Viorst, Milton, 60

Waltz, Kenneth, 17, 182, 192
Washington Post, 111
West Point speech (Bush, G.W.), 2, 3, 5

Weymouth, Lally, 46
Whitehead, John, 46–47
Wittes, Tamara, 133, 137
WMD, possession of as reversible, 12, 161,
    198n76
  See also specific country
World War II, 181–82
Wright, Claudia, 72–73
Wright, Robin, 142

Yom Kippur War, 59

Zaa'faraniyah nuclear facility, 132
Zakaria, Fareed, 157

CPSIA information can be obtained
at www.ICGtesting.com
Printed in the USA
LVHW111747081020
668327LV00004B/22/J